DATE DUE

Cat. No. 23-221

BRODART, INC.

PUT ANOTHER NICKEL IN

Put Another Nickel In

A History of Coin-Operated Pianos and Orchestrions

by

Q. David Bowers

BONANZA BOOKS • NEW YORK

DC2S

Contents

Credits

When I first contemplated writing PUT ANOTHER NICKEL IN several years ago the main problem was finding sufficient material to make a book exclusively about coin-operated pianos and orchestrions worthwhile. Unlike many historical fields there is no basic source for research information concerning these machines. Much of the material in this book was gathered bit by bit, catalogue by catalogue, from many different coin piano enthusiasts.

Harvey and Marion Roehl of the Vestal Press have aided greatly with this book. Harvey, author of the best-selling "Player Piano Treasury," has corresponded with hundreds of different collectors since that book was published in 1961. This correspondence and the many photographs taken by the Roehls on their annual summer trips were made available for my use.

During my first visit to Otto Carlsen's home in Monrovia, California several years ago I saw a Wurlitzer PianOrchestra for the first time. My amazement upon seeing and hearing this orchestrion must have been akin to the feeling that the Wurlitzer brothers experienced sixty years earlier at the Leipzig Trade Fair. The desire to learn more about the PianOrchestras led to intense research concerning the history of European and American orchestrions . . . and finally to the writing of this book.

Special thanks go to the following for assistance in various ways with this book: William Allen, Joseph Bacigalupi, Carl Baxter, Ted Behymer, Tom B'hend, Sen. Charles Bovey, Morris Bristol (of the Wurlitzer Company), Otto Carlsen, Ed Clark, Murray Clark, Jerry Cohen, Jocko Conlon, J. C. Daggs, Jacob De Bence, Bill Dodson, Jerry Doring, Harry Dring (superintendent, California Maritime Museum), Ed Freyer, Frederick Fried, Larry Givens, John Gourley, Leonard Grymonprez, Leslie Hagwood, Roy Haning, Terry Hathaway, Tom Herrick (of the Seeburg Corporation), Clay Holbrook, Frank Holland (British Piano Museum), Robert Horn, Robert Johnson, David Junchen, Lloyd Kelley, Walter Knott (Knott's Berry Farm), Steve Lanick, John and Mary Lemmer, Edwin A. Link (son of E. A. Link of the Link Piano Company), Little Falls Felt Shoe Company, Lyle Martin, Ray and Pat Merena, George Messig, Floyd Miles (Miles Mountain Musical Museum), Michael Montgomery, Milo Nellis (historian, St. Johnsville, N. Y.), Marg Paape, Stan Peters, David Rockola (president, Rock-Ola Manufacturing Corporation), Harvey and Marion Roehl, James F. Ruddy, Gary Sage, Arthur Sanders (Musical Museum, Deansboro, N. Y.), Pete Schaeble, Richard

Schlaich, N. Marshall Seeburg (son of Justus P. Seeburg, founder of J. P. Seeburg Piano Co.), Harold Shaner, Richard Simonton, Charles Smallwood, Spring Mills Hotel, Andy "Swede" Subwick (curator, Sutro's — San Francisco), Al Svoboda, A. Valente, H. E. Van der Boom, Reed Van Gorder, August VonKleist (son of Eugene DeKleist), Neal White, Oswald Wurdeman, Farny Wurlitzer (chairman of the board, the Wurlitzer Company), Ed Zelinsky.

Special credit goes to Mr. Farny Wurlitzer. Through his generosity I had access to the Wurlitzer archives — a file of catalogues, advertisements, photographs and other information relating to that firm's business in the coin piano field during the early decades of the twentieth century. During several visits with Mr. Wurlitzer in his North Tonawanda, New York offices Harvey Roehl and I discussed the early operations of the Wurlitzer Company and thereby learned much that might have been otherwise lost to history.

Upon leaving Mr. Wurlitzer's office during one of our visits Harvey Roehl noticed a bulky package wrapped in brown paper. On the outside was marked "AUTOMATIC MUSICAL INSTRUMENTS — OUTSIDE COMPANIES." Responding to our interest, Mr. Wurlitzer untied the package. What a treasure trove it held! Sometime before 1920 someone had gathered together several dozen catalogues issued by the Wurlitzer Company's competitors. Catalogues of Seeburg, Hupfeld, Welte, Frati, Mills Novelty Company, North Tonawanda Musical Instrument Works — these and many other firms were represented. These were added to the wealth of information already furnished by Mr. Wurlitzer. Without his assistance this book could not have been written.

Last, but not least, credit goes to my wife, Mary, and to my children. They are the ones who listen to endless hours of "shop talk" with visiting collectors and enthusiasts . . . and who share our home with a collection of orchestrions and other music makers.

In their day coin-operated pianos and orchestrions contributed to the fun of life. Today they are just as enjoyable to those who share the enthusiasm of the hobby. If you enjoy this book even a fraction as much as I enjoyed writing it I will be amply rewarded.

Q. David Bowers

The Hupfeld Helios IV — a representative example of an early 20th century German orchestrion.

Chapter 1

It's a warm evening in early October, 1904. The breeze is coming into San Francisco from the bay tonight bringing with it wraithlike swirls of fog. The prevailing atmosphere in the crowded city streets is gaiety and happiness.

Down at Charlie Weber's saloon, one of the town's brightest night spots, the revelers are packed in shoulder-to-shoulder. Music makes the drinks taste better . . . the time go faster . . . the company seem more convivial. There's no exception here tonight. Music and laughter prevail.

As usual the crowd is a mixed one. In addition to the Saturday night regulars there are a dozen or so sailors from the coastal steamship *Indian Empress* which docked only yesterday, six or eight clerks from nearby stores, and a few dozen other patrons . . . all gathered to have a good time.

You elbow your way up to the bar and order a drink. Just then someone says, "Put a nickel in the piano!"

You turn to the wall opposite the carved mahogany bar. There, under an oil painting of a Gold Rush scene, is the electric piano with *Tonophone* neatly painted on the front in Gothic lettering. Into the slot goes a nickel. There is a whirring sound. Then the piano comes to life! Out come the lively strains of the *Maple Leaf Rag*.

Another nickel, then *Smoky Mokes*. Another nickel, and then a slower tune, *My Old Kentucky Home* . . . and so on, far into the night.

Most saloons are doing well now if they have one coin piano. Charlie Weber knows a good thing when he sees and hears it, so now he has two of them. The jaunty little *Tonophone* with its gay repertoire of ten different tunes stands near the door, its familiar melodies drawing people in by the dozens. Further back in the saloon is an awe-inspiring and magnificent machine, the huge Wurlitzer *PianOrchestra*.

After realizing that his $600.00 *Tonophone* had paid for itself several times over, Weber paid $3,500.00 for the *PianOrchestra,* hoping that it would turn a similar profit. It is his pride and joy . . . and the conversation piece of the neighborhood.

Reaching into your pocket you find a nickel. Into the beckoning slot it goes. Suddenly the *PianOrchestra* becomes a living thing.

Near the top, over ten feet up from the floor, a large jeweled bulb begins to rotate, throwing sparkling and brilliantly colored rays of light from the many facets of the circular mirror behind it. From within the huge ornately-carved cabinet a mechanical orchestra composed of a dozen different instruments strikes up the racy march tempo of *Midnight Fire Alarm*. First the piano, then the drums, chimes, flutes, piccolos, saxophones and a host of other instruments join in harmony. All eyes in the saloon turn to the illuminated machine with its dazzling oriental splendor. Charlie Weber's business never had it so good!

Just a few short miles away at the seaside Cliff House the general manager, J.M. Wilkins, notes with amazement that his two electric coin pianos, costing him $650.00 each, have paid for themselves nickel-by-nickel in just a few months!

In 1904 the story was much the same in other places. In New York, St. Louis, Chicago, New Orleans, everywhere — America was discovering the charm and thrill of mechanical music. The latest in ragtime hit tunes, marches and waltzes all came to life with the drop of a nickel in the coin slot.

By 1904 the music machines which delighted the patrons of public places were fairly well developed. To trace the beginnings of automatic musical instruments we turn the clock back to several centuries earlier, in Europe.

The Renaissance brought with it an interest in mechanical things. In the years from about 1500 to 1700 a variety of automata were produced. Mechanical birds which chirped simple tunes, dancing musical dolls which moved in rhythm to a melody, even life-size figures which mechanically uttered simple sentences — the manufacture of all of these was attempted, some with failure but others with a surprising degree of success. Most of these devices were one-of-a-kind and were made for royalty or others who could afford them. In the sixteenth century mechanical dolls which fought battles to the accompaniment of mechanical trumpets and drums amused Charles V.

The first mechanical music makers produced on a quantity basis were simple music boxes playing a short tune. First built in the 18th century, these boxes were made by watchmakers and other ar-

1

ORCHESTRION,

WITH TWELVE

BARRELS

PREPARED FOR

SETTING.

BARRELS NOW READY.

No. 1.

CONCERTO

BY

KALLIWODA.

No. 2.

OVERTURE

TO

EGMONT,

AND FINALE TO

FIDELIO

BY

BEETHOVEN.

No 3.

OVERTURE TO

WM. TELL

BY

ROSSINI.

IMHOF & MUKLE,

GERMAN ORGAN BUILDERS,

PIANOFORTE MANUFACTURERS,

Music Publishers and Importers,

EUTERPEON ROOMS,

547, OXFORD STREET,

LONDON, W.C.

SELF-ACTING INSTRUMENTS have been constructed for centuries past, but have always borne the impression of the general knowledge of mechanism and music of the time being. Instead of simplicity of action, the most complicated and awkward designs were used, and therefore, would have better been termed motionless, instead of self-acting Instruments; but self-acting Instruments are as sure to act as perfectly as other machines, if properly constructed on scientific principles, which is proved by the great successes we have achieved in our Instruments, and particularly in our ORCHESTRION and all our Instruments of later years, which are more durable than any Pianoforte or Church Organ, even in tropical climates, which we can prove by testimonials.

The ORCHESTRION, constructed for the INTERNATIONAL EXHIBITION of 1862, contains the most perfect scale to produce varieties of tone and orchestral effects. It is capable of giving expression to the music played, with greater ease and precision, than any other Instrument ever made. All the music is arranged by Messrs. I. & M. themselves: the quantity of machinery used is less than one-half the amount used in other Instruments of even smaller size; and instead of winding up in five or six places, as in other large self acting instruments, this has only two windings—both on the same side of the Instrument—and it winds so easily that a child can work it, which is another important success; nevertheless, there is an abundant supply of wind. The pipes are so placed that the whole can be tuned from the sides, without removing a single pipe, and are not liable to get out of tune, as they all have free speaking room. The barrels can be conveniently removed in or out from the front, which is an important saving of the additional space required for Instruments of other manufacturers. The barrels are marked in a seperate machine, independent of the ORCHESTRION, and these barrels can be used in all other Instruments of the same size. An additional time regulator is attached to the main machinery, which obtains the "rallentando" and "accellerando," so necessary in music, and removes all the mechanical stiffness.

Should the frame-work stand uneven, or give way; the key frames are so connected with the machinery that they will follow in their proper places, and thus insure proper playing at all times. This supersedes the old mistaken principle of building all in a supposed perpetual way. There are no levers attached to the bellows, because such levers are always liable to cause clicking and noise, and also requires continual oiling. The mechanism of the ORCHESTRION will be found to work without the slightest noise, and is warranted to remain so.

Johns & Son Printers, 7, Great St. Andrew Street, Bloomsbury, London, W.C.

Early Imhof & Mukle advertisement for a cylinder-operated orchestrion.

tisans who encased the mechanical works in snuff boxes and other small containers. The tinkly music which issued forth was produced by a series of pins protruding from a small cylinder. When the cylinder was turned slowly the pins would strike the prongs of a musical comb in a specific sequence, thus producing the melody.

By the early 1800's larger machines utilizing cylinders made of wood were developed. These were essentially mechanical pipe organs. The pipes played when small levers were actuated by the cylinder pins.

The next evolutionary step was the addition of drums and various other percussion instruments in imitation of a small orchestra or band. These early *orchestrions* (as they later came to be known) were the playthings of kings and queens at the beginning of the 19th century. Perhaps the most famous of the early orchestrions was the *Panharmonicon* built by Johann Maelzel about 1812. The composer Ludwig Von Beethoven was so enamored of the *Panharmonicon* that he wrote a special composition, *Wellington's Victory,* especially for it. This crashing symphony commemorating Wellington's 1813 defeat of Napoleon utilized the drums, pipes and other orchestral effects to good advantage. Maelzel was somewhat of a showman and later, during the 1820's and 1830's, toured America with a traveling exhibit of automata including a mechanical chess player (later proved to be a fraud...a human was concealed within) and a mechanical trumpet player.

The *Panharmonicon* lived on. Until its untimely demise during a World War II conflagration it reposed in the Industrial Museum in Stuttgart, Germany.

During the early decades of the 19th century mechanical organs and orchestrions became very popular. The business of making them was centered in Germany. There were many engaged in the trade, and it became quite competitive.

In 1862 Imhof & Mukle, a leading German organ and pianoforte manufacturer with distribution outlets throughout Europe, was advertising that its new orchestrion was:

"...more durable than any pianoforte or church organ, even in tropical climates, which we can prove by testimonials. The orchestrion constructed for the International Exhibition of 1862 contains the most perfect scale to produce varieties of tone and orchestral effects. It is capable of giving expression to the music played, with greater ease and precision than any other instrument ever made... It winds so easily that a child can work it... The mechanism of the orchestrion will be found to work without the slightest noise, and is warranted to remain so."

This early Imhof & Mukle advertisement further noted that a repertoire of twelve different cylinders was available, including one pinned with Rossini's familiar *William Tell Overture.*

Showroom of Ludwig Hupfeld, A.G. of Leipzig, Germany. Note the six large orchestrions against the wall on the right side. The windmill on the front of the machine in the foreground was mechanical and revolved as the music played.

During the following years great progress was made with the refinement of these machines. Beginning in 1887 pinned cylinders started to give way to perforated paper rolls. Cylinders were expensive, often costing $50.00 to $100.00 or more each, and were large and unwieldy. By contrast, perforated paper rolls playing the same musical arrangement cost just a few dollars each and could be stored easily in a small space. To be sure, the pumps, bellows and other components which were pneumatically operated when air passed through the roll perforations were more complicated than the simple levers used by the cylinder machines, but the low cost and convenience of paper rolls more than compensated for the difference.

Other improvements were developed and widely copied by all of the various manufacturers. By means of opening and closing shutters and varying air pressure the orchestrions could be made to play either loudly or softly, with expression, thus more closely imitating a human orchestra. From a visual standpoint the appeal of the machines was enhanced by elaborate carvings, gargoyles, etc. to blend with even the most ornate Victorian sur-

The "Pepita" was one of several dozen different popular Hupfeld orchestrion styles. Like most other firms Hupfeld advised its customers that special case designs could be made to order for a nominal extra charge. A circa 1913 Hupfeld catalogue priced orchestrions from about $1000.00 to $12,000.00 f.o.b. Leipzig. It was noted that even larger orchestrions could be made on special order!

This photograph taken in the Hupfeld factory about 1910 shows many orchestrions in various stages of construction. As was the case with most large European and American orchestrions Hupfeld machines had the piano in the bottom section of the case toward the back so that it could be removed easily for tuning. Toward the front of the bottom were the various pressure and vacuum pumps and reservoirs. The top part of each machine usually contained the pipes, drums, xylophone and other instruments.

roundings. As if that were not enough, moving effects such as revolving windmills, cascading waterfalls and dancing waves were developed.

Although there were many engaged in the business of orchestrion and mechanical piano building during this time the German houses of Ludwig Hupfeld of Leipzig and M. Welte & Sons of Freiburg dominated the scene. Both firms were well diversified in the field and each had an extensive line of automatic musical products.

Among Hupfeld's best sellers were the *Dea, Solophonola, Triphonola* and *Animatic* pianos. These were widely marketed throughout continental Europe and England and, to a smaller extent, in America. Many of these pianos were of the *reproducing* variety. They not only played the melody but reproduced the exact nuances of expression, attack and style used by the original recording artist who was usually a famous pianist. Reproducing pianos found their way mainly into the homes and salons of the wealthy.

On the other end of the scale were the Hupfeld orchestrions. In the field of orchestrions Hupfeld was second to none . . . the machines were simply breathtaking. Some were so large as almost to defy description. The huge Hupfeld *Helios* and *Pan-Orchestrion* styles were so large that they resembled small buildings more than musical instruments! Most gigantic of all was the *Helios V* which measured *fifteen feet high* and *twenty feet wide*. Within its roomy interior were housed approximately fifteen hundred pipes, a xylophone, glockenspiel, five drums, triangle, tambourine, castanets and other effects . . . enough to represent an orchestra of one hundred and twenty men!

Most of the Hupfeld orchestrions were of a more modest scale and provided music for German beer halls and roller rinks. Some of the later models featured a glass-enclosed (visible for all to see) accordion as part of the instrumentation.

One Hupfeld optional "extra" available on its orchestrions was a complex double ferris wheel type of roll changing device which permitted up to one hundred and forty tunes to be played without interruption or repetition! Although other manufacturers developed roll-changing mechanisms none ever surpassed the Hupfeld double changer.

More of a novelty than anything else was the Hupfeld *Phonoliszt-Violina.* This machine imitated a human violinist by playing three or six (depending on the model) real violins by means of a mechanical bow and pneumatically-operated levers. The making of an automatic violin player represented an outstanding feat. Only a handful of firms over the years ever succeeded in perfecting one, although many tried.

The Hupfeld double roll-changer permitted up to one hundred and forty tunes to be played without interruption or repetition. When the roll on one side ended and started to rewind the next roll in line on the other side would begin playing. Other types of roll-changing mechanisms did not provide for continuous music but had periodic moments of silence when the roll rewound.

Helios in einem Restaurant der französischen Schweiz.

This young lady demonstrates the ease of changing a roll to restaurant patrons. The dog appears bored and diffidently looks in the opposite direction.

Helios in einer Rollschuhbahn in Le Havre.

This LeHavre roller-skating rink featured the latest in skating music provided by a Hupfeld Helios orchestrion. The machine shown is the mammoth Helios IV.

Hupfeld Riesen-Orchestrion Helios V.

Monster-Orchestrion Helios V.   Orchestrion géant Helios V.

Modell geschützt.

Höhe: 4,50 m, Länge: 6 m, Tiefe: 2,50. — Height: 14'9", width: 19'9", depth: 8'2". — Hauteur: 4,50 m, largeur: 6 m, profondeur: 2,50 m.

Artistic walnut case; also in Oak or Mahogany, or other style to order.

This gigantic piece of work is the largest orchestrion ever constructed. Its 49 registers embrace about 1500 pipes representing all the instruments of a military and concert band of about 100 to 120 Performers. The effects of the music are stupendous, reproducing all the charms of an orchestra, full of harmonies and tone-shadings. Alternately the leading melodies change with the secondary ones and the combined play of all the instruments is of such extraordinary and surprising evenness and exactness, only heard in a first class and well-conducted Orchestra. Owing to the all-round excellency of the instrumentation and especially the rhythmical accuracy and splendid artistic arrangement of the music rolls, this Orchestrion is equally well adapted for both Concert and Dance music.

The position of the registers is so arranged that all parts of the pipes are easily accessible for the purpose of tuning &c.

The 49 registers consist of 7 for bass, 9 for accompaniment, 22 for melody, and 11 for solo, and secondary parts.

In addition a complete outfit of drums, properly tuned &c. has been provided, including 1 large drum, 2 kettle drums, 2 military drums, cymbals, triangle, tambourine, castanets and chiming bells.

The different registers can be switched on or off and the force of the music so reduced so as to correspond with an orchestra of 30 to 50 Performers.

The huge Helios V was appropriately named the "Monster Orchestrion." Although several different manufacturers each claimed that their largest orchestrion was the "world's largest" it is doubtful if any regular orchestrion model was larger than this Hupfeld Helios V. Containing about 1500 pipes it represented a band of up to 120 performers!

Helios in einem Etablissement Cairos.

Helios in einem Leipziger Restaurant.

Helios in einem Ausflugsort bei Wiesbaden.

The above illustrations taken from a circa 1913 sales catalog show various Hupfeld orchestrions "on location." One cannot help but wonder what kind of activities were carried on in the Cairo "establishment" shown in the top picture.

In the United States Hupfeld products were sold by the E. Boecker Organ and Orchestrion Company of New York City, a firm which also handled machines made by Frati, Imhof & Mukle and other German manufacturers.

In 1849 (or in 1848; accounts differ) Michael Welte exhibited a mechanical orchestra which had taken him three years to build. From this beginning, and a magnificent beginning it was — the machine was nearly twenty feet high and contained eleven hundred pipes plus an array of orchestra instruments — the Welte firm went on to the ultimate heights of the mechanical music business. Their products became known in every corner of the world. The Khedive of Egypt had a Welte orchestrion, as did the Sultan of Turkey. From Adelaide to Zelienople, Welte was a familiar name.

Throughout the "age of orchestrions" which lasted approximately from 1850 to 1930 the chief claim of these machines was their similarity to human orchestras. Countless testimonials to the imitative ability of orchestrions were obtained. An early Welte admirer was composer V. Lachner who wrote (in 1849):

"It is not merely mechanical performance, without life or soul, that reaches the ear of the hearer; no, he fancies that he is listening to the work of living human forces, conscious of their artistic aim."

This theme was later expanded, echoed and re-echoed many times by others in the trade. The Capitol Piano and Organ Company of New York wrote in its advertisements seventy years later, around 1920, that the only way to appreciate the Capitol coin-operated *Symphony Orchestra* orchestrion was to... "Imagine a human orchestra of twelve or fifteen pieces playing in perfect harmony under a skilled director and you get a fair conception of this music... People will flock to hear this wonderful orchestra."

Concerning one of its large orchestrions the Rudolph Wurlitzer Company wrote (circa 1915):

"The Wurlitzer PianOrchestra is so nearly a 'human' as to defy detection. There is nothing of the mechanical in its playing. Seated in another room, and not knowing of the existence of this instrument, you would never question but that this is a real flesh and blood organization of ten trained musicians..."

Michael Welte, later to become the firm of M. Welte & Sons, prospered. In 1865 Emil Welte, eldest son of Michael, started a branch in New York City to tap the lucrative American market. In the following decades Welte orchestrions found their way into the homes of the wealthy. One well-to-do Pittsburgh, Pennsylvania gentleman had a large Welte

THE HOUSE OF MICHAEL WELTE

IT was in the year of 1827 that a bright, ambitious young man, reared in the house of his uncle, a scholarly Catholic priest, came to Joseph Blessing at Unterkirnach, a small place in the Black Forest, famous at that time for his musical clocks, to become his apprentice.   Through five years the young mechanic patiently worked at his bench, learning every detail of the intricate mechanism of those clocks, every particle of which had to be made by hand, and drawing and inventing new improvements during his few spare hours in the evening and night.   Then he bade his master farewell, and in a tiny little workshop of his own at Voehrenbach, far from the main roads of commerce, he started out for himself.   Soon his name became known through the accuracy of his work and the startling improvements he had made.   Orders came from all parts of Europe, though he employed no salesmen, but the quality of his instruments was their best advertisement.   The workshop had long been enlarged and grew from year to year.   The clock attachment had become of but secondary importance, and gradually, as the musical value of the instruments was enhanced by new inventions and improvements, disappeared entirely.

In 1849 Michael Welte exhibited for the first time one of his new instruments, on which he had worked patiently for three years, and which public opinion termed "orchestrion," because it successfully imitated a many-voiced orchestra of artists in Karlsruhe.   It was a wonder of mechanical perfection, containing eleven hundred pipes that were brought to playing by thousands of small pins, representing the harmonies and melodies of musical compositions thus "written" on three large wooden cylinders, that moved with a startling precision as had been thought impossible before.

The fame of the new invention drew people from near and far; the Grand Duke of Baden himself came to hear and see it, and then, proud of this achievement of his country's industry, presented the inventor with an album, in which he wrote the following tribute:

> I share with all those who are enjoying your instrument in their admiration of your work, while, furthermore, I am particularly gratified at having an opportunity, my dear Mr. Welte, to express to you my satisfaction that it was a citizen of Baden whose artistic instinct and perseverance succeeded in accomplishing something so exquisite and beautiful.
>
> Karlsruhe, April 30th, 1849.   LEOPOLD, Grand Duke of Baden.

Vincent Lachner, the famous composer, also came to hear the new orchestrion, which in the meantime had received the highest award of the exposition, a gold medal, and then wrote:

> It is not a merely mechanical performance, without life or soul, that reaches the ear of the hearer; no, he fancies that he is listening to the work of living human forces, conscious of their artistic aim.
>
>   V. LACHNER, Director of the Court Orchestra.

News of the instrument had traveled in the meantime through all Europe, and from Frankfurt, where, in the Church of St. Paul, the North German "Bundestag," a representative body of most German States, held its sessions, the request came to show the new invention before it was delivered to its purchaser.   The request was complied with, and princes, savants, famous statesmen and dignitaries wrote their appreciation in the album of the Grand Duke of Baden, which still is one of the most cherished treasures of the descendants of Michael Welte.

Other equally perfect instruments followed this first one, and wherever they were shown during the great industrial and world expositions, in London 1862, Paris 1867, Munich 1885, Vienna 1892, Chicago 1893, Paris 1900, St. Louis 1904, Berlin 1906, Mailand 1906, Seattle 1909, Rotterdam 1909, Leipzig 1909, Turin 1911, and other smaller ones, they received without exception always the highest award.

Business was growing rapidly.   In 1865 the oldest son of the founder, Mr. Emil Welte, set out for America to start a branch there and open a new vast field.   His success was instantaneous.   The instruments, still more perfected from year to year, created the same sensation as in the old world, and many of the most prominent men soon belonged to the enthusiastic patrons of the new concern, among them:

Charles Chesebro	General Daniel Butterfield	H. B. Plant	P. T. Barnum
Henry Disston	John H. Starin	Col. Richard Lathers	John Pettit
James P. Kernochan	Jesse Seligman	Thomas Dolan	Samuel Horner

This success in both hemispheres made a further enlargement of the home factory necessary, and as Voehrenbach was too far away from the main road of traffic for the steadily growing important trade of the house the whole establishment was transferred to Freiburg i-B in 1872.

Eight years later Michael Welte closed his eyes forever, but his inventive genius survived in his three sons, Emil, Berthold and Michael.   In 1887 a patent of Mr. Emil Welte startled the world, and this invention, *the use of paper music-rolls in connection with a pneumatic action*, revolutionized the trade, as it did away with the expensive, bulky wooden music cylinders and gave to the instrument an unlimited repertoire.

Protected by patents in all countries, and for years absolutely without any competition, the financial success of the new idea, which now is imitated in every piano player, organ and orchestrion all over the world, was splendid,

"The House of Michael Welte" is the title of this short history printed in one of that firm's sales catalogues.

and paved the way to the greatest achievement of the house of M. Welte & Soehne, the invention of the Welte-Mignon by Edwin Welte, the grandson of the founder, and Karl Bockisch, his brother-in-law.

The phonograph already had made it possible to preserve the sound of the voice and the playing of instruments, but only the former in a successful way, while the tone quality and resonance especially of the piano was entirely lost in reproduction, on account of the structural differences. The Welte-Mignon, however, reproduces the playing of the great pianists of our day on their very instruments in absolute photographic likeness.

Shade, accentuation, expression, all the nuances, even the most subtle, all the charm of personality and force of mentality; in fact, everything that characterizes the individuality of the artist is faithfully and literally produced.

When the Welte-Mignon appeared first on the European market, in 1906, it created a sensation, and all great pianists, composers and critics united in a chorus of enthusiasm, for the Welte-Mignon meant the fulfillment of their dreams.

The incomparable "WELTE-MIGNON" Art Piano has opened an eventful future before the musical world. Henceforth the piano player will be on a level with the productive artist in regard to the imperishability of his work, since he will live for all time in his work. What a loss it means to us not to have had "THE WELTE-MIGNON" long ago! But what a blessing will it prove to future generations!
JOSEF HOFMANN.

The enthusiasm of Josef Hofmann has filled every great pianist that stood, as Gustav Mahler said, "marvelling and admiring" before our instrument.

I should not have thought it possible. "THE WELTE-MIGNON" is without doubt the most remarkable musical invention of our age,

writes Walter Damrosch, and Richard Strauss adds: "It is the only one among all similar mechanical devices which may lay claim to artistic importance."

It is unnecessary here to add the other glowing tributes of men like Tolstoi, Grieg, Paderewski, Busoni, d'Albert, Leschetitsky, Reisenauer, De Pachmann, Mottl, Humperdinck, Pugno, Santi Saens, Alfred Hertz, Teresa Carreno, Bloomfield-Zeisler, Weingartner and numberless others; our patrons know these tributes and know through their acquaintance with our instruments that they are rightly deserved.

It was an artistic and financial success. In order to introduce the new instrument in America a company was formed here in 1906 by the inventors and owners of the patents, the grandsons of Michael Welte, among themselves. A building was leased on Fifth Avenue for exhibition purposes. Concerts were given, and the Welte Studio, within a few months, became the Mecca of all music students and lovers.

Since then, as in Europe, we have been unable to fill the rapidly growing demand, and the building of a factory here in America has become an absolute necessity, not only for the Welte-Mignon, but also for our large line of orchestrions and organs, the development of which has led, *with the application of the Mignon principle*, to the construction of Philharmonic Autograph Organ. This factory is now completed and is located at Poughkeepsie, N. Y., while a large addition has been built to the factories at Freiburg. As with the Welte-Mignon, the field that this new invention has opened cannot be judged to its fullest extent at present. The first exhibition of it at the International Exposition at Turin, during the last year, brought us the highest award, a grand prize, and before it was possible to exhibit it in our New York Studio we had received already several orders.

The organ, "the pope of all instruments," as Berlioz called it on account of its supreme spiritual power in comparison with the orchestra, the emperor, has always been the instrument of the upper 400, whose large palatial residences and country-seats its noble character, its richness and beauty of tone and its impressive lines fitted more adequately than any other instrument. It will be more so with our Philharmonic Autograph Organ, which, as the Mignon reproduces the playing of our great pianists, will bring to present and future the noble messages of the greatest living organists of our time.

The irony of fate has willed that one of the greatest, Felix Alexandre Guilmant, passed away before we were ready. We had made all arrangements with him, who knew our Mignon and was enthusiastic about the possibility of having also his beloved art preserved in the same lifelike form that he admired in our records.

But other great organists live, and we have lost no time to record their art for our instrument before it might be too late, as in this case.

A new phase of modern musical life has been preserved for posterity, a new source also been found for the artistic delight of our present generation; love of music and all things beautiful is spreading rapidly, and in the region of music the Welte-Mignon and the Welte Philharmonic Autograph Organ represent the highest development of art and technic.

No. 9 Concert-Orchestrion

contains all the striking devices, Castanet, Carillon, two small drums.

Height 13 ft. 1 inches.
Width 11 ft. 1 inches.
Depth 5 ft. 3 inches.
Price, including 12 music rolls . . **$ 7000.—**
Extra music rolls, each . . **$ 20.—**

No. 10 Concert-Orchestrion

contains all the striking devices, Castanet, Carillon, two small drums.

Height 14 ft. 5 inches. — Width 16 ft. 8 inches. — Depth 9 ft. 9 inches.
Price, including 12 music rolls . . **$ 10000.—**
Extra music rolls, each . . . . . **$ 20.—**

Larger Orchestrions built to order.

This page from a Welte catalogue numbers the sultans of Turquey and Sumatra among Welte orchestrion owners.

10

Introduction

As the inventors, and for over seventy-five years the manufacturers of various kinds of musical instruments, it has always been the most sincere endeavor of our house to combine in our products the best musical effects with the very best workmanship and material. That these efforts have given great satisfaction is shown by the most flattering testimonials we have received from Reigning Princes and Members of the most eminent musical bodies, as well as from the adjudicators at all Exhibitions since 1849.

Orchestrion in the Castle of Adelina Patti

When we brought on the market in 1887 organs and orchestrions built on the Pneumatic System we were the only manufacturers who were building such instruments with paper music-rolls, and, being protected by patents, remained so for years. Recognizing that we are living at present in an age of progress, we not only endeavor to cope with the increase in trade, but also to meet all the modern demands, and are continually introducing improvements. We now beg to put before you our latest catalogue displaying an assortment of the latest patterns of Orchestrions used for Shows, Merry-Go-Rounds, etc., and trust it will meet with your approval.

The magnificent orchestrion installed in the castle of Adelina Patti-Nicolini must have been one of Welte's most proud accomplishments for it was featured in many Welte advertisements. During a visit to England in 1963 we obtained a "lead" on the Patti orchestrion. A correspondent stated that it had been moved from Craig-y-nos Castle shortly before 1920 and had been relocated at a summer camp near Douglas on the Isle of Man. Our hopes were high as we envisioned finding the orchestrion, shipping it to America and then setting it up to play once again! Finally we learned from the piano tuner who serviced the summer camp that (in his words): "I have tuned the pianos at the holiday camp for over thirty years and am sorry to say that the orchestrion in question is no longer in existence. It met with a series of accidents. First it was flooded. Then it caught fire because of the lighting system. The cost of repairing it was too much. After many meetings the directors of the camp had it broken up. The whole orchestrion was burned in the boiler house furnace shortly after World War II."

At the right: Illustration of Michael Welte's first orchestrion. This picture is evidently miscaptioned with the date "1845." Most other Welte catalogues place the date as 1849.

orchestrion built into his mansion . . . and another somewhat smaller Welte installed on his Great Lakes pleasure boat. In suburban Bridgeport, Connecticut, P.T. Barnum, America's most flamboyant showman, relaxed by listening to Welte music.

Early Welte orchestrions were operated by means of pinned cylinders, as were the machines of its competitors. In 1887 it was Welte who introduced the paper-roll-operated pneumatic system to orchestrion manufacturing, and thereby revolutionized the industry. Previous purchasers of cylinder-operated Welte orchestrions were given the opportunity to have their machines converted to roll operation at no extra charge (thereby creating more customers for Welte rolls). About 90% of the owners of cylinder machines took advantage of this opportunity.

Early Welte orchestrions were divided into two main groups, the *Cottage Orchestrions* and *Concert Orchestrions*. The *Cottage Orchestrions* were the "smaller" machines in the line . . . and ranged *only* up to eight or nine feet high! The *Concert* models were made mostly on special order and were usually of immense proportions. Many of these custom installations were literally "built in" and were not enclosed in cabinets but were in wall recesses separated from main areas by shutters or louvers.

Later Welte catalogues divided Welte orchestrions into other groups, the *Brass Band Orchestrions* and the *Piano Orchestrions*. The former types resembled band organs or carousel organs and were used mainly in amusement parks and skating rinks. The *Piano Orchestrions* included many models with

The large and first orchestrion
Built by
MICHAEL WELTE IN 1845
from which the name Orchestrion
was derived

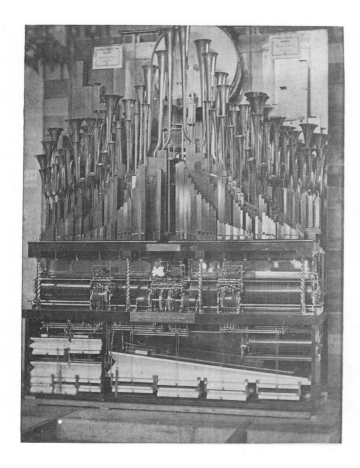

Grand Hotel, Trinidad, Colo.

William Kramer's Sons' Atlantic Garden, Bowery, N. Y. City
Largest Orchestrion ever built, taking the grand prize at the Chicago World's Fair

The above photograph is of an early Welte orchestrion begun in 1852 and completed in 1857. In later years the Welte firm reacquired it from the original owners and displayed it at their salon in Freiburg, Germany. It was totally destroyed during World War II. Dick Simonton of North Hollywood, California, who furnished the photograph, explored the ruins of the bombed-out Welte factory after the war. He found parts of this orchestrion in the rubble. Mr. Simonton was a close friend of the Welte family in later years and furnished us with much of the Welte information and illustrations in this book.

American installations of Welte orchestrions. The machine in the Grand Hotel shared its room with a bank of gambling machines and a coin-operated peep show.

Piano Orchestrion
BRISGOVIA BI

Specifications

The instrument contains a first-class overstrung piano with pedal, loud and soft, in accompaniment with pipes representing:

Violin	Bass Horn with Xylophone
Flute	Snare Drum
Cello	Bass Drum
Viola	(imitation Kettle Drum)
Horn	Cymbals and Triangle
Clarinet	
Trumpet	
Bourdon	

Further, a very effective crescendo arrangement, producing a most refined effect of an orchestra of about ten pieces.

Dimensions
Height, 9 ft. 11 in.   Width, 7 ft. 4 in.
Depth, 3 ft. 8 in.

Case in modernized Renaissance, finished in gray oak, with brass ornaments and electric light fixtures. The picture is a German landscape, representing a mountain gorge spanned by a railway bridge, under which is a waterfall. While the instrument is playing the picture is illuminated. The water begins to move, a train crosses the bridge and disappears into the tunnel, and an airship approaches slowly in the air, executes some manuevers, and disappears again. Nothing can be imagined more attractive than this elegant case and wonderful living picture.

Piano Orchestrion
BRISGOVIA C

Specifications—Duplex Player

The instrument contains a first-class overstrung piano with pedal, loud and soft, in accompaniment with pipes representing:

Violin	Contra Bass with Xylophone
Flute	Snare Drum
Cello	Bass Drum
Trumpet	(imitation Kettle Drum)
Piccolo	Cymbals and Triangle
Clarinet	
Bass Horn	
Bassoon	

Further, a very effective crescendo arrangement, producing a most refined effect of an orchestra of about twelve pieces.

Dimensions
Height, 11 ft.   Width, 7 ft. 6 in.
Depth, 4 ft.

Case in modernized Oriental style, of gray stained oak, the grain of the wood filled with white. On either side two bronze statues holding electric lights. In the middle a painting representing an Oriental landscape. A desert with an oasis surrounded by palms. In the distance pyramids and a sphinx. A Bedouin with a camel is resting, while a native woman is carrying water from the neighboring fountain. When the instrument is playing the picture is illuminated, a caravan is seen passing on the horizon, while the sun slowly sets.

Two of the many different styles of Welte Piano Orchestrions.

"THE MULTITONE"

MOTION PICTURE AND CABARET MIDGET ORCHESTRA

OPERATED BY A SINGLE MUSICIAN OR WITH MUSIC ROLL AUTOMATICALLY

THERE has been such a demand of late for a Piano with Mandolin and various DRUM TRAPS suitable for Moving Picture and Cabaret use that we have added three new styles to meet these requirements. In these Instruments the Piano and ALL THE EFFECTS can be PLAYED BY HAND, or played AUTOMATICALLY by means of paper music rolls.

A great number of the Picture Houses throughout the United States use only Piano Player and Drummer, and these musicians are only able to play about one-third of the time the show is on. With our instrumen it is possible to have music all the time. Any ordinary Piano Player can play it, with the drums and all the effects, and follow the pictures equally as well and in as satisfactory a manner as a ten or fifteen-piece Orchestra. It does not require an Expert Organist to play this Instrument, as with most of the other so-called Photo Players or Picture Show Instruments. It is impossible for a Piano Player to play continuously for hours, so that with the music rolls it can be played Automatically part of the Show, and the Piano Player play for the balance of the Show, THUS GIVING A VARIETY OF CONTINUOUS MUSIC THROUGHOUT THE ENTIRE PROGRAM.

M. WELTE & SONS
273 FIFTH AVENUE, NEW YORK

American Factory

At Poughkeepsie, N. Y.

(on the Hudson)

CASE: The case is as fine an example of the artist's design and master cabinet-maker's art as can be found. It is carved with the most original designs with rich decorations of gold and beautiful French art glass panels. DIMENSIONS: Height—5 feet; Width—5 feet 4 inches; Depth— 2 feet 6 inches.

"MULTITONE"

Style TWO

CONTAINS a strictly high-grade Piano built to withstand constant, regular usage. Equipped with rewind music mechanism, with rolls containing either 5, 10, 15 or 20 tunes which re-roll automatically after last selection has been played, although any piece can be repeated by means of pneumatic push buttons provided, which will re-roll the piece to any desired part and another button will start it playing again. A feature not found in any similar instrument. Roll can be changed instantly. Coin 20-point contact magazine slot playing from 1 to 20 times, included, when requested.

ORCHESTRATION: Contains Piano playing Automatically full 88 notes, Automatic Mandolin Attachment, Bass Drum, Kettle Drum, Snare Drum, Triangle, Cymbal, and full scale Xylophone with tremolo effect. Piano and all these Attachments play Automatically and can also be played by the Piano Player as shown by the accompanying picture in which can be seen buttons and pedals for their operation.

Brass Band Orchestrion
WALLHALL

Replacing a military band of about fourteen pieces.

Specifications

1st and 2d Cornet	Oboe
1st and 2d Clarinet	Flute with Xylophone
Trumpet	Snare Drum
Alto	Bass Drum
Trombone	(imitation Kettle Drum)
Contra Bass	Cymbals and Triangle
Bourdon	
Piccolo	

Dimensions

Height, 10 ft. 6 in.   Width, 8 ft. 3 in.
Depth, 4 ft. 7 in.

Case is of Renaissance design of solid, dark oak. The upper middle panel is a hand-painted picture representing a mythological scene of "Hope"; when illuminated depicts a temple on a high eminence throwing a strong searchlight. An iridescent rainbow appears and a rocky falls shows rushing waters. These effects are obtained by means of electric light devices behind the picture.

ADDED ATTACHMENTS

For Styles ONE and TWO

"MULTITONE"

BY means of an Auxiliary KEYBOARD and FOOTBOARD, placed adjacent to the Piano, additional attachments can be played by the Piano Player. The Auxiliary keyboard can be turned aside and the Piano played as it ordinarily would be. The Piano can be played alone, or each of the other Instruments can be played alone, or in combination, as desired.

ATTACHED KEYBOARD PLAYS:

ORCHESTRA BELLS
PARSIFAL BELLS
XYLOPHONE
CATHEDRAL CHIMES

ATTACHED FOOTBOARD PLAYS:

DOOR BELL	CASTANETS	LOCOMOTIVE WHISTLE
TELEPHONE BELL	HORSES' HOOFS	WIND SIREN
FIRE GONG	AUTO HORN	BABY CRY
LOCOMOTIVE BELL	SLEIGH BELLS	CANARY BIRD
TAMBOURINE	CHINESE CYMBAL	LION ROAR
	STEAMBOAT WHISTLE	

Brass Band Orchestrion
WOTAN

Replacing a military band of about twenty pieces.

Specifications

1st and 2d Cornet	Bourdon
1st and 2d Clarinet	Piccolo
Trumpet	Oboe
Alto	Flute with Xylophone
Trombone	Snare Drum
French Horn	Bass Drum
Baritone	(imitation Kettle Drum)
Bass	Cymbals and Triangle
Contra Bass	
Saxophone	

Dimensions

Height, 12 ft. 9 in.   Width, 9 ft. 3 in.
Depth, 4 ft. 10 in.

Case of dark gray-green oak with three illuminated glass scenes, the middle representing the fire scene from the Walküre picturing Siegfried and Brunnhilde. On each side panel are scenes from Switzerland, showing waterfalls. By means of special mechanism the water appears to be rushing continuously.

Above: The Welte "Multitone" was identical in internal appearance and instrumentation to the Coinola X and Empress Electric Y orchestrions. In all probability the Multitone machines were made by the Operators Piano Company of Chicago and marketed by Welte.

Top Right: Welte's American factory at Poughkeepsie, N.Y.

Center Right: Two different Welte Brass Band Orchestrions. Orchestrions of this style did not have pianos and sounded like military band organs. Their recommended use was for fairs, carnivals and merry-go-rounds.

Bottom Right: A large self-contained Welte theatre pipe organ which provided music to accompany silent movies.

An Orchestra and Organ in ONE

THE GREATEST INVENTION FOR INCREASING PICTURE HOUSE RECEIPTS

Playing Automatically, by Means of Paper Rolls, Reproducing all Orchestral Effects, or can be Played by Hand with Keyboard, so as to Accompany a Singer

ELIMINATE EXPERIMENTS

WHEN you purchase a Welte instrument you eliminate experiments. Your value is represented in every detail. Built to endure severe tests. Built to satisfy a discriminating public, and conceded by artists as being musically correct, as is attested by being in the homes of the wealthiest and most representative people in the world.

EIGHTY YEARS OF SUCCESS

A Welte instrument represents eighty years of successful building of Automatic Musical Instruments, backed up by a concern whose product has been sold in practically every nation on the globe, a house whose integrity is beyond question, and whose product has captured first and grand prizes at all world's exhibitions for over fifty years.

MUSIC ROLLS FOR WELTE INSTRUMENTS

The House of Welte cuts the largest repertoire of music rolls of any manufacturer of automatic musical instruments in the world, and their collection of higher grade music, such as the classics, overtures and sacred music is unparalleled. The latest popular Broadway hits are constantly being made.

intricate scenic effects. One model (the Welte Bris-govia BI) portrayed a "German landscape, representing a mountain gorge spanned by a railway bridge, under which is a waterfall. While the instrument is playing the picture is illuminated. The water begins to move, a train crosses a bridge and disappears into the tunnel, and an airship approaches slowly in the air, executes some maneuvers, and disappears again..."

Among the smaller machines manufactured by Welte were the famous *Welte-Mignon* pianos which reproduced faithfully the very soul and expression of leading pianists of the day. When the *Welte-Mignon* was first introduced, right after the turn of the century, it created a sensation. Business was so good that a separate company to manufacture Welte instruments was formed in America by the grandsons of Michael Welte and by principals of the Rudolph Wurlitzer Company (which had a 49% ownership interest plus the right to use Welte expression devices and controls in Wurlitzer coin-operated pianos and orchestrions). A showroom was leased on New York's fashionable Fifth Avenue. Welte's American business, especially the sales of *Welte-Mignon* pianos, was excellent.

World War I essentially ended Welte's American operations. All Welte assets in this country were seized by the Alien Property Custodian and were sold. The American orchestrion market was left to Wurlitzer, Seeburg and a host of new companies. Aeolian's *Duo-Art* and the American Piano Company's *Ampico* captured the lion's share of the reproducing piano sales.

In Germany, the Welte business continued for two more decades. It met its end when the Welte factories at Freiburg were leveled during Allied bombing raids during World War II.

Although Welte and Hupfeld were the dominant forces in the European orchestrion market there was sufficient business that Frati, Philipps, Blessing, Weber, Dienst, Popper and several dozen other manufacturers each made and sold a wide variety of machines.

In America most German-origin pianos and orchestrions imported in the 1880's and 1890's were sold to financiers, industrialists and others for use in their homes. Only a few were sold to business establishments. The omnipresence of razz-a-ma-tazz piano and orchestrion music in public places awaited the beginning of the twentieth century... and the aggressive merchandising of American manufacturers.

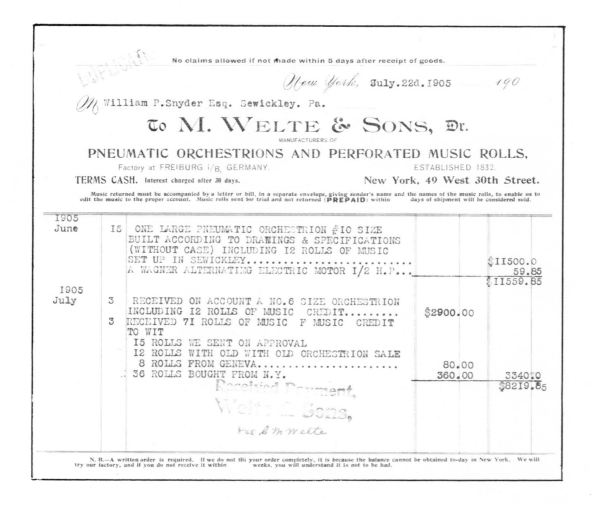

Welte invoice addressed to William P. Snyder of Pittsburgh, Penna. Only the very wealthy could afford luxuries such as orchestrions and reproducing pianos in their homes. Their cost in terms of present-day dollars was staggering.

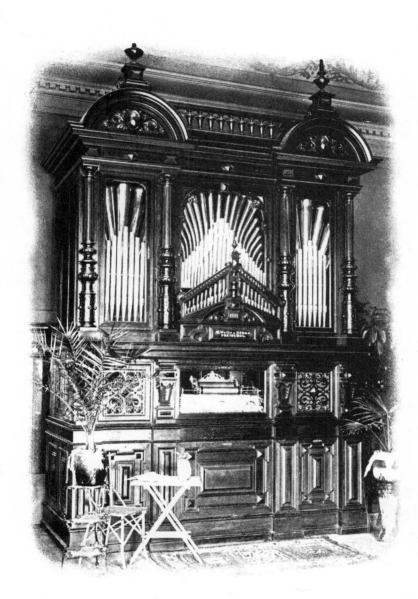

No. 7
Concert-Orchestrion

Contains all the striking devices.

Height 11 ft. —
Width 8 ft. 3 inches. —
Depth 4 ft. 7 inches.

Price, including 12 music rolls . . . $ **4300.**—
Extra music rolls, each . . . . . . $ **10.** —

No. 8
Concert-Orchestrion

Height 12 ft. 10 inches. — Width 10 ft. 1 inches. —
Depth 4 ft. 10 inches.
Price, including 12 music rolls . . $ **5500.**—
Extra music rolls, each . . . . . $ **15.**—

Page from a Welte catalogue circa 1907.

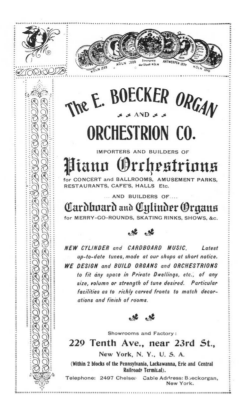

Trompeter von Saeckingen.
Piano Orchestrion.

Height 9 feet.   Width 6,10 feet.   Depth 39 in.
Price, with Motor complete, $2,400.

Walkuere.
Piano Orchestrion.
THE GRANDEST INSTRUMENT EVER PRODUCED

Oak, Walnut or White and Gold.

Height 12,10 feet.   Width 10,10 feet.   Depth 66 in.
Price, with Motor complete, $3,800.

Tell.
Piano Orchestrion.
OAK OR WALNUT.

Height 11,4 feet.   Width 8,9 feet.   Depth 60 in.
Price, with Motor complete. $2,750.

The E. Boecker Organ and Orchestrion Company of New York City imported German machines and sold them in America. Machines made by Imhof & Mukle, Frati, Hupfeld and others were distributed by this firm. Illustrated above are a few interesting German-built machines from an early Boecker catalogue.

In einer deutschen Wirtschaft in Buenos-Ayres geht es lustig zu beim Klange eines Dienst - Orchestrions.

Mühsam werden Dienst's Orchestrions in den steilen Bergen Chiles auf Maultieren transportiert.

Interesting sketches from a Dienst (of Germany) orchestrion catalogue. Dienst Piano Orchestrions could be delivered anywhere ... and they meant ANYWHERE. Note the Dienst Piano Orchestrion being carried over the Chilean Andes by muleback!

Pneumatic Piano-Orchestrion „GLADIATOR" No. 2 driven by electricity and played by means of paper tune-rolls which roll back automatically. Elegant and modern oak-case with rich electric light-effects. „Gladiator" contains a first-class overstrung piano with mandoline, xylophon, orchestra bells, additional instruments, striking piano and forte, as well as ten different pipe-registers. **Recognised equivalent to military band by military band-masters.**

Height . . . . about	307 cm
Width . . . . abdut	363 cm
Depth. . . . . about	158 cm
Gross weight . . . . about	2000 kg
Net weight . . . . . about	1300 kg

Height with gallery . . about	405 cm
Height without gallery about	345 cm
Width . . . . about	400 cm
Depth . . . . about	190 cm
Net weight . . . . about	2700 kg

Symphony Orchestrion „GOLIATH" No. 2. A most beautiful case of refined taste, supplied with solid columns, very tasteful candle-stick holders (fastened on the columns) and containing at the top an electric light-arrangement of striking effect. The centre pictures, (divided into three framed parts) give an exceedingly beautiful impression by its fine striking electric lighting effects. All the various musical instruments combined in the „Goliath" Nr. 2 are arranged chromatically to reproduce the most complicated compositions in the original key and arrangement. The specially patented construction of the windchest produces a most exact repitition, f. i. the deepest Bass repeats just as easy as the highest Treble. The bellows work absolutely noiseless, and the softest instruments are to be heard without any unpleasant noise. The combination of the various instruments in the Orchestrion is as follows: Bass Flute, Salicet Bass, Violon Bass, Vioncello, Cello, Flageolett-Flute, Echo Flute, Muted Strings, Violo, Flageolett, Saxophone. For the dominant melody the following combination-effects may be used: 2 Solo Violins with „Tremolo", Violin I, Reed, Principal, Horn, Clarinet, Piccolo Flute, Oboe, Solohorn, Vienna Flute, Bass Oboe and furthermore: Bass Drum, Side Drum, Kettle Drum, Cymbals, a complete patented instrument of percussion, (to produce the finest piano and forte effects), Castanets, Triangle, Tambourine, Orchestra bells Xylophone (for p. and f.) A combined Piano (Bass and Treble divided), can be used for Solo playing as well, this instrument is necessary for the various instrumentation-effects. The construction is specially arranged, so that the accompaniment-instruments can be changed into the dominant melody, whilst the main Piano accompanies or plays another Theme. The whole construction and the combined Piano afford the reproduction of single Instrumentation Soli with Orchester — or artistic Piano accompaniment, f. i.: Violin, Flute, Trumpet, Piccolo or Xylophon Soli etc. The work contains two independent Swell Organs and an Echo Device. A great number of stops for Swellers, Modulation and Couplers are at disposal, so that incomparable effects can be easily produced! The Musicrolls are arranged artistically by first class Musicians.

Although little is known of the firm today, Poppers of Leipzig was a dominant force in the automatic piano and orchestrion industry in its day. A catalogue issued about 1910 featured several dozen different models . . . including the two mammoth machines illustrated above.

„Fratihymnia"

No. 7.

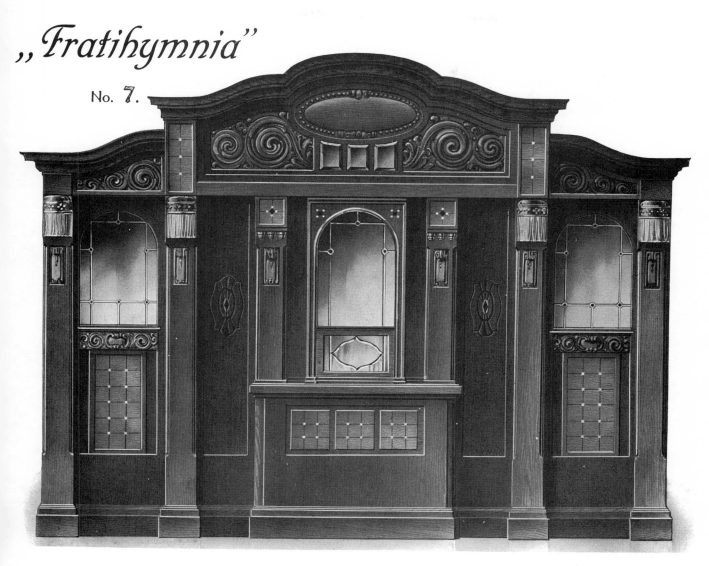

Artistic Playing Orchestrion „Fratihymnia"

No. 7.

In contradistinction to the preceding instrument of the same type, this Fratihymnia 7 contains all instruments of a **complete military band**, with trombones, trumpets, horn, saxophone, tuba, cornet-à-pistons, piccolo, cornets, clarinets, flutes, bassoon, oboe, forte and piano beating big and little drum, with cymbals, kettledrum, castanets, anvil, triangle, chimes, etc. etc.

A tremendous volume of sound is produced by this orchestrion, the demand for a substitute for a military band is excellently met. The playing produces an enthusiastic effect and the percussion is of an excellent precision. Even the largest room is filled with music by this monster-ensemble.

The instrument is adapted like the preceding one for **concert and ball rooms**.

It can be supplied in natural oak, stained in any colour. If desired, the front spaces or squares can be filled with animated pictures or with any other desired equipment, the extra price for which to be specially agreed upon.

Height about 3,15 m	Width about 4,15 m
Depth about 1,30 m	Weight about 1200 Ko.

The Fratihymnia No. 7 was one of the largest orchestrion styles built by Frati, a leading German manufacturer. The description, "monster-ensemble," is at least a different term for an orchestrion. Note that animated features could be supplied at extra cost. The illustrations in most German catalogues, those of Frati included, were intended as suggestions. The purchaser of an orchestrion could have appropriate scenic effects, architectural accoutrements, etc. added to suit his whim or fancy.

Auch in Südamerika sind schon Dienst's Orchestrions aufgestellt.
Obiges Bild zeigt den Transport mittelst Flußdampfers.

A scene from Huckleberry Finn? No, a Dienst Piano Orchestrion being delivered via sidewheel steam-
boat to somewhere in the Amazonian jungle!

Chapter 2

American manufacturing activity in the coin-operated piano field was pioneered by the firm of Roth & Engelhardt (later to operate as F. Engelhardt & Sons, Peerless Piano Player Company and finally, after bankruptcy and re-organization, as the National Electric Piano Company) of St. Johnsville, New York.

Beginning with their small style D in 1898 this firm marketed several dozen different models under the names of *Peerless* and *Engelhardt*. The machines ranged in size from a small cabinet-style piano playing a range of only forty-four notes to large orchestrions consisting of upright pianos with case extensions containing many instruments added on top.

Alfred Dolge, historian of the piano business in America and a close personal friend and business associate of the Engelhardts (Dolge's factory, in nearby Dolgeville, N.Y., provided many raw materials and accessories for the *Peerless* products), wrote in 1913:

MODEL "WISTERIA"
Plays 88 notes. Equipped with set of Pipes (either Violin or Flute), Castanets, Triangle. For full description see Bulletin No. 7.

PEERLESS AUTOMATIC PIANOS HAVE PLAYED THEIR WAY THROUGH ALL PUBLIC PREJUDICES

THERE was a time when a favorite argument against the Automatic Piano was that the individuality of the performer was lost. Some daring and original souls discovered, and with much simplicity and the courage of their convictions, asserted that the individuality of the average performer was a good thing to lose. The truth of this statement came home to many an employer, and a tide set in in favor of the Automatic Piano.

There is nothing more trying nor tiring than to endeavor to dance to uncertain and fluctuating measure, and the faultless time of the Peerless is an inspiration to rhythmic movement, whether it be in the gymnasium or ball room. The demand is for real music correctly rendered and in the creation of the new type depicted above, the purchaser has what he has been looking for all these years.

As an economical and satisfactory substitute for an individual performance for all public amusements, the arguments in its favor are too obvious to require mention. The PEERLESS pays for itself in a short time, and immediately becomes an appreciable profit-compelling asset.

A NICKEL DOES THE TRICK

MADE BY THE

PEERLESS PIANO PLAYER COMPANY

General Offices: 316 South Wabash Avenue, Chicago
Factories: St. Johnsville, N. Y.

Advertisement for the Peerless Wisteria orchestrion. The above text is unusual in that it states that the Peerless DOES NOT attempt to copy the human performer. Most other advertisements took a different tack: the piano or orchestrion was said to be indistinguishable from the human player. Most Peerless machines were made in St. Johnsville, New York, however certain pianos made by the Niagara Musical Instrument Company and certain Electrova machines were also sold under the Peerless label.

The PEERLESS ORCHESTRION

PEERLESS ORCHESTRION
Model Arcadian

IN OAK OR
CIRCASSIAN WALNUT

SPECIFICATIONS

Measurements	HEIGHT	WIDTH	DEPTH
	6 feet	5 feet 4 inches	34 inches

Mechanism Containing the well-known *Peerless* pneumatic player action playing the *entire key-board* of piano—88 notes. Equipped with re-wind music drawer mechanism holding perforated rolls containing fifteen (15) selections. Rolls can be changed instantly. After last selection has been played, it stops, re-winds automatically, and begins with first piece.

    Contains magazine coin slot mechanism, holding upward from one to twenty coins.

Orchestration Full Piano—88 notes. Set of wood pipes, thirty-two in number (either violin or flute, optional with the purchaser). Bass and snare drums, cymbal and triangle. Tympani and crash cymbal effects. Set of castenets. Solo mandolin. All orchestral effects are produced automatically and correctly direct from the perforated roll and true to the composer's interpretation.

Case Fumed Oak or Circassian Walnut. Brass trimmed throughout. Art glass panels (Arcadian scene) with upright standards bearing artistic lamps. Electric lights illuminate interior of instrument when playing.

Music Using rolls containing fifteen (15) selections, which re-roll automatically after last selection has been played, although any piece can be repeated by means of pneumatic push buttons provided, which will re-roll the piece to any desired part and another button will start it playing again. A feature not found on any similar instrument.

    Music rolls for all Peerless instruments made in our own factories from original masters.

    Rolls available for the Model Arcadian Orchestrion are listed in the 20,000 series. See supplementary Music Bulletins.

ORCHESTRION
Style "O"
Model De Luxe

SPECIFICATIONS

Measurements	Height	Width	Depth
	7 feet 7 inches	5 feet 3 inches	34 inches

Mechanism Containing the well-known pneumatic player action playing the *entire key-board* of piano—88 notes. Equipped with re-wind music drawer mechanism holding perforated rolls containing fifteen (15) selections. Rolls can be changed instantly. After last selection has been played, it stops, re-winds automatically, and begins with first piece.

    Contains magazine coin slot mechanism holding upward from one to twenty coins.

Orchestration Full Piano—88 notes, seventy-two wood pipes producing effects of violin, flute and cello. Bass and snare drums, cymbal and triangle. Tympani and crash cymbal effects. Set of castanets. Solo mandolin. All orchestral effects are produced automatically and correctly direct from the perforated roll and true to the composer's interpretation.

Case Fumed oak, wax finish. Brass trimmed throughout. Art glass panels with gold torches bearing flaming globes. Electric lamps illuminate interior of instrument when playing.

Music Using rolls containing fifteen (15) selections, which re-roll automatically after last selection has been played, although any piece can be repeated by means of pneumatic push buttons provided, which will re-roll the piece to any desired part and another button will start it playing again. A feature not found on any similar instrument.

    Music rolls for all instruments made in our own factories from original masters.

    Rolls available for the Model De Luxe Orchestrion are listed in the 20,000 series.

"Among the pioneer makers of coin-operated electrical self-playing pianos, F. Engelhardt and Sons have earned a reputation for their products. With the laudable ambition to out-do one another in creating something new, or to improve the old, the members of this firm have introduced perhaps more novelties in their particular line than any other house. Starting with the simple automatic player having one music roll, they are now building fourteen different models, among them being the *Peerless Orchestrion* with an entire keyboard of eighty-eight notes equipped with a rewind music drawer mechanism holding perforated rolls containing fifteen selections. The instrument is furthermore provided with thirty-two wood pipes to produce either violin or flute effects, bass and snare drums, cymbal and triangle, tympani and crash cymbal effects, sets of castanets and solo mandolin. All of these orchestra effects are produced automatically and correctly directly from the perforated roll, true to the composer's interpretation.

The factories of the concern, located at St. Johnsville, New York, are of the most modern construction, and are in charge of Walter L. Engelhardt, while Alfred D. Engelhardt attends to the business end of the enterprise, under the guidance of their father.

At the great expositions at Buffalo, 1901, St. Louis, 1904, Portland, 1906, Jamestown, 1907, and Seattle, 1909, their player-pianos and orchestrions received invariably the highest award for excellence."

In this book are illustrated several of the larger *Peerless* orchestrion styles. However, the few shown are just a fraction of the total number of different models made. In addition to the multitude of styles made at St. Johnsville a number of coin-operated pianos made by the Niagara Musical Instrument

DID you ever hear of the London tailor who noticed that when a street piano came under his window and played "God Save the Queen" the machines of his operators slowed down to keep time with the music?

It took him just about a minute to size up the situation.

He hired a man by the day to play good, rollicking, *swift* tunes, with the result that the work of his shoproom trebled itself. This was a natural, though unconscious, result, an instinctive compliance with the demand of the musical tempo.

Does your enterprise need a stimulant?

Give it some *Peerless* tonic and watch it brace up. The *Peerless* is a business booster of the Big Bull Moose variety. It will change the entire atmosphere of your establishment and put backbone into the most spineless employee. It will give *you* an optimistic viewpoint that by natural attraction will induce patronage.

The *Peerless* will advertise you. It never gets tired, doesn't belong to the union, works overtime without extra pay, never gets sulky or dopey, has no bad habits, and is always "fit" and ready for business.

The *Peerless* stimulates the appetite, increases the thirst, lightens the feet and the spirits, and loosens the strings of the pocketbook.

It's a coin-coaxer, a money-wheedler, a nickel-winner.

It's the *big thing* for which you have been looking.

Do your requirements call for a single piano or an orchestra?

The *Peerless* supplies either—in fact, two, three, four or five instruments in one.

Try it! Put one in your establishment, bait it with a nickel and watch the people bite. The next nickel and the next and all the rest will come out of your customers' pockets.

Make it easy for them—have the slot connections where they can't help but see them. The suggestion is all that's needed.

Tell us what you need, and we will recommend the right instrument.

Mail communications will have our immediate attention.

THE PEERLESS PIANO PLAYER CO.
F. ENGELHARDT & SONS, Proprietors
ST. JOHNSVILLE, N. Y.
NEW YORK   CHICAGO

Above: Does your enterprise need a stimulant? If so, a Peerless automatic piano fills the bill exactly — according to the above advertisement.

At the left: Peerless Arcadian and DeLuxe orchestrions. Peerless cases and art glass were among the industry's most attractive.

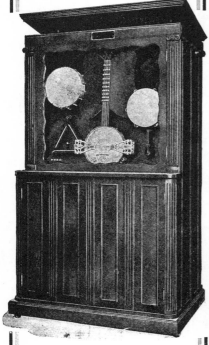
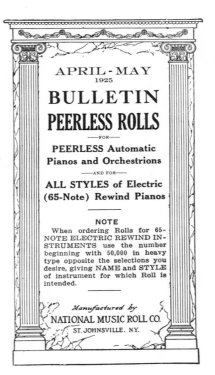
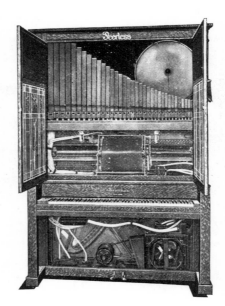

Company of North Tonawanda, N.Y. were sold under the Engelhardt label and were evidently manufactured under contract.

Not withstanding Alfred Dolge's glowing 1913 report, F. Engelhardt & Sons went into bankruptcy several years later. The old Engelhardt factories still stand today in St. Johnsville, on the main line of the New York Central Railroad. There is no trace, not even a weathered sign, to indicate the former glory of these buildings and the part they played in America's musical heritage. The order of things has changed. Modern America's economy has new needs, goals and aspirations. In St. Johnsville

scarcely anyone remembers what was once the town's main industry . . . and the Engelhardt buildings which once hummed with the activities of roll cutting and orchestrion manufacturing are now converted to a shoe factory.

When the Engelhardts entered the coin-operated piano business in 1898 they did not have the field to themselves for very long. Just a year later, in 1899, the Rudolph Wurlitzer Company of Cincinnati marketed the *Tonophone*, a piano operated by a ten-tune pinned cylinder, manufactured under contract by Eugene DeKleist of North Tonawanda, New York.

Violin Rhapsodist

Coin-operated Electric Piano
with Violin Pipes, Xylophone and Mandolin Attachment.
Playable by hand or with Perforated Roll.

Orchestration
Full 88 Note Piano, 37 Violin Pipes of the highest quality that perfectly imitate the Violin Soloist, 25 bar Professional Rosewood Xylophone, and Solo Mandolin effect. Three small levers on the side of keyboard enables you to shut off anyone of the effects that you do not wish to play.

Description
Double veneered, mission oak case, with illuminated art glass panels, two illuminated art lamps and beveled mirror, seven and one-third octaves, overstrung full copper wound bass, three unisons throughout. Full iron frame. Brass flange action, German felt hammers. Finest grade ivory keys, polished ebony sharps.

Equipped with magazine slot that plays one to twenty nickels, and our Patented Re-wind Machine that is considered the best on the market and practically eliminates the many troubles others are still battling with.

This instrument is equipped with the highest grade of motor, in either A. C. or Direct Current. Can also be furnished with ten cent slot if so desired, without extra charge.

Rhapsodist Orchestra

A perfect Orchestra, to be operated by Perforated Roll or by hand. A very desirable Instrument for Moving Picture Theaters and other places of Amusement.

NOTICE

Do not confound these two instruments with the ordinary electrically-operated Instruments.

Remember, that either of these Instruments can be played by hand, producing the full Orchestral effect.

If interested, write at once as the demand is heavy and it may take some little time to fill your order.

Orchestration
Full 88 Note Piano, 37 Violin Pipes that are a perfect imitation of the Violin, 25 bar Professional Rosewood Xylophone, Solo Mandolin, Base Drum, Snare Drum, Crash Cymbal and Triangle. Small levers on the right side of keyboard enables you to cut out any of the instruments that you do not wish.
The entire combination of above Orchestra can be played by hand, or Automatically with Perforated Roll.

Description
Double veneered, mission oak case, three illuminated art glass panels, two illuminated art lamps, seven and one-third octaves, overstrung full copper wound bass, three unisons throughout. Full iron frame. Brass flange action, German felt hammers. Finest grade ivory keys, polished ebony sharps.
This instrument is equipped with Automatic Mandolin Attachment.
Our patented Re-wind Machine makes it an automatic wonder. Supplied with either A. C. or D. C. Motor. When playing, automatically the current is turned off and on with an electric switch, we can however supply it with Magazine Slot Attachment, if so desired, without extra charge.

Above: Two machines from the "Rhapsodist" line manufactured by the Player Piano Manufacturing Company which variously listed its address as Cincinnati, Ohio and Covington, Kentucky. This firm also sold a large Rhapsodist theatre instrument somewhat similar in appearance to the self-contained Welte pipe organ shown at the bottom of page 13. Evidently only a few Rhapsodist pianos and orchestrions were sold for they are virtually unknown in collections today.

At the left: Ephemera relating to Peerless products taken from various advertisements from about 1918 to 1925. The Engelhardt Banjorchestra was also sold as the Connorized Banjorchestra. The unearthing of the Engelhardt and Connorized Banjorchestra advertisements was one of the major finds made during the compilation of material for this book. Previously the Banjorchestra was unknown to modern day mechanical music aficionados.

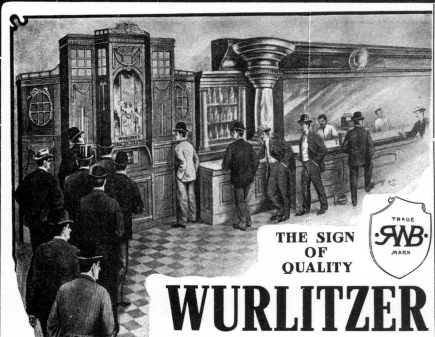

Wurlitzer advertisement. The Billboard, March 21, 1908.

Compliments of the

Niagara Musical Instrument Mfg. Co.
NORTH TONAWANDA, N. Y.

DINNER MENU

SERVED WITH MUSIC

DINNER

5:30 to 8:30

BLUE POINTS		LITTLE NECKS
CELERY	SALTED ALMONDS	OLIVES

CONSOMME PRINCESSE · · · · CREAM OF CORN

BROILED SHAD ROE WITH BACON
BAKED STUFFED BLUEFISH

CHICKEN PATTI, A LA REINE · · · · BANANA FRITTERS
ORANGE SHERBERT

ROAST TURKEY-CRANBERRY SAUCE
LARDED TENDERLOIN OF BEEF · · · ROAST SIRLOIN OF BEEF

GRILLED SWEET POTATOES · · · · BOILED POTATOES
FRENCH PEAS · · · · STRING BEANS

GRAPE FRUIT SALAD

CHOCOLATE ECLAIRS · · · · HOT MINCE PIE
PISTACHIO ICE CREAM · · · · FRENCH PASTRY
ASSORTED CAKES

ROQUEFORT · · · CAMEMBERT · · · AMERICAN
TOASTED CRACKERS

DEMI-TASSE

MUSICAL PROGRAM

5:30—*Overture-Tannhauser* - - - - *Wagner*

5:45—*Put on Your Old Grey Bonnet* - · - - *Wenrich*

6:00—*By the Light of the Silvery Moon* - - *Edwards*

6:15—*The Palms* - - - - - - *Leybach*

6:30—*I've Got Rings on My Fingers* - - - *Scott*

6:45—*By the Blue Lagoon* - - - - *Kern*

7:00—*The Anvil Chorus* - - - - *Verdi*

7:15—*Lady Love* - - - - - - *Gumble*

7:30—*Military Mary Ann* - - - - *Hirsch*

7:45—*Dixie* - - - - - - *O'Donnell*

8:00—*Cubanola Glide* - - - - *Von Tilzer*

8:15—*Grand American Fantasie* - - - - *Bendix*

THE ABOVE PROGRAM RENDERED ON THE
EN-SYMPHONIE

The EnSymphonie manufactured circa 1911 by the Niagara Musical Instrument Company was essentially a pipe organ which played from regular 65-note home player piano rolls. The above menu was part of a promotional kit for the EnSymphonie. The EnSymphonie was available in two basic models; with keyboard and without.

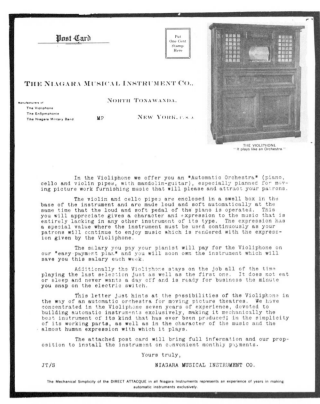

THE NIAGARA MUSICAL INSTRUMENT CO.,

NORTH TONAWANDA.

Manufacturers of
The Violiphone
The EnSymphone
The Niagara Military Band   NP   NEW YORK, U.S.A.

THE VIOLIPHONE
"It plays like an Orchestra."

In the Violiphone we offer you an "Automatic Orchestra" (piano, cello and violin pipes, with mandolin-guitar), especially planned for moving picture work furnishing music that will please and attract your patrons.

The violin and cello pipes are enclosed in a swell box in the base of the instrument and are made loud and soft automatically at the same time that the loud and soft pedal of the piano is operated. This you will appreciate gives a character and expression to the music that is entirely lacking in any other instrument of its type. The expression has a special value where the instrument must be used continuously as your patrons will continue to enjoy music which is rendered with the expression given by the Violiphone.

The salary you pay your pianist will pay for the Violiphone on our "easy payment plan" and you will soon own the instrument which will save you this salary each week.

Additionally the Violiphone stays on the job all of the time playing the last selection just as well as the first one. It does not eat or sleep and never wants a day off and is ready for business the minute you snap on the electric switch.

This letter just hints at the possibilities of the Violiphone in the way of an automatic orchestra for moving picture theatres. We have concentrated in the Violiphone seven years of experience, devoted to building automatic instruments exclusively, making it mechanically the best instrument of its kind that has ever been produced; in the simplicity of its working parts, as well as in the character of the music and the almost human expression with which it plays.

The attached post card will bring full information and our proposition to install the instrument on convenient monthly payments.

Yours truly,

JT/S   NIAGARA MUSICAL INSTRUMENT CO.

The Mechanical Simplicity of the DIRECT ATTACQUE in all Niagara Instruments represents an experience of years in making automatic instruments exclusively.

The Violiphone used a ten-tune style "A" roll . . . the same standard coin piano roll used by several dozen other manufacturers.

The beginning years of the twentieth century were good ones for the coin-operated music business. From an obscure beginning in a Sedalia, Missouri cafe a new style of music, ragtime, grew until it became America's favorite. *The Buffalo Rag, Original Rags, Sunflower Slow Drag,* the *Brownie's Rag* . . . all became familiar tunes.

At the same time the new marches of John Philip Sousa and George M. Cohan were being hummed and whistled everywhere.

What better way was there to hear all of this music and learn the latest hit tunes than by listening to a honky-tonk coin piano?

Saloons, candy stores, billiard parlors and, yes, even brothels — none were quite complete without a coin piano near the door to lure in the customers.

The market for coin pianos and orchestrions widened with the advent of motion pictures. To attract paying customers to the theatre box office there was no substitute for having an orchestrion playing nearby. Inside the theatres a new breed of automatic musical instrument, the photoplayer, kept up the musical pace.

Nearly every manufacturer of coin-operated pianos in business in the 1905 to 1925 years also had a line of photoplayers. These photoplayers, marketed

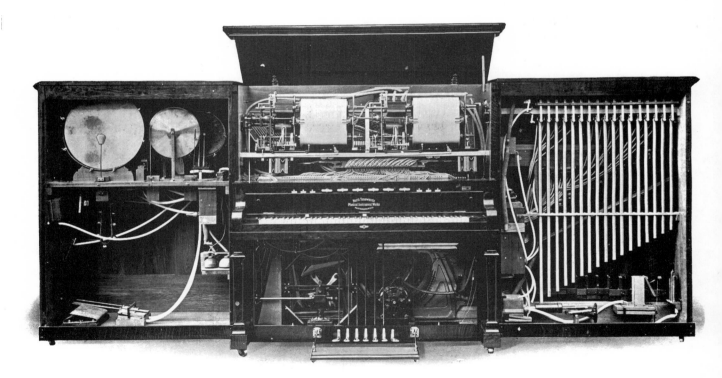

Interior of the "Ideal" Moving Picture Orchestra
Style "G"

Style G Moving Picture Orchestra (photoplayer) manufactured by the North Tonawanda Musical Instrument Works. From about 1900 to 1930 North Tonawanda, New York and Chicago, Illinois were the manufacturing centers of the coin piano, orchestrion and photoplayer industry. More firms were located in those two cities than in any others.

under such names as *Photo-Orchestra* (Engelhardt), *Pipe-Organ Orchestra* (Seeburg), *Fotoplayer* (American Photo Player Company) and *One Man Orchestra* (Wurlitzer), usually consisted of a piano, several ranks of pipes plus assorted traps and percussion instruments housed in side chests. The most interesting features of these machines were their sound-effects gadgets. For example, the *Fotoplayer Style 50* (an immense machine which measured twenty-one feet wide!) had such effects as: fire gong, auto horn, automobile exhaust, Chinese cymbal, bird whistle, cowbell, wind, waves, telegraph key, crackling flames and horse's hooves...plus other miscellaneous appropriate noises.

By pulling handles, pushing buttons and stepping on footpedals the photoplayer operator could orchestrate the fast-changing movie scenes by providing march music, romantic interludes, funeral dirges...or whatever the flickering screen demanded.

While coin-operated pianos and photoplayers were different types of machines and filled different musical needs, they were inalienably intertwined. Usually the same firm made both types of machines using basically the same parts, the same mechanical systems and often the same type of paper rolls. For that reason we describe and illustrate on these pages a few of the many dozens of different photoplayers of the early years of the silent screen.

Seeburg Pipe-Organ Orchestra, Style "V"

As the instrumentation shows, this is an exceptionally "complete" combination of a pipe organ and orchestra. As a pipe organ it gives results as satisfactory as an exclusive organ costing more money than this complete instrument. In addition to the full organ, it supplies the orchestral tones, including a magnificent set of **twenty chimes,** and all the necessary sound effects. The piano is equal in tone to the average grand. When played by the music rolls—either 88-note piano or orchestrated—the art of world-famous musicians is perfectly reproduced. The organ can be coupled to the piano keyboard so that both instruments may be played from the one keyboard. By an ingenious arrangement the music can be made to exactly fit the picture. Because any of the several selections can be played as wanted, the roll can be run forward or back to a sentimental or rag selection to conform with the action of the picture.

The **crescendo** pedal in this instrument is of wonderful advantage to the musician. By its use all of the different sets of pipes (full organ) can be thrown on instantly, or each set of pipes individually. The different tone combinations can be thrown on by means of stops, and by the crescendo pedal as described. Equipped with the Seeburg **SOLO**-effect features and hand arranged rolls containing ten selections.

Height 5 feet 2½ inches. Width 3 feet 7½ inches. Length 13 feet 1 inch.
Weight boxed for shipment about 2000 pounds.

INSTRUMENTATION, "PO"	
Organ-Piano	Castanets
Violin	Triangle
Flute	Tom Tom Effect
'Cello	Bird Whistle
Bass Melodia 8'	Wind Siren
Vox Humana 8'	Telephone Bell
Tremolo	Door Bell
Bass Drum	Fire Gong
Snare Drum	Horse Trot
Cymbal	Tympani Effect
Octave Coupler	Organ Swell
Crescendo Pedal	Tambourine
Piano 88 Notes	

An almost unlimited variety of effects may be obtained from key-board, such as: Cuckoo, Scotch Bag-pipe Effect, etc.

Xylophone   Mandolin

Successfully Solves the Theatre Music Problem

This Seeburg Pipe-Organ Orchestra, Style V, from a Seeburg booklet entitled "The Soul of the Film," was one of several dozen different Seeburg photoplayer styles. This particular style featured two roll mechanisms...a not uncommon arrangement which permitted continuous playing. The top roll was a regular 88-note home player piano roll such as could be purchased in any music store. The bottom roll was a special roll... a special Seeburg style "H" (also known as "SSS") or a style "MSR" roll, depending upon the particular model. The large number of foot pedals operated the various sound effects...one pedal for each effect such as the bird whistle, horse trot, etc.

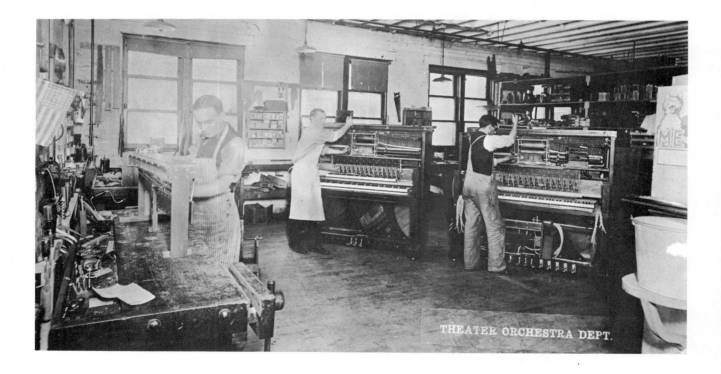

These photographs taken in March, 1919 at the Rudolph Wurlitzer Company's North Tonawanda factory show work in progress on Wurlitzer photoplayers, known as "One Man Orchestras." Keen observers of minutia will note that the right-hand machine in the lower photograph features a Welte-style roll drive. The Rudolph Wurlitzer Company owned a 49% interest in Welte's American operations and was authorized to use certain Welte systems and devices in its machines. Other pictures from the March, 1919 photographic tour of the factory appear elsewhere in this book.

In Chicago Lyon & Healy provided a school for the student aspiring to be a photoplayer operator. Much skill was needed to properly correlate the Chinese gong, locomotive whistle, crockery smash, antelope mating call or whatever with the action on the screen. The Fotoplayer, a photoplayer manufactured by the American Photoplayer Company (later to become the Robert Morton Organ Company), featured rope pulls rather than the usual foot pedals. An old-timer who used to repair Fotoplayers (a miserable job as most theatres operated from early morning until late at night . . . leaving only the wee hours of the morning available for repair time — according to him) told us that in the trade this type of machine was known as the "cow photoplayer" because of the dangling pull knobs.

After finishing his Lyon & Healy course the successful student would find a job in a theatre such as this one. Among theatre organ buffs the photoplayers are known today as "pit organs" as they were located below the screen in the orchestra pit. Photoplayers were generally found in theatres of medium size. Very small theatres would have a regular home player piano and large theatres would have a pipe organ instead.

Practice makes perfect . . . Clarence Eddy, famous theatre organist of the 1920's, was evidently trying his skill on a Fotoplayer located somewhere in a wareroom. The ornate machine in the background is an Orchestrina manufactured by the North Tonawanda Musical Instrument Works (see illustration on page 55).

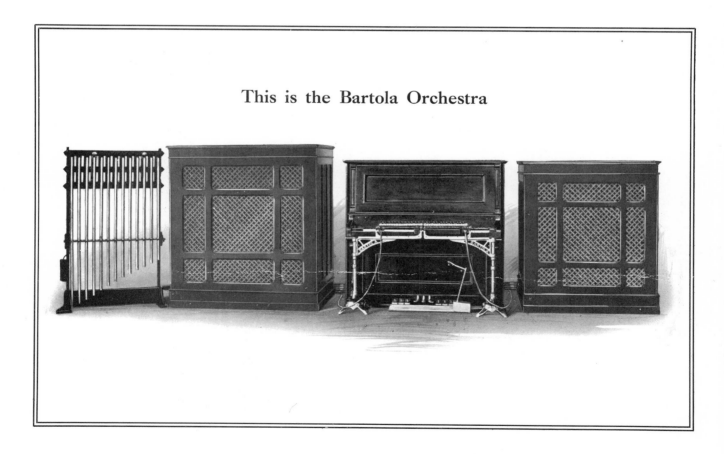

This is the Bartola Orchestra

The Bartola Orchestra was a photoplayer invented by Daniel Barton of Oshkosh, Wisconsin. Starting with a basic piano, Mr. Barton experimented with various additions such as chimes and pipes. A limited number of Bartola photoplayers, all consisting of a piano with various gadgets added, were made. Later Daniel Barton became well known as a manufacturer of theatre pipe organs.

The advent of the twentieth century saw many new firms join the mechanical piano fray. The J. P. Seeburg Piano Company, under the aegis of Justus P. Seeburg, entered the game in 1907. Aided by a good sense of business coupled with quality machines and appealing advertising the J.P. Seeburg Piano Company was soon firmly established. Within four years Seeburg had a wide line of products on the market, including their previously-mentioned *Pipe-Organ Orchestra* photoplayer, the large *Style G, H, J and L* orchestrions and several varieties of smaller coin-operated pianos.

Seeburg promoted its products in many ways. One of the early Seeburg catalogues was a lavishly illustrated color presentation entitled *Art and Music*. We quote from the introduction to this (circa 1918) catalogue . . . and let Seeburg tell its own story:

"We live in a remarkable age. Forty years ago the telephone was being laughed at as an inventor's dream, the typewriter was unheard of, the electric streetcar was unknown.

Twenty years ago the automobile was in the first stages of experiment, the incandescent electric light was undergoing development, the

STYLE G—Art Style
ORCHESTRION

HEIGHT 6 ft. 5 in.   Length 5 ft. 6 in.   Depth 2 ft. 4 in.   Contains 2 sets of pipes, violin and flute, bass and snare drum, Cymbal, Triangle, Tympani, Mandolin, loud and soft effect piano, giving the effect of an Orchestra of 6 men. Can be regulated and shut off any one instrument not desired to play. New and original scale of seven and one-third octaves, overstrung bass and three unisons throughout. Ornamental full iron plate. Nickeled tuning pins. Imported music wire and copperwound bass strings. Brass flange action, highest grade imported wool hammers. Best grade ivory keys and ebony sharps. Double veneered hardwood case. Roll fall-board with continuous nickeled hinges. Double casters. Early English mission finish. Magazine slot registering 20 coins. Roll contains from 10 to 20 selections on rewind system.

Exclusive Agents for This Territory

J. P. SEEBURG PIANO CO.,   MANUFACTURERS, CHICAGO

One of the earliest case designs of the Seeburg Style G "Art Style" orchestrion. Taking the style G (also known as "SS") roll this orchestrion simulated an orchestra of six men. From about 1911 to 1926 or 1927 the Seeburg G orchestrion was manufactured with at least three main styles of art glass. The earliest style (illustrated above) was the only G with hanging lamps on the front. The two outer front glass panels were mirrors surrounded with art glass inlays; the two center panels depicted exotic birds. The second style pictured allegorical muses playing musical instruments with scenes of sailing ships above. A Seeburg G of this style is pictured on page 34 (the third machine from the left). The final G style, and the main style if one may judge from the machines surviving today, is the design pictured on page 40.

talking machine was a dream, the moving picture did not exist, the automatic musical instrument was hardly thought of.

Today *all* of these revolutionary inventions are common factors of our everyday life, bringing profit, comfort, safety, efficiency, convenience, amusement, instruction, pleasure and recreation to millions of people every hour, and forming the basis of great industries giving employment to millions of persons and using thousands of millions of capital.

In common with all these inventions, Seeburg Automatic Instruments have gone through the periods of invention, development and improvement, until now, when they are recognized as the *standard*, by which all automatic musical instruments are judged. In one city

Illustration of the Seeburg factory and showroom from "Art and Music," a catalogue of Seeburg automatic musical instruments issued about 1918. From the firm's very beginning in 1907 the J. P. Seeburg Piano Company was a leader in the coin-piano and orchestrion industry.

STYLE "H"—"Solo Orchestrion"
Piano; xylophone; 68 pipes, giving violin, piccolo, flute, and clarinet effects; mandolin attachment; bass drum; snare drum; tympani; cymbal; triangle, and castanets.

Seeburg Style H orchestrion; the largest and most expensive orchestrion in the Seeburg line. Machines of this type were manufactured continuously from about 1911 to 1926. The H used a special (type H or SSS) roll which permitted solo effects to be played. As a point of interest, the term "nickelodeon" as applied today to coin-operated pianos and orchestrions is strictly a modern usage. In the "good old days" these machines were called "coin pianos," "automatic orchestras," or similar names. The term "nickelodeon" referred to a moving picture theatre which charged 5¢ admission. Literally "nickelodeon" is a combination of "nickel" and "odeon" ... the latter being the Greek word for "theatre."

alone over two thousand Seeburg automatic instruments are giving regular continous service, with complete and constant satisfaction to their purchasers and with profit to the dealers who have sold them.

The preeminent position attained by the Seeburg Automatic Instruments is due not merely to superior manufacturing ability and facilities and greater experience, but — like every other product which has achieved a special success, the prime reason has been in giving to customers a product which will be certain to deliver satisfactory service.

In every line of manufacture there is always one product which is so universally recognized as of superior character, that it becomes a standard. Consequently in all lines we invariably hear other goods spoken of as 'Just as good as' the standard — the leader. This universal comparing phrase of 'just as good' is the frequent unconscious tribute which is invariably paid to the article of such superior merit that it has established itself as a standard in its particular field of operation.

View of a special display room which Seeburg set up to show its various instruments. Many of the machines are illustrated elsewhere in this book. From left to right they are: (1) "A" roll coin-piano, style unknown; (2) Style F coin-piano; (3) Style G orchestrion; (4) Style J orchestrion; (5) Seeburg "Pipe Organ Orchestra" photoplayer somewhat similar to the machine pictured on page 29, but with only one roll mechanism; (6) Style H orchestrion; (7,8,9) Different styles of Seeburg photoplayers. Note the foot pedals which operate the various sound effects. This room seems to have been set up to display photoplayers, as evidenced by the movie screen in the center background. In correspondence with the author Mr. N. Marshall Seeburg, son of J. P. Seeburg, noted that "The Seeburg photoplayers were introduced about 1912. In order to demonstrate them we had to buy a nickel theatre and install the instruments ..."

Distinctive and– Complete

STYLE L AUTOMATIC ORCHESTRA

SEEBURG Automatic Instruments

THE LEADING LINE

Distinctive because of pronounced artistic superiority in design.   Every SEEBURG instrument incorporates individuality of style and instrumentation.

Complete mechanically—complete musically—complete throughout the entire line

Seeburg Style L orchestrion. Machines of this style are extremely rare today, indicating that only a few must have been made. Using a G roll the Style L Automatic Orchestra contained a piano, mandolin effect, bass drum, tympani, snare drum, cymbal, triangle and one or two ranks of pipes. A machine presently in the collection of Roy Haning and Neal White (Troy, Ohio) uses an "A" roll and contains a piano, mandolin bar and pipes ... indicating that the Style L case was also originally used for machines other than orchestrions. Do not confuse this Style L machine with the Seeburg L of the 1920's ... a small cabinet-type piano with mandolin effect.

Photographic views showing installations of J. P. Seeburg Automatic Pianos
as a highly profitable investment for many lines of commercial endeavor.

A page from the "Art and Music" Seeburg catalogue.

Photographic views showing installations of J. P. Seeburg Orchestrions as a highly profitable investment where quality in music and refinement always reign supreme.

Seeburg orchestrions in use. From the "Art and Music" catalogue.

With the recognition of Seeburg Automatic Instruments as the standard, that name on an instrument thus becomes a policy of insurance of satisfaction to the purchaser. It insures a high quality in the music produced, a perfection in tone, an accurancy of mechanical operation and thorough durability, which qualities mean pleasure to the hearers of the instrument and a lasting and profitable investment to the purchaser . . ."

The J.P. Seeburg Piano Company merchandized its coin-pianos and orchestrions aggressively. "There is a SEEBURG piano or orchestrion for every purpose!" — so proclaimed another sales brochure of this firm. There is no doubt that practically every commercial establishment in America was visited at one time or another by a Seeburg salesman . . . for Seeburg machines became a familiar sight everywhere.

Style	Retail	Wholesale	Special
A	650.00	300.00	275.00
B	750.00	325.00	300.00
C	850.00	350.00	325.00
E	950.00	400.00	375.00
F	1050.00	425.00	400.00
G	1500.00	650.00	600.00
H	2500.00	850.00	800.00
J	1800.00	700.00	650.00
K	650.00	275.00	260.00
L	1350.00	550.00	500.00
M	2850.00	1250.00	1125.00
O			
P	950.00	475.00	450.00
Q	1250.00	625.00	600.00
R	4000.00	2000.00	1800.00
S	1950.00	975.00	950.00
Cab.	350.00	150.00	150.00

1918 price schedule of Seeburg automatic instruments showing retail prices, regular wholesale prices and special wholesale prices. Although styles changed over the years it seems probable that the machines listed are as follows: A and B — keyboard coin-pianos with mandolin attachment; C — piano with mandolin effect in elaborate art case; E — keyboard piano with mandolin and xylophone; F — see description below; G and H — the orchestrions described previously; J — the orchestrion pictured on page 41; K — cabinet style with piano, mandolin and xylophone (or pipes); L — the orchestrion pictured on page 35; M, P, Q, R, S — Pipe Organ Orchestra photoplayers; Cab. — the small cabinet-style piano with mandolin effect . . . known in later years at the Style L (see illustration on page 39).

Scenes at the Seeburg factory, probably taken circa 1910-1915 judging from the early model piano in the top picture.

STYLE F
Case Design Patented
INSTRUMENTATION:
PIANO, VIOLIN AND MANDOLIN, OR PIANO, FLUTE AND MANDOLIN

Massive appearing artistically designed case, 6 inches higher than an ordinary piano, but no larger in the length or width. Featuring a row of small art glass panels at top and elaborate coppered art glass illuminated panels and colonial art lamps hanging at sides. Double veneered hardwood case finished in mission oak. Equipped with automatic mandolin and pipe attachments, loud and soft lever, and tempo regulator on outside below key-bed. Any instrument can be shut off at will. Magazine slot registering 1 to 20 coins. Music roll "S" contains from 10 to 20 selections on Seeburg rewind system. Art glass design subject to change without notice. When ordering specify whether violin or flute pipes are desired. Height—5 feet 6 inches. Width—2 feet 4 inches. Length—5 feet 4 inches. Weight boxed for shipment about 1050 pounds.

Seeburg Style F coin-operated piano with mandolin attachment and violin or flute pipes. The retail price of this machine was $1050.00 . . . a sum which could easily be recouped in a year or two if the machine were in a good location.

Style "L"—Smallest Electric Piano made. Also
has Mandolin Attachment. Uses Standard 65-
Note Music Roll. Dimensions—Height: 51½";
Width: 36½"; Depth: 23½"

STYLE "A"—"The Sturdy Performer
Piano with mandolin attachment.

STYLE "B"—"The Artistic Automatic"
Piano with mandolin attachment.

Style "C"—Piano; Xylophone, Mandolin. Uses
Standard 65-Note Music Roll.
Dimensions—Height: 56½"; Width: 40";
Depth: 26".

STYLE "E"—"The Automatic Master"
Piano, xylophone, and mandolin attachment.

STYLE "X"—"Expression"
Straight piano, reproducing expression, almost human in accomplishment.

STYLE "E SPECIAL"—"The All-Purpose Orchestrion
Piano, mandolin attachment, xylophone, bass drum, snare drum,
tympani, cymbal, triangle, castanets, tambourine, Chinese block.

STYLE "KT SPECIAL"—"The Matchless Orchestrion
Piano, xylophone, mandolin attachment, bass drum, snare drum, tympani,
cymbal, triangle, castanets, tambourine, Chinese block.

STYLE "K"—"Midget Orchestrion"
Case design patented
Piano, mandolin and xylophone.

STYLE "KT"
Same as the Style "K" with the added attractiveness of castanets, triangle, and tambourine. Uses Style "G", 65-note, ten-selection music roll.

An array of Seeburg machines from the 1920's.

STYLE "G"—"Art Style Orchestrion
Piano, two sets of wood pipes (violin and flute), mandolin attachment,
bass drum, snare drum, tympani, cymbal and triangle.

Seeburg Style G orchestrion. The multi-colored art glass of this machine made the Style G one of the most attractive models in the Seeburg line. Many of these and other coin-operated machines of their era were sold on a time payment plan. The owner of a restaurant or other public place would invest only a small down payment, with the balance to be paid over a period of time adjusted to the receipts of the machine. In some localities the machines were not owned by the public places but were owned by route operators who placed them on location. With such an arrangement the owner of the establishment would be paid a percentage of the receipts . . . similar to the practice prevalent in the coin-operated juke box industry today. Most often coin-operated pianos and orchestrions were equipped with a nickel slot although occasionally a dime slot was used. Most machines featured an accumulating mechanism in the coin box which permitted up to twenty nickels to be dropped into the slot at one time.

At least a part of Seeburg's success was due to its standardization of models and the rolls which they used. While most other firms changed designs and styles practically every year or two, J.P. Seeburg offered essentially the same models year after year. A purchaser who bought a *Style G — Art Style* orchestrion in 1911 would find it to be virtually identical to a *Style G* produced in 1925, for instance. The art glass designs varied but the interiors remained the same.

Seeburg pioneered the use of the "A" roll (designated as an "S" roll in the earlier years) which later became the industry standard and was used by dozens of other firms. This particular roll was used on most Seeburg coin-pianos having a piano, mandolin effect and sometimes an extra instrument such as a xylophone or set of pipes. The Seeburg "G" roll (earlier called an "SS" roll) was likewise an industry standard. The "G" roll was used on orchestrions and had perforations to operate drums, triangle, cymbal and other effects. Later, the "G" rolls were used in orchestrions made by Nelson-Wiggen, Western Electric and a few others. The style "H" roll (earlier known as "SSS") was an exception; it was mainly used on the Seeburg *J* and *H Solo Orchestrions* and on several different types of Seeburg photoplayers.

Judging from machines which survive today (unfortunately, the early records of the J.P. Seeburg

This pre-Prohibition era photograph shows a Chicago tavern replete with a Seeburg G orchestrion to provide patrons with the latest music. This photograph, loaned to us by A. Valente of Hillside, Illinois, was acquired by him from a Seeburg representative many years ago. Note that this same photograph was used as part of the catalogue page shown on page 37.

Piano Company have been lost to history) the twilight years of the coin piano business in America, the 1920's, were Seeburg's best. The lively *KT* orchestrion and the slightly larger *KT Special*, the little *Style L* (affectionately called the "Junior Seeburg" by collectors today) cabinet piano with a mandolin attachment, the *Style E* which was available either with a xylophone or with violin pipes — these and several other Seeburg styles were all good sellers.

STYLE J—"Solo-Orchestrion"
Case Design Patented
INSTRUMENTATION WITHOUT DRUMS:

New and original scale piano of seven and one-third octaves and three unisons throughout, with mandolin attachment, 68 pipes giving effects of violin, piccolo, flute, obo and clarinet, triangle, castanetes, and xylophone. The rolls used on this instrument are hand arranged and play wonderful solo effects. Equipped with tempo regulator on outside below key-bed. Any instrument can be shut off at will. Magazine slot registering 1 to 20 coins. Music roll "SSS" contains 10 selections on Seeburg rewind system. Art glass design subject to change without notice. Height—6 feet ½ inch. Width—2 feet 7½ inches. Length—5 feet 7½ inches. Double veneered hardwood case finished in circassian walnut. Weight boxed for shipment, about 1200 pounds.

Seeburg Style J orchestrion. This machine used the style H ("SSS") roll and played music with melodic solo effects. Unlike the G and H orchestrions which were manufactured well into the late 1920's the Style J was discontinued about 1920.

The Clark Orchestra Roll Company was the leading manufacturer of coin-piano and orchestrion rolls. With the outstanding exceptions of Link, Wurlitzer, North Tonawanda Musical Instrument Works, Engelhardt and the Operators Piano Company (who made all or most of the rolls used on their machines) most manufacturers were not in the roll manufacturing business. Many of these concerns used Clark rolls on their machines. The 65-note rewind roll, known as the "A" roll, was the most widely used type of roll in the business. The listing of manufacturers at the right indicates the widespread use of the "A" roll. Although the "A" rolls were Clark's bread and butter business this firm also made G, 4X (interchangeable with G rolls, but featuring arrangements primarily intended for the xylophone), M, O, XP and other coin-operated musical instrument rolls. Clark also made rolls for other firms on a contract basis. The Automatic Music Roll Company, a Seeburg subsidiary, actually manufactured no rolls itself but designed them and had them cut by Clark. The Clark firm managed to stay in business until the 1940's by which time the market for coin piano rolls had dwindled to virtually nothing.

Western Electric Piano Co.

429 West Superior Street   CHICAGO, ILL.

Selectra Model "B"

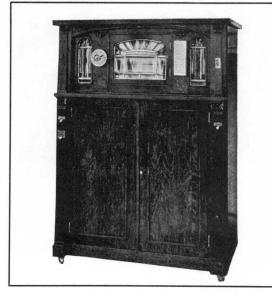

Height 62 inches   Width 46½ inches   Depth 22½ inches
Oak Finish   Other Finishes To Order

Select Your Own Tune

Piano, Mandolin and Xylophone

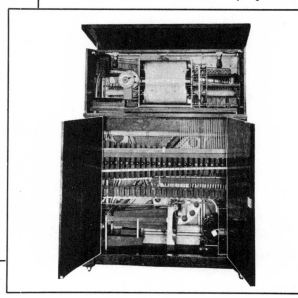

The Standard Ten Tune Music Roll

THE original design of case, with beautiful art and bevel glass panels, will appeal to lovers of art and meets the demand of high class business houses and amusement parlors.

Instrumentation

Piano, mandolin and new type xylophone with expression control.

Selection Controlled

The latest and *finest* of all coin operated pianos. You can select any tune that you desire, in addition to having it play in rotation, without any special music roll.

FEATURES — expression control, music roll on top, dependable transmission, improved re-wind, slow moving bellows, hand adjusted links, no knocking in driving mechanism, operates without any noise, patented spring motor base, large and specially made money box.

THE Selectra is the very latest and most modern coin-operated electric piano. The new tune selection device will positively increase its money making power.

THE MOST PLEASING AND PROFITABLE MEANS OF PROVIDING PUBLIC ENTERTAINMENT

The Western Electric Piano Company manufactured a popular line of several different coin-operated piano styles. Mr. N. Marshall Seeburg, who kindly assisted us by furnishing previously unpublished information concerning the J.P. Seeburg Piano Company, provided us with an interesting revelation. In Mr. Seeburg's own words: "One interesting sidelight is the fact that we (the J.P. Seeburg Piano Company) bought and owned the Western Electric Piano Company. It was necessitated by our desire to stimulate more competition among the Seeburg dealers who had exclusive territories and really needed competition. That is why none of our officers appeared on our board in order to cover up the ownership. The Blackhawk Street address (Western Electric's later address — see page 70 — Ed.) that you give for the Western Electric Piano Company was actually our building and today it serves as an employee entrance to the Seeburg factory." Before the Seeburg purchase the directors of Western Electric also were officers of the Marquette Piano Company, another leading manufacturer of coin pianos and orchestrions. In the course of doing research for this book the author interviewed dozens of people, traveled countless miles, read every historical account and studied every original advertisement and catalogue he could find. Without the generosity of Mr. N. Marshall Seeburg, Mr. Farny Wurlitzer and others once connected with the trade not to mention the many collectors and enthusiasts who loaned printed material this book would not have been possible. We have learned well that information concerning the operations of these early firms is often harder to track down today than are the machines they made!

In Binghamton, New York, E. A. Link produced a variety of coin pianos, orchestrions, photoplayers and pipe organs which were sold under the Link label. The Link Piano Company its beginning in 1915 when the assets of the bankrupt Automatic Musical Company of Binghamton were acquired. The latter firm had produced coin-operated pianos and the *Hiawatha* self-playing xylophone and had sold them, evidently without great success, mainly in the New York state and Pennsylvania area.

In the early 1920's the Link Piano Company employed fifty to seventy-five men and was one of Binghamton's most thriving industries. A contemporary account *(History of Broome County, N. Y.,* published in 1924) tells us:

> "In their product the best features of the piano player and the automatic piano are combined and the resilience and singing quality of the tone are brought out. Holding a roll of fifteen tunes ... this instrument has gained wide popularity as a substitute for a small orchestra.... Flute and harp tones can be brought out giving a richly beautiful trio effect ... The theme of the composer is interpreted with fidelity hitherto unknown in the automatic piano, placing the Link product in a class by itself ..."

Style A-X—Piano, Mandolin, Marimbaphone, Snare Drum, Triangle, Tom-tom, Tambourine, Chinese Wood Drum

Style A-X, one of the dozen or so different models made by the Link Piano Company of Binghamton, New York. Note the endless-type roll on the shelf at the top of the machine.

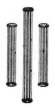

This sign displayed in a tavern window or hung on the front of a piano induced the patron to part with a "nickle" (typesetters weren't always perfect then, either!) to hear the latest hit tunes.

Chicago's Marquette Piano Company earned an excellent reputation for quality with its *Cremona* line of machines. Many of the *Cremona* pianos and orchestrions had interiors lined with finely finished bird's eye maple. The various pneumatics, striker actions and other components were often made of high grade mahogany, a sharp contrast to the unfinished pine used by many other manufacturers.

Certain of the *Cremona* machines incorporated a tune selector, a rare refinement which permitted the choosing of a favorite tune on a particular roll, rather than the usual practice of having to hear whatever came next in succession.

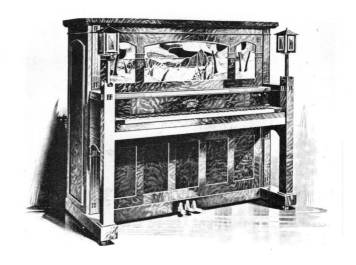

No. (Style A Art)

THE MARQUETTE PIANO COMPANY.
Address of Offices and Factories—1608-1622 S. Canal St., Chicago, Ill.
Established—1905.
Capital Stock—$100,000.
Capacity of Factory (Annually)—1,000.
Names of Pianos Owned and Controlled—Marquette, Cremona.
Numbers of Styles Now Manufactured—
  Uprights, B, C.
  Upright Player-Pianos, D, E.
Established Retail Prices (Freight Charges to Be Added)—
  Uprights, $275 to $350.
  Upright Player-Pianos, $500 to $650.

Special Construction Features—Player-pianos using our own special Marquette player action and improved air motor. Coin-operated pianos principal product.
Names of Proprietors or Officials—C. S. Morse, president; B. C. Waters, vice-president; A. F. Larson, vice-president; C. A. Scott, secretary-treasurer.
Name of Traveling Representative—J. C. Cox.

Marquette statistics from an early trade journal.

An early Cremona piano which used the style "A" roll. Cremona machines were exceedingly well built compared to the products of most other manufacturers. The Marquette Piano Company evidently lacked an effective distributorship set up as surviving Cremona machines are virtually unknown in certain sections of the United States. On the other hand, areas which had active Cremona dealers offer good hunting grounds for the collector today. For instance, we learned of five Cremona pianos in different locations in Bridgeport, Connecticut during searching there in 1964. However, the likelihood of such finds is steadily decreasing as more and more collectors scramble to acquire a steadily diminishing supply of these fascinating music makers!

ANATOMY OF CREMONA STYLE 20

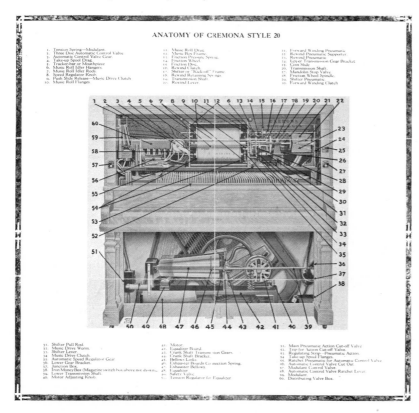

1. Tension Spring—Modulant.
2. Three Disc Automatic Control Valve.
3. Automatic Control Valve Gear.
4. Take-up Spool Drag.
5. Tracker-bar or Mouthpiece.
6. Music Roll Idler Hangers.
7. Music Roll Idler Rods.
8. Speed Regulator Knob.
9. Push Slide Release—Music Drive Clutch.
10. Music Roll Flanges.
11. Music Roll Drag.
12. Music Box Frame.
13. Friction Pressure Spring.
14. Friction Wheel.
15. Friction Disc.
16. Rewind Clutch.
17. Shifter or "Kick-off" Frame.
18. Rewind Retaining Springs.
19. Transmission Shaft.
20. Rewind Lever.
21. Forward Winding Pneumatic.
22. Rewind Pneumatic Supporter.
23. Rewind Pneumatic.
24. Upper Transmission Gear Bracket.
25. Coin Slide.
26. Transmission Shaft.
27. Mandolin Stop Valve.
28. Friction Wheel Spindle.
29. Shifter Pneumatic.
30. Forward Winding Clutch.

31. Shifter Pull Rod.
32. Music Drive Worm.
33. Shifter Lever.
34. Music Drive Clutch.
35. Automatic Speed Regulator Gear.
36. Lower Gear Bracket.
37. Junction Box.
38. Iron Money Box (Magazine switch box above not shown.)
39. Lower Transmission Shaft.
40. Motor Adjusting Knob.
41. Motor.
42. Equalizer Board.
43. Crank Shaft Transmission Gears.
44. Crank Shaft Bracket.
45. Bellows Links.
46. Exhauster Boards Connection Spring.
47. Exhauster Bellows.
48. Equalizer.
49. Safety Valve.
50. Tension Regulator for Equalizer.
51. Main Pneumatic Action Cut-off Valve.
52. Trip for Action Cut-off Valve.
53. Regulating Strip—Pneumatic Action.
54. Take-up Spool Flanges.
55. Ratchet Pneumatic for Automatic Control Valve.
56. Automatic Control Valve Cut Out.
57. Modulant Control Valve.
58. Automatic Control Valve Ratchet Lever.
59. Modulant.
60. Distributing Valve Box.

Relating to the Tune Selecting Device

The Cremona tune-selector, **fully protected by Letters Patent**, is the only perfect tune-selecting instrument. It does not require additional expense for separate music rolls, as it uses a **single multiple piece 88 note roll**, same as used on standard Cremona instruments.

The method of operation is very simple: one merely inserts the coin and turns the indicator to the number of the piece desired. The **mechanism automatically selects its piece** by winding or rewinding at a high rate of speed, always in the proper direction, until the number at which the indicator is set is reached when it slows down to the proper speed and begins to play.

In case the indicator is changed, even while the machine is winding forward or re-winding, the machine will either reverse or continue in the same direction, as the change may require, until the number last indicated is reached and **by no manipulation of the indicator** whatever can the instrument be made to miss or play its own selection.

When it is desired to have the instrument play the selections in **rotation**—as does the ordinary automatic instrument—the indicator is simply set on the letter "R" at either side of the dial. If a distant slot box is used it will always play in rotation when coins are inserted—no matter how the indicator is set, but will play selectively again as soon as the piano slot is used.

Another strong feature of this device is the **combination automatic and manual control speed regulator**. The automatic speed regulator controls the speed automatically and is the only one in use which insures **absolute uniform tempo** for every piece on the roll. This result is effected without bringing parts in contact with the music roll. This method of control has been found objectionable on many speed regulators, due to the tearing of the paper, which objection is eliminated with this device.

The instrument is **beltless**, being equipped throughout with **direct noiseless gear, shaft transmission**, and is absolutely reliable; extremely simple in principle and constructed of the highest grade of material and workmanship.

THE MARQUETTE PIANO COMPANY
CHICAGO, U. S. A.

The Cremona tune selector enabled the patron to select his favorite tune. After the selection was made the roll would race ahead or rewind to the start of the tune desired. The Marquette Piano Company did not promote its tune selector actively. Only a few Cremona advertisements even mentioned it. Likewise, only a few Cremona machines were ever equipped with it. Perhaps the intricate mechanism was beyond the comprehension of the average tavern owner or routeman who had to service it!

Cremona — Style A Art

The original lines of this Art style appeal to lovers of the beautiful and meet the approval of the most exacting. The piano may be played automatically or by hand when desired. An attractive instrument for ice cream parlors and similar locations.

CASE—Arts and Crafts case, built from original exclusive designs by our own designers. Regularly furnished in mission oak finish. Mahogany finish if desired. Illuminated art glass panels and hanging lamps. Rolling fallboard with continuous hinge. Empire top.

CONSTRUCTION—Piano is full 7⅓ octaves. New improved overstrung scale—International pitch. Three stringed unisons. Double copper wound bass. New type double repeating action with patent brass flanges. Ivory keys. Imported felt hammers.

FEATURES—

Mandolin Attachment—Which may be cut in or out manually or automatically, or may be set for continuous playing.

Modulant—The latest improved automatic expression device; varies the tonal expression from very loud to very soft without impairing the perfect rendering of the music.

Distant Control—When desired can be equipped for operation from a distance, either by push button or wall boxes.

Magazine Slot—For coin operation. Instrument is furnished with or without as desired. Slide to take nickel, dime, quarter or other coin, as ordered. From one to twenty coins can be registered at a time. Our coin slide eliminates defective and odd size coins and steel slugs.

Multiple Tune Music Rolls—Plays standard music rolls of ten, fifteen or twenty pieces.

Bellows—Cremona Slow Speed Bellows. New-born calfskin lining. Stationary centerboard. Phosphor bronze bearings.

Coin Boxes—Iron Coin Boxes with substantial locks are used.

Motor—Special type quiet running piano motor—voltage and current as desired.

DIMENSIONS—Height 57 inches; Width 64½ inches; Depth 28½ inches.

WEIGHT—Boxed for shipment 1,040 pounds.

THE MARQUETTE PIANO CO.   CHICAGO

One of the most popular instruments of the Cremona line. Piano can be played manually or with roll; the roll is orchestrated and will select its own instrumentation, or the instrumentation may be selected manually. For cafes, buffets, dance halls and large candy stores this model is particularly fitted.

CASE—Specially designed colonial case of quarter cut oak. Will stand hard service. Regularly furnished in mission finish; mahogany if desired. Three beautiful art glass panels of geometric design in top frame. Fitted with two handsome brass trimmed art lamps. Both panel and lamps illuminated when piano is playing. Full Empire top.

CONSTRUCTION—Piano is full 7⅓ octaves. Decorated bronzed plate. New improved overstrung scale, International pitch. Imported music wire. Three strings in unison. Double copper wound bass. New type double repeating action with Billings patent brass flanges. Ivory keys. Imported felt hammers.

INSTRUMENTATION—Piano, Mandolin and Flute Pipes (or Violin Pipes if preferred). The Pipes and the Mandolin may be played either singly or together with piano accompaniment, as desired.

FEATURES—

Modulant—The latest improved automatic expression device; varies the tonal expression from very loud to very soft without impairing the perfect rendering of the music.

Tempulator—A new device by which the time of the music when played automatically can be varied to suit the nature of the piece, or to secure the fine time variation required for the modern dances.

Distant Control—When desired can be equipped for operation from a distance, either by push button or wall boxes.

Magazine Slot—For coin operation. Instrument is furnished with or without as desired. Slide to take nickel or other coin, as ordered. From one to twenty coins can be registered at a time. Our coin slide eliminates defective and odd size coins and steel slugs.

Multiple Tune Music Rolls—Plays standard music rolls of ten, fifteen or twenty pieces.

Coin Boxes—Iron Coin Boxes with substantial locks are used.

Motor—Special type quiet running piano motor—voltage and current as desired.

DIMENSIONS—Height 67½ inches; Width 64 inches; Depth 28½ inches.

WEIGHT—Boxed for shipment 1,190 pounds.

THE MARQUETTE PIANO CO.   CHICAGO

Cremona—Theatre Orchestra, Solo Style O

Cremona styles A and G and the Solo Style O photoplayer.

Cremona — Orchestral, Style J

A perfectly balanced orchestra; self-contained in a single instrument, occupying the same floor space as a piano. Especially adapted for use in cafes, candy kitchens, dance halls and similar locations of the best sort. For dancing purposes this instrument is furnished with an encore device.

CASE—Finest grade carefully selected quarter sawed white oak. Mission finish. Illuminated colored colonial art glass panels in artistic and harmonious designs.

CONSTRUCTION—Piano is full 7⅓ octaves. Decorated bronzed plate. New improved overstrung scale—International pitch. Three stringed unisons. Double copper wound bass. New type double repeating action with patent brass flanges. Ivory keys. Imported felt hammers.

INSTRUMENTATION—Piano, Mandolin, Flute Pipes, Violin Pipes, Bass and Saare Drums, Cymbal, Triangle, Xylophone, (choice of unatone if desired) and tympani.

FEATURES—

Modulant—The latest improved automatic expression device; varies the tonal expression from very loud to very soft without impairing the perfect rendering of the music.

Tempulator—A new device by which the time of the music when played automatically can be varied to suit the nature of the piece to secure the fine time variation required for the modern dances.

Distant Control—When desired can be equipped for operation from a distance, either by push button or wall boxes.

Magazine Slot—For coin operation. Instrument is furnished with or without as desired. Slide to take nickel, dime, quarter or other coin, as ordered. From one to twenty coins can be registered at a time. Our coin slide eliminates defective and odd size coins and steel slugs.

Multiple Tune Music Rolls—Plays special 88-note orchestrated music rolls of ten, fifteen or twenty pieces.

Bellows—Cremona Slow Speed Bellows. New-born calfskin lining. Stationary centerboard. Phosphor bronze bearings.

Coin Boxes—Iron Coin Boxes with substantial locks are used.

Motor—Special type quiet running piano motor—voltage and current as desired.

DIMENSIONS—Height 80 inches; Width 65 inches; Depth 29 inches.

WEIGHT—Boxed for shipment 1,455 pounds.

THE MARQUETTE PIANO CO.   CHICAGO

Cremona — Orchestral K

A late development in the Cremona Orchestral is the Style K. Altogether a wonderful instrument full of remarkable musical results. Built especially for high class trade desiring a superior instrument.

CASE—A new and original Grecian design, made of the finest quarter sawed oak. Regularly furnished in mission oak; other finishes to order. Beautiful art glass panels in top frame. Two brass trimmed art lamps. Design subject to change without notice.

CONSTRUCTION—Piano is full 7⅓ octaves. New improved overstrung scale. Three string unisons, double copper wound bass. New type repeating action with patent brass flanges. Ivory keys. Imported felt hammers.

INSTRUMENTATION—Three sets of pipes for effects of flute, piccolo and violin, piano, mandolin, triangle, tambourine and castanets.

FEATURES—

Modulant—The latest improved automatic expression device; varies the tonal expression from very loud to very soft without impairing the perfect rendering of the music.

Expression Shutters—Automatically controlled.

Distant Control—When desired can be equipped for operation from a distance, either by push button or wall boxes.

Piano Mute—Operated by knob on side of piano.

Tempulator—A new device by which the time of the music when played automatically can be varied to suit the nature of the piece or to secure the fine time variation required for the modern dances.

Magazine Slot—For coin operation. Instrument is furnished with or without slot as desired. Slide to take nickel or other coin, as ordered. From one to twenty coins can be registered at a time. Our coin slide eliminates defective and odd size coins and steel slugs.

Multiple Tune Music Rolls—Plays 88-note specially orchestrated music rolls.

Coin Boxes—Iron Coin Boxes with substantial locks are used.

Motor—Special type quiet running piano motor—voltage and current as desired.

DIMENSIONS—Height 67½ inches; Depth 30½ inches; Width 64 inches.

WEIGHT—Boxed for shipment about 1,295 pounds.

THE MARQUETTE PIANO CO.   CHICAGO

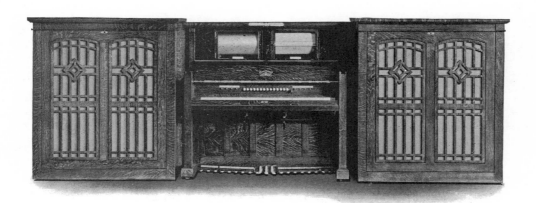

Cremona Orchestral K and J orchestrions and the M3 photoplayer.   Cremona—Theatre Orchestra, Solo Style M3

The largest machines in the *Cremona* line were the *Orchestral* models; the *Orchestral K* and *Orchestral J* which featured many different instruments and played from a special *M* roll.

From records extant today it is evident that the Marquette Piano Company's production in the 1920's was on the order of 1,000 to 2,000 machines per year. In 1924 Marquette executives, B.C. Waters and A.F. Larson established the Western Electric Piano Company and continued as officers of both firms. Like Marquette the Western Electric company offered machines with a tune-selecting device. In the mid-1920's Western Electric was purchased by the J.P. Seeburg Piano Company. Western Electric continued as an autonomous division. Most of Western Electric's productive efforts were concentrated on small cabinet-style machines taking an *A* roll. If machines surviving today are any indication one of the most popular of the Western Electric pianos was the *Selectra Model B* which featured a piano, mandolin effect, xylophone and the aforementioned *Selectra* tune selector.

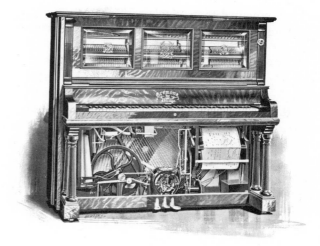

Cremona No. 3
With lower panel removed, showing perfect accessibility of motor and mechanism, and easy, instantaneous insertion of music rolls.

Cremona Style 3. Note the elaborate belt-driven drive mechanism. Extant Cremona machines today indicate that Marquette never did standardize its roll and pump drive system as there are many different types. Music roll insertion was hardly "instantaneous" as the above description would lead the reader to believe. At least two or three minutes were required to take the old roll off of the machine, remove the metal spool from the roll, put the spool on the new roll, insert the spool back into the machine, thread the leader over the tracker bar and adjust the tracker bar holes to align them properly with the roll perforations.

Cremona
STYLE 20—Tune Selecting

Especially adapted for coin operation. Piano can be played by hand or automatically, as desired. Music roll is placed above, being very easy of access. Any tune can be selected and played at will.

SPECIFICATIONS

CASE—Best selected quarter sawed oak case. Regularly furnished in mission oak finish; other finishes as desired. Illuminated art and plate glass panels with coppered bars. Design subject to change.

CONSTRUCTION—Piano is full 7½ octaves. Decorated bronzed plate. New improved overstrung scale—international pitch. Imported music wire. Three strings in unison. Double copper wound bass. New type double repeating action with patent brass flanges. Ivory keys. Imported felt hammers.

FEATURES.

Tune Selecting Device—Plays selectively or in rotation as desired. Automatic or manual speed control.

Transmission—Beltless shaft drive. Noiseless—dependable.

Mandolin Attachment which may be cut in or out manually or automatically or may be set for continuous playing.

Modulant—The latest improved automatic expression device; varies the tonal expression from very loud to very soft without impairing the perfect rendering of the music.

Distant Control—When desired can be equipped for operation from a distance, either by push button or wall boxes.

Magazine Slot—For coin operation. Instrument is furnished with or without as desired. Slide to take nickel, dime, quarter or other coin, as ordered. From one to twenty coins can be registered at a time. Our coin slide eliminates defective and odd size coins and steel slugs.

Multiple Tune Music Rolls—Plays special 88 note orchestrated music rolls of ten and fifteen pieces.

Coin Boxes—Iron Coin Boxes with substantial locks are used.

Motors—Special type quiet running piano motors—voltage and current as desired.

DIMENSIONS—Height 57 inches; Width 64 inches; Depth 28½ inches.

WEIGHT—Boxed for shipment 1,000 lbs.

Cremona
Style 20

This Style is equipped with **tune-selecting mechanism** and is designed and built expressly for coin-operating service, in which field it stands as the greatest achievement by manufacturers of automatic musical instruments.

It plays 88 note music;

    is beltless;

    is noiseless;

    has music roll above keyboard;

    has shaft drive;

    requires no adjustment of bearings;

    has beautiful combination plate and art glass panels, affording view of mechanism when operating;

    has motor and bellows mounted together, permitting ease of removal for inspection or for other purposes;

    is equipped with the **modulant,** by means of which the expression is controlled automatically and which can be adjusted manually to produce music from very loud to very soft, as may be desired, or to suit the room and service in which placed;

    has combination automatic and hand-controlled speed regulator;

    has **Cremona quality** throughout;

    is a **real** musical instrument.

Read the specifications.

THE MARQUETTE PIANO COMPANY
CHICAGO, U. S. A.

Above Left: Title page from a 1925 price list of rolls for Cremona pianos and orchestrions. Cremona electric pianos used an "A" roll; orchestrions, a special "M" roll with solo perforations; photoplayers, a special "S" roll 134 perforations wide.

Above Center and Right: Description of Cremona Style 20. Although the Style 20 was a piano with mandolin attachment which would normally have used an "A" roll it used an 88-note "M" roll as this type of roll had special perforations for the tune-selecting device cut into it. Needless to say the various "M" roll perforations for drums, triangle, castanets and other effects were not used.

From the standpoint of sheer listenability few machines equalled the *Coinola* series of pianos and orchestrions manufactured by the Operator's Piano Company of Chicago. The *Coinola* orchestrions used the style *O* roll which had a special solo section, permitting orchestra bells, xylophone bars or pipes to play a counterpoint melody in accompaniment to the tune being played by the piano. A similar solo arrangement was used by certain other orchestrion rolls such as *H, M* and certain types of Wurlitzer rolls. In contrast, most types of coin piano rolls did not have solo sections — the piano, pipes, xylophone and other effects all played the same notes at the same time.

Not only did the *O* rolls feature a solo section, they featured superb arrangements. Many of these rolls had toe-tapping syncopated arrangements unusual for perforated paper music.

The standard *Coinola* orchestrion was the style *X*. Like other Operator's Piano Company products the Coinola X was marketed under several different names including *Seltzer* (sold by the Seltzer Piano Company of Pittsburgh, Penna.), *Multitone* (sold by M. Welte & Sons) and *Empress Electric Style Y* (sold by Chicago's large Lyon & Healy house). The *Coinola X* was billed as "the most popular orches-

trion that has ever been made" although the scarcity of surviving examples today belies this.

Unfortunately for collectors today the two largest *Coinola* orchestrion styles, the *CO* and the *SO*, were not introduced until about 1920, by which time the market for the larger orchestrions had largely disappeared. As a result these particular models are extremely rare at the present time.

The Operator's Piano Company also made the *Reproduco* series of piano-pipe organs for theatre and funeral parlor use. These machines produced melodious tones with an almost haunting ethereal sound. An original *Reproduco* brochure stated that with good care one of the machines should provide about twelve years' worth of service . . . which gives some idea of the original life expectancy of this type of instrument.

One of the most curious Operator's Piano Company products was the tiny *Profit Sharing Player Piano* sold under the *Rock-Ola* name. In essence this machine was a glorified slot machine which provided gamblers with the latest in snappy tunes while it took in their money! Despite advertised claims that the *Profit Sharing Player Piano* was "Declared Legal Everywhere" it was quite illegal in most places. Hence, only a few were ever sold.

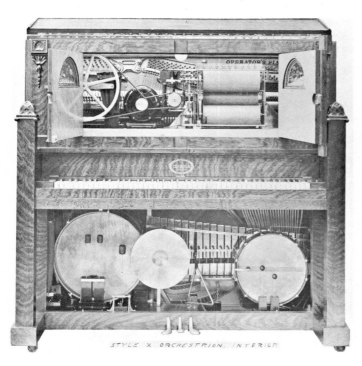

The Coinola Style X was one of the most beautiful-sounding of all orchestrions. The metal orchestra bells with their repeating mechanism played solo melodies cut into the "O" roll used by this machine. Instrumentation of the Style X consisted of a piano, mandolin bar, orchestra bells, bass drum, cymbal, tympani, triangle, wood block, snare drum single beat and snare drum roll. The Coinola X was also sold (with external case design variations) as the Welte Multitone Style 2 and as the Empress Electric Style Y. Although collectors today consider the "O" roll used in Coinola orchestrions to be the most desirable of all standard orchestrion rolls the Operators Piano Company never mentioned the superior "O" roll arrangements in its advertising.

Coinola Style CO orchestrion. Introduced circa 1920 the CO was the largest Coinola keyboard orchestrion. Instrumentation consisted of a piano, mandolin attachment, bass drum, snare drum, tympani, xylophone, flute pipes, wood block, triangle, cymbal and tambourine. The list price was $2200.00.

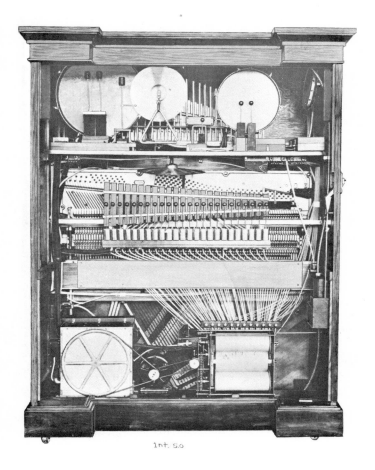

Int. SO

Style SO

Coinola SO — the largest Coinola orchestrion. Costing $2300.00 the SO featured all of the instruments of the CO plus a rank of violin pipes and a 15-inch Chinese crash cymbal. The above illustrations of the SO exterior and interior plus the X and CO photographs are from a portfolio or salesbook used by an Operators Piano Company salesman during the 1920's. Many of the "O" rolls were manufactured by the Capitol Roll and Record Company, a subsidiary of the Operators Piano Company.

———— REPRODUCO PIPE ORGAN ————

The Reproduco
The Giant In Musical Production
The Price within the reach of all

The Operators' Piano Company
Chicago, Illinois

The Reproduco piano-pipe organ was intended for two main markets, the mortuary trade and the theatre. Most found their way into theatres where they were used as a small pipe organ to provide music to accompany silent films. The duplex roll mechanism permitted two rolls of differing music...a roll of romantic tunes and a roll of marches, for instance...to be on the machine at the same time. By depressing appropriate small levers to the left and right of the top keyboard music could be played as desired from one roll or the other, in keeping with whatever action was on the screen. Most Reproducos used special "OS" or "NOS" rolls containing ten tunes each. To aid the Reproduco operator the nature of the music on each roll was usually stated at the top of the tune list. "Light Dramatic," "Very Heavy Dramatic," "Oriental Interludes" and "Comedy Rags" are examples.

The Super Reproduco

REPRODUCO PIPE ORGAN

Specifications

Created by the demand for larger instruments that would embody the successful features of the Reproduco Organ

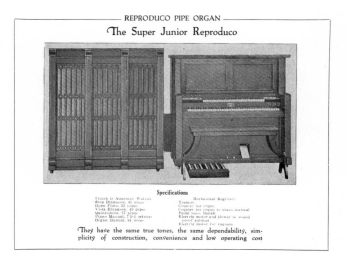

The Super Junior Reproduco

REPRODUCO PIPE ORGAN

Specifications

They have the same true tones, the same dependability, simplicity of construction, convenience and low operating cost

Two of the larger Reproduco models featuring side chests which housed organ pipes. The Reproduco played very harmonious, almost ethereal, music which made very pleasant listening.

The New and Improved
Rock-Ola Player Piano
THE ONLY AUTOMATIC PIANO MADE WITH SLOT MACHINE FEATURES
The Musical Marvel—It Pays While it Plays
OVERCOMES ALL OBJECTIONS—DECLARED LEGAL EVERYWHERE
OPENS THE DOOR OF OPPORTUNITY

No Promise of Rewards   No Colors or Emblems   No Spinning Reels
Plenty of Thrill   Lots of Excitement   Wonderful Repeater
THE POSSIBILITIES ARE UNLIMITED, IF YOU ARE A LIVE WIRE
OPERATION

The operation is simple and easily understood. A coin is deposited in the coin slot, located at the center near the top of the piano front, this starting the piano mechanism, playing a complete 2½ minute tune. Each coin deposited for music affords the player an opportunity to participate in the profits which are immediately declared, if due, in the form of the familiar brass tokens. These are delivered to the player at the right hand side of the piano and each token is plainly marked "Good for Music Only." Profit payments range from 2 to 20 tokens and distribution is controlled automatically by the piano mechanism and is governed by the patronage the piano receives.

COIN DEPOSITED HERE

Last Coin Played Shown Here

4-Way Switch on Back of Piano.

Return Profit Cup

CABINET QUARTER SAWED OAK

PROFITS RANGE FROM 2 TO 20 TOKENS.

GOOD FOR PLAYING THE PIANO

METAL TRIMMINGS

DULL FINISH

54 NOTE PIANO

SPECIAL FEATURES

Continuous operation of the piano is cared for by the exclusive Rock-ola coin slide, which permits continuous play without waiting for the termination of the 2½ minute tune. Each coin deposited participates in the profits if due; also registers on the piano for its tune. This permits continuous play without waiting or delay. It is also possible to declare all profits in coin where this is permitted. Made for 5 cent or 25 cent play.

The Rock-ola Profit-sharing Player Piano photographed herewith is one of the most beautiful, practical, staunch and sturdy instruments ever put on the market. Every line and detail has been designed specially for this type of instrument. The case is of quarter sawed oak in a hand rubbed, dull finish. The lines are simple but elegant, an ornament in any location. The action is built by one of the leading automatic player action manufacturers, standard 54 note range, playing ten tune rolls. All parts are easily accessible. Instrument is operated on any 110-volt electric current. Size of case 52 in. high, 25 in. wide, 38 in. long; shipping weight 665 lbs.

Special Price $550   *Write for Quantity Prices, Terms and Territory Available*
BARGAIN—4 Rock-Ola Profit Sharing Player Pianos
Rebuilt Like New—Including 3 Music Rolls—While They Last—**Price $275 each**

COINOLA MIDGET ORCHESTRIONS
In addition to the regular line there was a Coinola Midget Orchestrion series. These small keyboardless cabinet-style machines also utilized the Style O roll. Priced from $875.00 to $1250.00 they were made to order in any of the following combinations, according to a Coinola catalogue:

(1) With piano and mandolin only.
(2) Piano, mandolin and set of orchestra bells.
(3) Piano, mandolin and choice of flute or violin pipes or both.
(4) Piano, mandolin, snare drum, bass drum and cymbal.
(5) Piano, mandolin, snare drum, bass drum, cymbal, two-octave range set of steel orchestra bells with vibrating pneumatics.
(6) Same as (5) but with xylophone instead of orchestra bells.

At the left:
The Profit Sharing Player Piano was one of the most curious of all coin-operated pianos. Mr. David Rockola, president of the Rock-Ola Manufacturing Corporation of Chicago, told us that: "The Profit Sharing Player Piano was developed in 1926-1927. We bought these pianos from the Operators Piano Company and developed a profit-sharing mechanism so that the customer would receive a return on the profits that were made. A total of fifty of these pianos were purchased by us and the mechanism was manufactured and installed by us. For a time we operated a number of them and later on we prepared a circular and sold them in different parts of the country..."

50

The Mandolin Piano

Bottom board removed to display effects

Front panel open to display pipes

Combination of Flute and Violin Pipes

The Violin Pipe Piano

Front panel open to display bells

The Bell Piano

Bottom board removed to display effects

The Drum Piano

The Little Empress Electric Cabinet Player

Piano with Complete Orchestral Effects

Front panel open to display pipes

The Flute Pipe Piano

Empress Electric
Pianos
LYON & HEALY
CHICAGO

The Empress Electric pianos and orchestrions marketed by Lyon & Healy of Chicago were Coinola machines with differing exteriors. They were sold mainly in the Chicago area. The Little Empress Electric Cabinet Player contained a roll mechanism and pneumatic stack and played a regular upright piano by clamping on to the keyboard as illustrated. The Operators Piano Company made an even larger type of similar machine, the Orchestrion Cabinet. This tall cabinet contained a bass drum, snare drum, set of orchestra bells, cymbal, wood block and triangle plus a piano-playing mechanism. The whole outfit operated properly when attached to an ordinary upright piano. Note that the cata- logue description of the Empress Electric Style Y mentions that the piano has an "88-note range." Although the tracker bar had 88 holes only 66 holes were for different piano notes; the other holes were used for the drums, cymbal, triangle, soft pedal and other devices. Another interesting Empress Electric machine was the Twin-Tracker Solo Expression Piano (not illustrated above) which featured a double-width roll, one side of which played when the roll was going forward, the other side of which played when the roll was going backward — an ingenious system which enabled the machine to play uninterruptedly. A similar device was used by Nelson-Wiggen on certain mortuary organs.

One of the earlier entries in the coin-operated piano field was the Berry-Wood Piano Player Company of Kansas City, Missouri. This firm made and marketed over a dozen styles of coin pianos and orchestrions. The latter machines were known as *Auto-Orchestras*. Berry-Wood advertisements stressed the quality of their product. Such deluxe features as imported hammer felts, double veneered cases, German silver action rails, best-grade ivory keys, etc. were pointed out to the prospective buyer. In step with other manufacturers a (circa 1913) catalogue stated that "We will also add moving picture organs and players to the line in a short time." Whether too much emphasis was placed on quality and not enough on low price, or whatever, will never be definitely known. The firm went out of business before 1920.

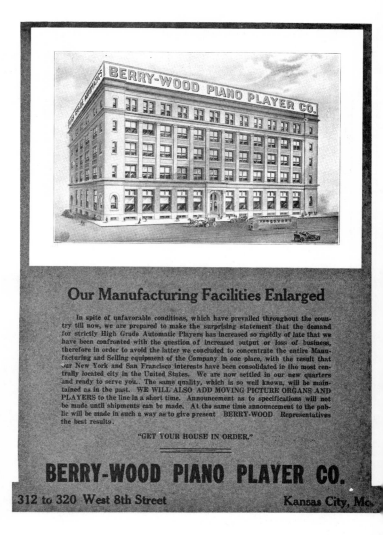

Our Manufacturing Facilities Enlarged

In spite of unfavorable conditions, which have prevailed throughout the country till now, we are prepared to make the surprising statement that the demand for strictly High Grade Automatic Players has increased so rapidly of late that we have been confronted with the question of increased output or loss of business, therefore in order to avoid the latter we concluded to concentrate the entire Manufacturing and Selling equipment of the Company in one place, with the result that our New York and San Francisco interests have been consolidated in the most centrally located city in the United States. We are now settled in our new quarters and ready to serve you. The same quality, which is so well known, will be maintained as in the past. WE WILL ALSO ADD MOVING PICTURE ORGANS AND PLAYERS to the line in a short time. Announcement as to specifications will not be made until shipments can be made. At the same time announcement to the public will be made in such a way as to give present BERRY-WOOD Representatives the best results.

"GET YOUR HOUSE IN ORDER."

BERRY-WOOD PIANO PLAYER CO.

312 to 320 West 8th Street   Kansas City, Mo.

Styles C. and L.

STYLE C contains Endless Roll Eighty-eight Note Player Seven and one-third Octaves, Ivory Keys, Full Iron Frame, Three Veneers on Wrest Plank, Three Strings to Bass, Bushed Pins, Imported Hammer Felt, Nickel Action Brackets, German Silver Action Rail, Rich Design of Case, Double Veneered.
Style L contains rewind roll eighty-eight note player. Same mechanical specifications otherwise as Style C.

The above are both equipped with Magazine Slots.

Motors furnished with instruments for any current. Cases furnished in Polished Oak, Mission Oak and Mahogany.

Above: Note that the above piano could be obtained with either the rewind or endless type of roll. Certain Peerless pianos offered the buyer the same option.

Top right: The illustration of the Berry-Wood factory is captioned with the announcement that the firm is consolidating its sales and manufacturing facilities in Kansas City and is closing its New York and San Francisco interests.

Bottom right: This interesting engraving from a Berry-Wood catalogue shows longhair musicians contemplating a Berry-Wood A.O.W. orchestrion which evidently has replaced them!

UNION BANK NOTE CO KANSAS CITY

Style 15

THIS beautiful instrument is built exclusively for use with our *Hand-Played* *Music Rolls* and is beyond a doubt the finest production ever offered to the trade. The music rendered by this player is an exact reproduction of the interpretation of the artist, and all mechanical effects are eliminated completely. Made as a plain Automatic Piano or with Flute or Violin Pipes. Music rolls are exactly as played by an artist and contain from four to eight selections. Eighty-eight Note Scale. Rewind Music. Magazine slot.

In ordering state whether wanted as Piano alone or with Flute or Violin Pipes.

Style A. O. S.

CONTAINS eighty-eight note Piano Player, one set of Flute or Violin Pipes, Bass Drum, Snare Drum, Cymbal and Triangle. Coupler system giving greater range to pipe scale. A fine instrument in a beautiful case. Moderate in price and substantial. Eighty-eight Note Scale. Music rolls contain eight selections for rewind and five for endless. Magazine slot.

In ordering state whether Flute or Violin Pipes are wanted, also whether rewind or endless roll.

Style F.
In Rewind Music Only

CONTAINS Celebrated Berry-Wood Eighty-eight Note Player Action, Thirty-seven wood Flute or Violin Pipes. All mechanism contained in a rich Teak-wood finished case, Beautiful Swell front center Art Glass Panel, Two Oval Side Panels of Harp Design, Double Veneered Case, Full Iron Plate, 7⅓ Octaves. Full Extension Automatic Music Desk, Three Strung Unisons; imported German Wire, Full Copper Wound Bass Strings, Built-up Pin Blocks of Rock Maple Double Repeating Action, Billings Brass Flanges, Best Ivory Keys, Fourteen Pound Hammers.
Magazine Slot
In ordering state whether Flute or Violin Pipes are wanted

Style A. O. W.
In Rewind Music Only

CONTAINS Celebrated Berry-Wood Rewind Player. Case six feet high, ordinary width. Mission Design and Finish. Beautiful Art Glass Panels and Lamps. Has Thirty-four wood Flute Pipes, Thirty-four Violin Pipes, Coupler giving Ninety-two Pipe Tones. Twenty-five Steel Bells, Twenty-five Bar Xylophone, Kettle Drum, Castinets, Crash Cymbal, Triangle, Bass and Snare Drum, Cymbal, Device for drumming on rim; also Tambourine and Mandolin. Equivalent to a ten piece orchestra.

Four of the many different Berry-Wood styles. The A.O.W. was the largest machine in the Berry-Wood line. Introduced in 1912 this style was said to have been "particularly adapted for use in moving picture houses." Moving pictures were the public entertainment highlight of the day and the coin piano manufacturers rushed to get whatever share they could of the profits.

One of the leading manufacturers of the day was the North Tonawanda Musical Instrument Works. Formed shortly before 1908 by dissident Eugene DeKleist employees the North Tonawanda Musical Instrument Works went on to develop and sell a full line of automatic musical instruments including coin pianos, orchestrions, theatre photoplayers and military band organs.

The best known product of this company was the *Pianolin*, a small arcade-type piano which utilized an endless roll. The endless roll was essentially a very long continuous loop of paper which was fed into one side of a storage box and drawn out from the other side. Certain Berry-Wood, Engelhardt and Link products also used the endless roll system.

The largest North Tonawanda nickel-in-the-slot machine was the *Mando-Orchestra*, an orchestrion standing an impressive nine feet high. The *Mando-Orchestra* was a latecomer to the orchestrion scene. Only a limited number of this model were sold after its introduction in 1921.

North Tonawanda Musical Instrument Works machines were also sold under the *Capitol* label by the Capitol Piano and Organ Company of New York City. The North Tonawanda Musical Instrument Works became a division of the Rand Company about 1920. Later, the original incorporators of the North Tonawanda Musical Instrument Works founded the Artizan Factories, Inc. which made band organs and calliopes in addition to office furniture and other items.

Military Band Organ . . . . No. 92	Military Band Organ . . . . No. 192
Bass and Snare Drums and Cymbal	Bass and Snare Drums and Cymbal
With Carved and Ornamented Wings	With Carved and Ornamented Wings
52 KEYS 9 TUNES	52 NOTES 18 TUNES
Operated by Pinned Cylinder	Operated by Perforated Paper Music

Automatic Keyboard Piano Style "L"

THE case is an Arts and Crafts design, made of fine figured quartered oak, and finished in either early mission, fumed or polished golden oak, double veneered inside and outside.

Two handsome art-glass panels, copper framed in the front.

New and improved scale of seven and one-third octaves, especially designed for high grade instruments of this class.

Overstrung bass and three unisons throughout.

Best quality ivory keys and ebony sharps.

Contains set of solo violin or flute pipes of extraordinary quality and considered by experts to be the closest imitation of the tones of these instruments of anything of the kind on the market.

The mandolin attachment on the piano is so designed as to produce the real tone of a mandolin, and with the pipes, on and off automatically in the perforated music, the monotony usually found in automatic instruments is entirely eliminated, and with the clever expression device, the music is rendered like that of a human artiste of high degree. This instrument is ideal for home use, lodge rooms, dancing, fine ice cream parlors, cafes, etc., also moving picture theatres, as any selection on the music roll may be played at will by using the re-wind and starting buttons in front of the instrument.

Dimensions:

Height, 4 ft. 5½ in.; length, 5 ft. 5½ ins.; width, 2 ft. 5½ in.

Instrumentation:

Piano, seven and one-third octaves, with mandolin attachment, loud and soft pedal.

Set of very fine violin or flute pipes.

Clever automatic expression device.

Fourteen selections on each music roll; two of which are included in the price of the instrument.

When ordering, please give data to the electric power to be used, namely, number of volts and cycles, also phases, so as to enable us to supply the correct kind of electric motor.

The Style 92 North Tonawanda Musical Instrument Works military band organ shown at the top right is representative of the many styles made by this firm. Style 92 featured a cluster of brass trumpets, making it especially desirable to collectors today. Below is shown a Style L piano with mandolin attachment and pipes. Early models of the Style L used a special 14-tune roll. Later models used a standard ten-tune "A" roll. The North Tonawanda Musical Instrument Works later changed its name to the Capitol Piano and Organ Company and was headed by James H. Rand. The present-day Sperry-Rand Corporation can trace part of its ancestry to various early Rand family enterprises including the North Tonawanda Musical Instrument Works.

What Users Say

PIANOLIN

Crown Candy Kitchen

COLLINGWOOD, ONT., July 12th, 1910.

Gentlemen: We are very much pleased with our PIANOLIN, and wish to say, that it has already paid for itself in the increased business it has brought us since we installed it last April. The people here are very fond of it, and we all think it the best instrument for the money in the world.

C. GEORGAS, Prop.

GRAND RAPIDS, MICH., July 19th, 1910.

Gentlemen: I received the PIANOLIN on Friday afternoon, and by 5.30 P. M. it was working fine. It is a splendid instrument, and I am pleased with it. My friends say that the music is the very best they have ever heard on an instrument of the size. We counted the cash it has taken since Friday (4 days) and it amounted to $31.65. It has also helped the bar trade wonderfully, and I would not part with it for the best electric piano on the market. Thanking you for all past favors, I remain,

Respectfully yours,

BERT WOSINSKI.

TONAWANDA, N. Y., August 31st, 1910.

Gentlemen: My PIANOLIN is doing great work, as it is averaging over $100.00 per month, and it has increased my bar trade from $5.00 to $8.00 per day, and I would not take twice what I paid for it if I could not get another one of them.

Respectfully yours,

WILLIAM KOLPACK.

ORCHESTRINA

The 44-note Pianolin is the most plentiful North Tonawanda Musical Instrument Works piano surviving today. Several dozen specimens are known. The elaborate Orchestrina was the same as the Capitol Symphony Orchestra (see page 57) and contained a full range of orchestra instruments. Note the carrying handles on the side of the Orchestrina. This was a common feature of North Tonawanda and Capitol instruments. The illustration of the factory shows two street cars nearby. Many such illustrations of buildings during this period featured street railway systems, implying that the factory was up-to-date with the latest in transportation service.

Pianolin "B"—49 Notes

Electrically Driven   Coin Operated

Pianolin "A"—49 Notes

Electrically Driven   Coin Operated

Mando-Orchestra—87 Notes

THIS instrument is considered a marvel by musicians; on account of its splendidly-balanced orchestration, the fine shading of expression in its music and its great carrying power. Moving picture theatres, dance halls, dining rooms, cafés, restaurants and all other places where orchestra music is needed demand an instrument of this kind.

The case is made of the best quality of quartered oak with piano finish, and with an elaborate, colored art-glass panel in the top part depicting a scene in Holland; while the two art-glass panels in the lower part show a western landscape; both of which are displayed to great advantage by electric lights inside the instrument when playing; the two outside art-glass lamps being lighted at the same time.

The stops are controlled by the perforated paper music, so that violin and cello solos are beautifully rendered.

Operated by an electric motor which, with two ten-piece rolls of music, is included in the price.

Dimensions:—

Height, 9 ft.; length, 5 ft.; depth, 3 ft. 4 in.

Instrumentation:—

80 cremona-toned pipes; representing one first violin, one second violin, one viola, "cello" and stringed bass; 44-note piano, with loud and soft pedal; 25-note mandolin, playing first and second parts; set drummers' traps, consisting of bass and snare drums with loud and soft stroke; cymbal, crash cymbal, Chinese wood drum, castanets, tom-tom and set of orchestra bells with resonators.

In ordering, it will be necessary to furnish us with data of the electric current to which the instrument would be connected—such as the number of volts, cycles and phases—which information can be obtained from the electric power company in your city. A book of instructions with each instrument.

Mando-Orchestra—87 Notes

20 Selections

The Pianolin contained a 44-note piano, mandolin attachment and a rank of flute and violin pipes. The Mando-Orchestra (identical to the Capitol Jazz Concert Orchestra — see page 58) was one of the largest orchestrions ever built in the United States.

Capitol Symphony Orchestra

**Electrically
Driven**

**Coin
Operated**

9 ft., 6 in. High   6 ft., 4 in. Long   3 ft., 8 in. Deep

THIS is a remarkably handsome instrument in both case design and musical quality. Imagine a human orchestra of twelve or fifteen pieces playing in perfect harmony under a skilled director and you get a fair conception of the grandeur of this music. It reproduces the music of two first violins, two second violins, 'cello, string bass, first and second clarinets, snare and bass drums, cymbal, castanets, and a set of orchestra bells. People will flock to hear this wonderful orchestra. A nickel will start the instrument and give you one complete selection of either classical, dance, or popular music; it can also be played by push button. This instrument is ideal for large hotels, restaurants, confectioneries, halls, dance halls, etc.

The Rolls used in the Capitol Symphony Orchestra are made in our own plant at North Tonawanda, N. Y., by expert musicians who are masters in their calling. Each roll contains ten separate pieces. Every month a bulletin listing the new orchestrations is sent to each instrument owner so an up-to-date repertoire may be maintained.

This instrument is ready to be played when received and may be instantly connected with any electric current. It will never require attention.

THE CAPITOL

"Music is the Life of the Nation"

PIANO and ORGAN CO.
Incorporated
251 West 34th Street   New York City

'Phone Longacre 7660
7661

The Capitol Symphony Orchestra. Note that the rolls were said to have been made "by expert musicians who are masters in their calling." As was the case with the other North Tonawanda Musical Instrument Works and Capitol large orchestrions only a few were sold.

It is Just Like a REAL Jazz Orchestra

This 1922 Capitol Jazz Concert Orchestra will

Crowd Your Place   Increase Your Business   Double Your Profits

SOMETHING ENTIRELY NEW!

Everybody Loves This New Orchestra

This Orchestra will Advertise Your Place

This Orchestra will Double Your Business

Notice !
If you have an old piano or organ, we will gladly take it in exchange.

This Handsome Jazz Orchestra Interprets
Classical and Operatic Music with the Same Human Effect

Attention

YOU want more business. This Jazz Orchestra will get you more business. People passing your doors will stop to listen to the sweet music and will drop in —spend their money and come again and again with their friends, which means—Big Crowds—Big Business—Big Profits.

Don't Delay — Every day you are without this trade winner, you are Losing Business.

This Capitol Jazz Orchestra is a 1921 Invention—entirely different from the old style electric pianos and organs you have seen in the past. This is a Real Musical Instrument that plays with Human Expression that the people want and enjoy.

It Pays for Itself

IN order to introduce this new Orchestra we will install it in your place at practically no expense.

Your customers will go wild about it and never stop dropping nickels into it to hear it play and in that way it will pay for itself.

If you cannot call, mail today the enclosed post card and we will tell you how you can get this wonderful business getter so that it costs you practically nothing.

Mail back the enclosed Postal and we will send you full Information FREE.

Capitol Bluebird Orchestra

Electrically Driven   **Coin Operated**

6 ft., 6½ in. High   4 ft., 2 in. Long   2 ft., 6 in. Deep

THE Capitol Bluebird Orchestra is handsomely and solidly designed, being constructed of highest grade quartered oak with art glass panels. It is designed to fulfill the needs of medium sized dance halls, cafes, restaurants, confectioneries, or anywhere high class music is required. It is free from all complicated mechanisms and will stand hard wear unusually well.

Beside the high grade piano there are 45 string-toned pipes representing first and second violins, viola and 'cello, mandolin and orchestral bells, castanets, and the sweetly singing bluebird occasionally chirps in an accompaniment.

The Rolls used in the Capitol Bluebird Orchestra are made in our own plant at North Tonawanda, N. Y., by expert musicians who are masters in their calling. Each roll contains twelve separate pieces. Every month a bulletin listing the new orchestrations is sent to each instrument owner so an up-to-date repertoire may be maintained.

This instrument is ready to be played when received and may be instantly connected with any electric current. It will never require attention.

THE CAPITOL
"Music is the Life of the Nation"
PIANO and ORGAN CO.
Incorporated
251 West 34th Street   New York City
'Phone Longacre 7660 7661

Capitol Midget Orchestra

Electrically Driven   **Coin Operated**

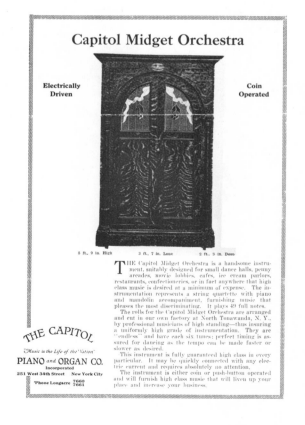

5 ft., 9 in. High   3 ft., 7 in. Long   2 ft., 3 in. Deep

THE Capitol Midget Orchestra is a handsome instrument, suitably designed for small dance halls, penny arcades, movie lobbies, cafes, ice cream parlors, restaurants, confectioneries, or in fact anywhere that high class music is desired at a minimum of expense. The instrumentation represents a string quartette with piano and mandolin accompaniment, furnishing music that pleases the most discriminating. It plays 49 full notes.

The rolls for the Capitol Midget Orchestra are arranged and cut in our own factory at North Tonawanda, N. Y., by professional musicians of high standing—thus insuring a uniformly high grade of instrumentation. They are "endless" and have each six tunes; perfect timing is assured for dancing as the tempo can be made faster or slower as desired.

This instrument is fully guaranteed high class in every particular. It may be quickly connected with any electric current and requires absolutely no attention.

The instrument is either coin or push-button operated and will furnish high class music that will liven up your place and increase your business.

THE CAPITOL
"Music is the Life of the Nation"
PIANO and ORGAN CO.
Incorporated
251 West 34th Street   New York City
'Phone Longacre 7660 7661

The copywriter who stated that the Capitol Jazz Orchestra would "Crowd Your Place" and "Double Your Profits" was hardly modest. However, introduction of this machine came too late. By 1922 a public place could buy a coin-operated phonograph or a more "modern" compact orchestrion such as a Seeburg KT for a fraction of the price. Had the Capitol Jazz Orchestra been introduced in 1910 instead of 1921 it undoubtedly would have been a tremendous success. The Capitol Bluebird shown below was also sold as the North Tonawanda Sextrola; the Capitol Midget Orchestra is identical interior-wise to the North Tonawanda Pianolin.

Sextrola "A" 52 Notes

Sextrola "A" 52 Notes

DESCRIPTION

THIS INSTRUMENT is designed and gotten up to fill a much needed want in Penny Arcades, Moving Picture Theatres, and also to furnish Orchestra music in Cafes, Restaurants, Ice Cream Parlors, Dance Halls and in places where people congregate for recreation, also in Railroad Stations, Waiting Rooms, Department and Tonsorial Parlors.

It is operated by electricity and controlled by a coin slot.

INSTRUMENTATION : This consists of 44 notes of Piano, with loud and soft pedal and with a Mandolin effect on and off automatically and 44 Cremona tone pipes representing a stringed quartette and also a set of Orchestra bells.

There is also a swell box in this instrument which works automatically, making soft and loud effects in addition to the loud and soft pedal, which adds very materially to the pleasing quality of the music.

On the outside of the case is a device with which the violins may be entirely shut off and also a mute for the Piano, which makes it play very soft in case necessity so requires and in addition to this, there is another device on the outside of the case, which is almost invisible and under the control of the owner, with which the coins may be dropped through the contact stopping the instrument instantly.

The case is made of a fine quality of hardwood having a fine grain effect, as shown in the cut and finished in Mission, Silver Gray or any of the other popular up to date finishes. The beautiful Art Glass in the upper front panels are shown off to good effect when the instrument is playing by the two electric lamps which are placed on the inside of the case and which light up when the coin is dropped in the slot that starts the music.

DIMENSIONS, . . Height, 6 feet 6½ inches ; Width, 4 feet 2 inches ; Depth, 2 feet 6 in.

The music is in the form of endless paper rolls, which, with our perfect steel tracker box and improved paper box, divided tracker bar and tempo regulating device, has proved to be the most reliable system on the market, which prevents the paper from getting out of track and does away with all of the objections to spooled paper music.

There are twelve selections on the SEXTROLA endless music rolls.

The workmanship and materials are fully guaranteed in our instruments, placing them in the lead of all other makes of instruments of like size and prices.

The connection to the electric line can be made from a regular lamp socket and in ordering, it will be necessary to furnish us with the data to the electric current to which the instrument would be connected, such as the number of volts, number of cycles and phases, which can be obtained from the Electric Power Company in your city.

The speed on the four way crank in the instrument should not turn faster than 78 to 80 revolutions per minute.

A book of instructions is sent with each instrument.

Sextrola "B"

A 52-Note Orchestrion

THE "Sextrola" is recognized by musicians and the trade to be a superior instrument for medium-sized picture theatres, dance halls, restaurants, cafés, ice cream parlors, etc.

The case is an arts-and-crafts design; built of first quality oak, satin finish, and with three fine, colored art-glass panels which are lighted up, when the music is started, by dropping a coin in the slot.

There is a knob on the outside of the case with which the pipes are shut off, and another one to soften the piano; also an almost invisible push button to drop coins through the slot when the music is not wanted during prohibitive hours. Tempo regulator inside of case to govern time of music.

The music is in the form of endless paper rolls (twelve selections to the roll), one of which is included in the price of the instrument and is passed through our patented steel tracker box which does not permit it to get out of track; therefore, no trouble is ever encountered with this perfect system.

The tracker bar is divided by a wire screen which catches all of the dust and dirt; thus preventing the clogging of the valves. Workmanship and material fully guaranteed.

Dimensions:—

Height, 6 ft. 6½ in.; length, 4 ft. 2 in.; depth, 2 ft. 6 in.

Instrumentation:—

Piano, 44 notes, with loud and soft pedal and with mandolin attachment; 44 cremona-toned pipes; representing first violin, second violin, viola and "cello"; set of orchestra bells. Swell box in rear to add expression to music.

When ordering, please furnish data to electric power—such as number of volts and cycles. Book of instructions with each instrument.

Sextrola "B"—52 Notes

12 Selections

North Tonawanda Musical Instrument Works' Sextrola style A and B. The Sextrola B was later sold as the Capitol Bluebird Orchestra as noted on the preceding page.

**Art
Design**

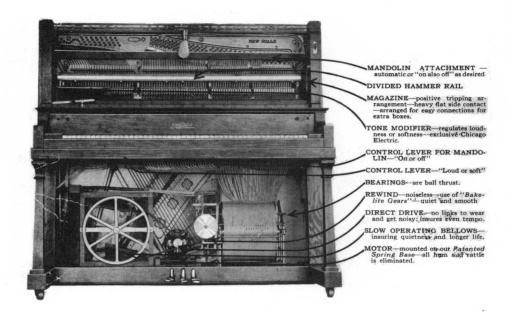

MANDOLIN ATTACHMENT — automatic or "on also off" as desired.

DIVIDED HAMMER RAIL

MAGAZINE — positive tripping arrangement — heavy flat side contact — arranged for easy connections for extra boxes.

TONE MODIFIER — regulates loudness or softness — exclusive Chicago Electric.

CONTROL LEVER FOR MANDOLIN — "On or off"

CONTROL LEVER — "Loud or soft"

BEARINGS — are ball thrust.

REWIND — noiseless — use of "Bakelite Gears" — quiet and smooth

DIRECT DRIVE — no links to wear and get noisy; insures even tempo.

SLOW OPERATING BELLOWS — insuring quietness and longer life.

MOTOR — mounted on our *Patented Spring Base* — all hum and rattle is eliminated.

The
CHICAGO ELECTRIC
MODEL K

*The
CHICAGO
ELECTRIC*

MODEL
EL-2

We are offering you the Chicago Electric Piano—coin operated—that furnishes music of the quality that pleases. The real quality of piano playing that people like. Especially popular with young people.

The Chicago Electric line was manufactured by Smith, Barnes & Strohber Company, a division of the Continental Piano Company of Chicago. A trade directory of the mid-1920's places the annual output of the firm at 15,000 pianos; however, only a small fraction of these must have been coin-operated models as Chicago Electric machines are very scarce today. The Chicago Electric models shown on this page used the standard "A" coin piano roll. Standard instrumentation of the K and EL-2 models consisted of a piano with a mandolin attachment. A xylophone was available at extra cost with the model K. According to a sales catalogue the Chicago Electric was "a modern electric piano of the highest order, constructed to serve without difficulty."

Many other manufacturing firms were active in the market. National, Electrova, Nelson-Wiggen, Rhapsodist, Niagara, Johnson, Chicago Electric and many others—about one hundred different major manufacturers and marketers in all — each claimed a share of the lucrative market. Some, like the Piano Player Manufacturing Company of Cincinnati, were strictly limited-production concerns. Others, such as Seeburg and Wurlitzer, were nationwide or even worldwide and produced tens of thousands of machines in many different styles, shapes and sizes.

Perhaps the most widely used method of advertising during this time was that of printing testimonials; probably on the theory that what's good for your neighbor is good for you too. What restaurant owner could resist the temptation that a competitor's *Seeburg H* orchestrion, costing $2,500.00, had paid for itself in just fourteen months? And if this statement were not enough, there were dozens of other testimonials ready to use.

Any resistance to the purchase of a new Seeburg orchestrion could easily be overcome when the Seeburg salesman presented this testimonial (from a Mr. Frank Wasikowski):

> "It gives me great pleasure to inform you that the orchestrion which I purchased from you last November has proven a great success. My business has increased 25 percent, which I attribute wholly to the Seeburg orchestrion style 'G'.

> I cannot express too highly my approval of the musical qualities of the Seeburg orchestrion, as well as the way the instrument has been running without getting out of order, considering that in the past eleven months there have gone through this instrument over thirty thousand (30,000) nickels.

> The receipts from the orchestrion have far surpassed my expectations. I now own this instrument, with only the expense to me of the initial down payment..."

Not only did coin pianos take in a torrent of nickels, they increased business as well. In Denver one J.H. Doherty (owner of a Wurlitzer coin piano) reported that, "...It took some careful consideration before making the investment, thinking that it would not pay me to do so. I now consider it to be the best investment I have made. I have had it six weeks and it has taken in, in nickels, $92.00, and it has increased my bar trade at least from $6.00 to $10.00 per day..."

We cannot help but wonder that the musicians' unions would say today about this one (from a German restaurant in New York City):

> "...It was my original intention to secure an orchestra of three musicians, but I can truthfully say that I am grateful to your representative for persuading me to do otherwise... The other day I figured that I have already saved $2,160.00 on musicians, besides being able to furnish my patrons with music at all times..."

The Mills Novelty Company of Chicago printed a booklet containing nothing but testimonials concerning its products. Among those writing to Mills over the years were the U.S. Commissioner of Patents, the mayor of Omaha, the governor of Idaho, the president of Cornell University, composer George M. Cohan and dozens of other luminaries.

The output of most companies was limited to coin-operated pianos and orchestrions. However, a few ventured into new areas. Seeking new fields of profit the American Automusic Company, also known as the American Automatic Banjo Company, marketed a coin-operated banjo, the *Encore*. Expanding on this theme the *Banjorchestra*, billed as "The Automatic Marvel of the Age," added a piano, tambourine, triangle, bass drum, kettle drum and castanets to accompany the banjo.

Wurlitzer's self-playing *Harp* with its dulcet tones was recommended for small places in which a piano might be too loud.

Self-playing xylophones, automatic buglers and trumpeters and many other types of mechanical instruments were experimented with and placed on

The Nelson-Wiggen Orchestra --- Style 5-X

IN selecting the best automatic musical instrument for your purpose you can be wisely guided by the practical considerations that influence the preference of so many owners and managers of public places.
The Nelson-Wiggen Orchestra, Style 5X, is as dependable and practical as it is beautiful and attractive --- so necessary in an instrument from which the most profits are expected.

Supplied in Walnut or Mahogany
Height: 68 inches
Width: 46 inches
Depth: 27 inches
Weight, boxed for shipment: about 800 lbs.
Furnished regularly with Curtains and supplied with Art Glass on special order

Contains piano, banjo attachment, set of Marimbas, snare drum and triangle. Plays a standard orchestrated ten-tune roll.

Formed in the 1920's by Oscar Nelson and Peter Wiggen, two former Seeburg superintendents, the Nelson-Wiggen Piano Company quickly achieved a reputation for well-built quality products. The 5-X orchestrion shown above used a regular G (or 4X) orchestrion roll. Other Nelson-Wiggen machines included several different styles of keyboard pianos and orchestrions and several cabinet styles including one with a xylophone and set of orchestra bells which played alternately by means of a special switching arrangement.

Mills Violano Virtuoso

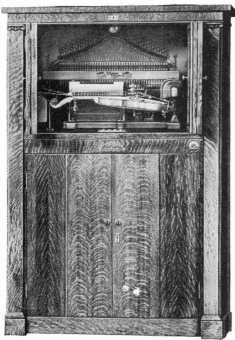

(Made with one or two Violins)

10 Reasons Why the Violano is Great for Any Business

1. World's Greatest Business Builder to Neighborhood or Small City Stores.
2. Increases Sales 10% to 100%.
3. Makes "Extra" Profit in Coins Dropped Into Coin Box—up to $200.00 a month.
4. Takes Place of Orchestra.
5. Livens up Store and Entertains Customers.
6. Puts Your Store Above Ordinary Competition.
7. Pays You Two-Way Profits—Increased Business—and in Nickels Dropped into Coin Box.
8. Furnishes Highest Quality of Music.
9. Lasts Practically a Life Time — Many of First Instruments Installed fifteen years ago are still rendering satisfactory service.
10. Can be Bought on Easy Monthly Payments.

Mills Violano Virtuoso

Like a 3 to 4 Piece Orchestra

This is a self-playing violin and piano. As each violin string has a separate bow, two or more strings are played at the same time, thus giving the effect of a three to four piece stringed orchestra.

Designated by the U. S. Government as "One of the Eight Greatest Inventions of the Decade"

So superior is the Violano to all other musical instruments that the U. S. Government designated it as "One of the Eight Greatest Inventions of the Decade," and exhibited it at Government expense at four of the greatest expositions in the United States.

Read These Proofs of Enormous Profits

$2,856.65 The First Year

"The Mills Violano Virtuoso has an earning power more than double any other instrument. My Violano has earned $2,856.65 during the first year."

Buckhorn Curio Store, Texas.

$130.00 A Month

"While the Mills Violano Virtuoso makes money for me up to $130.00 a month—it also draws people and increases my business. I would recommend the Violano to anyone because it is the best musical instrument you can get."

Chas. Mullen, New York.

Measures	Weighs
64x 43x31 inches	730 lbs.
163x110x79 centimeters	332 kgs.
Packed for shipment:	
78x 51x38 inches	1075 lbs.
199x130x97 centimeters	488 kgs.
5 Rolls of Music	

Measures	Weighs
	26 lbs.
	12 kgs.
Packed for shipment:	
27x19x14 inches	68 lbs.
69x49x36 centimeters	31 kgs.

The Mills Violano-Virtuoso was first introduced to the public at the 1909 Alaska-Yukon-Pacific Exposition. It was exhibited there as part of a U.S. Patent Office display of American inventions. The Violano was a great drawing card and attracted much attention. The Violano-Virtuoso was a refinement (with piano added) of the earlier Mills Automatic Virtuosa violin-playing machine. Unlike most other automatic musical instruments of the day the Mills Violano-Virtuoso was not pneumatically operated but worked instead by electromagnets. The paper roll was "read" by metal brushes and a contact roller, an advanced system for the time. The machine shown in the above 1929 Mills catalogue illustration is the Grand Model Violano Virtuoso which listed for $2000.00 but was available for $300.00 cash plus 25 monthly installments (including interest) of $68.00 each. The model with two violins cost $3000.00. As an attention-getter the Violano was matched by few other automatic instruments. They are no less interesting today. The several hundred remaining single-violin models and the two dozen or so surviving double-violin models are highly prized by collectors.

Mills Magnetic Expression Piano

All Electric ～ 1,000 Fewer Parts

Any air-operated piano has at least 1,000 more parts than the Mills! We'll prove it. Open up the Mills and look at the working mechanism. You can hardly believe it is a piano—so simple is the construction. All air apparatus is dispensed with. Every part of the mechanism is visible and every operation of every note can be seen and understood!

Here's all there is to The Mills; for every note a hammer, magnet, and string; a hammer rail for expression; a music roll, feeder, and motor; and a coin box; NOTHING COULD BE MORE SIMPLE. No sensible merchant, after seeing The Mills, could be satisfied with any other piano.

Measures	Weighs
65x56x28 inches	800 lbs.
166x143x72 centimeters	363 kgs.
Packed for shipment:	
78x63x33 inches	1200 lbs.
199x160x84 centimeters	544 kgs.

Mills Magnetic Expression Piano

Consider These 10 Special Features

1. The ONLY electric piano produced.
2. Absolutely no pneumatic apparatus.
3. Should last for twenty years.
4. Graduation of Expression over 65 notes.
5. A piano—nothing else.
6. A thousand fewer parts.
7. A $3,000 tone.
8. Exclusive sounding board.
9. Uses hand-played rolls—10 selections on every roll.
10. Quickly pays for itself.

Installed In A Moment

Just connect the piano with the current in your store (either Alternating or Direct) and the instrument is ready to play. The Mills has a range of Sixty-five notes—it can play every style of piano music with complete elaborations. Write for complete information regarding this wonderful piano and our easy payment plan.

Read These Letters from Successful Merchants

$85.00 Last Month

"I wouldn't be without good music in my store because it draws so many young people and increases my business. Your piano has cleared me $85.00 last month."

Chas. Schweppe, N. C.

$825.00 Last Year

"I am pleased to report that I have just checked up the earnings on my Mills Piano and find that it cleared me $825.00 clear profit last year."

Robert K. Crowe, N. Dak.

The Mills Magnetic Expression Piano was first marketed in the 1920's. Like the Violano-Virtuoso it was operated by electromagnets. Variations of the Expression Piano included the Mills Piano Orchestra (with drums and traps added) and the Race Horse Piano (see page 66). About four thousand Violano-Virtuosos were sold. However, no such success attended the Expression Piano. It is doubtful if more than a few hundred Expression Pianos were ever sold. Of all American automatic musical instrument manufacturers the only one that distributed its products widely in England was Mills. In 1908 a Mills Automatic Virtuosa toured England and received nearly two thousand newspaper notices! Mills evidently felt therefore that England would be a good place to market the Violano-Virtuoso. During your author's trips to England he has learned of many extant Mills machines, but virtually none of any other American manufacturers. Outstanding was the hoard discovered by Frank Holland of the Piano Museum, Brentford, Middlesex. This large group consisted of over a dozen Violano-Virtuosos, one Expression Piano and three Race Horse Pianos. They had previously been on a route of coin-operated machines owned by the Sampson Novelty Company of London. Several years earlier another hoard, this one consisting of nearly twenty Violano-Virtuosos still in their factory shipping crates, was located in England by Robert Johnson of Rossville, Georgia.

The Automatic
The BANJ

6 ft. 7 in. hig

THE USE OF THE BANJORCHESTRA

The Banjorchestra is a highly artistic automatic instrument which may be used in the place of the banjo orchestra, which has become popular in dancing salons, owing to its adaptability to the dance music of the day. Perfect rhythm for the modern dances has been worked out in the music rolls by which this instrument is operated. All the expression which is put into the music by the most extensive banjo orchestra is reproduced by this instrument. It may be used with great effect in high class dancing salons, and where cabaret entertainment is in vogue, and dancing is indulged in by the guests, at a saving of from $100 to $400 a week.

The Banjorchestra may also be used in ice=cream parlors, cafes and places of amusement as a coin operated instrument for profit.

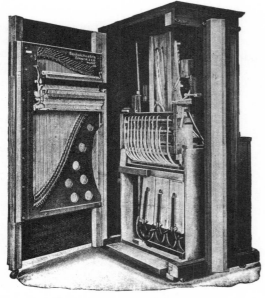

Banjochestra—Showing Accessibility for Tuning

WHAT

The Banjorchestra comprises an automatic
drums and castanets, accompanied by an a
may be attached to any ordinary electric soc
with or without a coin. If operated with a
and the instrument will continue to play u
artistic. It is finished in mahogany and the
in the upper door. It is equipped with a
for the piano, and an automatic muffler fo

PIANO
should investigate our liberal propositio

The CONNORIZED

The Banjorchestra was certainly one of the most interesting of the early automatic machines.

arvel of the Age
RCHESTRA

2 ft. 7 in. deep.

ACCESSIBILITY FOR REGULATION

All the controls are directly in front of the lower part of the instrument. The banjo is regulation size and equipped with wire strings. It may be tuned easily, by the use of four buttons which have been installed in the panel at the top of the instrument which sound the four notes of the piano to which the banjo should be tuned. The entire back of the instrument opens, so that the piano may be tuned with the greatest ease. By pressing a series of five buttons the traps may be cut off singly or as a group.

MUSIC ROLLS

Owing to their equipment and many years' experience as manufacturers of high-grade music rolls, the Connorized Music Co. is admirably well fitted to produce music rolls of artistic and attractive arrangement. Those for the Banjorchestra are specially prepared for dancing. The rhythm, expression and time which are all cut in the roll have been carefully and scientifically produced so that the greatest effect for dancing is had at all times. They have been cut and timed the proper length of the dance, and when rerolled commence over again for an encore. In fact, the Banjorchestra does what human hands have been doing at about one-tenth the cost.

Special rolls have been prepared for the Banjorchestra when used as a coin-operated instrument. Each roll comprises ten selections of the latest and most popular song and dance hits.

OMPRISES

ported by tambourine, triangle, bass and kettle piano. It is operated by an electric motor which alternating or direct current. It may be operated many as 20 coins may be inserted at one time, st coin has been used. Its case design is highly d traps may be seen through a large plate-glass tic rerolling device, automatic expression devices jo.

RCHANTS

are in the profits of this 20th-century marvel.

JSIC CO. 144th St. and Austin Place
NEW YORK

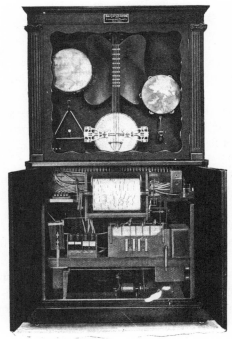

Banjorchestra Showing Mechanism and Controls

Race Horse Piano

Thrilling and Amusing—Big Money Maker

How It Operates

Six numbered horses line up at the minature judges stand and start off around the race track (as shown in the illustration). They disappear around the bend in the track only to appear a few seconds later dashing down the home stretch. It's thrilling—fascinating— keeps the crowd on their toes with excitement. They can't wait for the next race. They deposit nickel after nickel while the same piece is being played. A few seconds completes a race so the crowds can have ten or fifteen races while one piece of music is being played. Every time a nickel is deposited the horses start on another race so this instrument may take in 50c or 75c while a single selection of music is being rendered.

Friendly groups stand around trying to guess the winner each time. If their favorite doesn't win the first time, they are anxiluos for another race. They want to guess the winner, and they play it again and again. They not only drop nickel after nickel into the instrument, but also liberally settle their arguments with drinks, cigars, and other merchandise.

How Profits Are Divided

The Race Horse Piano is usually purchased by the dealer, but can be installed by operator on a commission basis, the dealer receiving from 25% to 40% of gross receipts for the use of his location.

Average Monthly Earnings $150.00 to $300.00

The Mills Race Horse Piano was a Mills Expression Piano with a diorama of racing horses added. The horses were jogged along by a moving belt below them. The winner varied from race to race and provided excitement for onlookers who, according to the catalogue, "also liberally settle their arguments with drinks, cigars and other merchandise." As the above description indicates the Race Horse Piano was primarily intended as a gambling device, with the musical feature being secondary. The Mills Novelty Company was mainly a manufacturer of slot machines and other gambling equipment, and was probably the largest concern in the field at one time. A 1931 Fortune Magazine article placed Mills' annual sales volume at $10,000,000.00. Among the firm's assets at that time was the yacht "Minoco," a name formed no doubt from a contraction of Mills Novelty Company.

the market, usually without great success. Many were one-of-a-kind and never reached production status.

The greatest success in the area of unusual machines was the famous *Violano-Virtuoso* produced by the Mills Novelty Company, a leading maker of arcade machines and gambling equipment.

The *Violano-Virtuoso* featured a real violin operated by a mechanical bow and small magnetically-worked fingers. Over four thousand of these machines were sold at prices up to $3,200.00 each. Much less successful was the Mills automatic *Viol-Cello* which imitated a string quartet.

Expositions and fairs were a major part of life in the early twentieth century. Each exposition presented hundreds of awards. Each event had a quota of coin-operated pianos on view, hoping to win

recognition. Few were disappointed as there was usually an award for nearly everyone.

A huge Welte orchestrion won a gold medal at the 1893 Columbian Exposition. Wurlitzer copped gold medals for its machines displayed at the 1901 Pan-American Exposition in Buffalo and at St. Louis' 1904 Louisiana Purchase Exposition. Engelhardt did likewise.

Many early machines carried decal reproductions of these award medals prominently displayed on the front.

At the Alaska-Yukon-Pacific Exposition held in Seattle in 1909 the Mills Novelty Company was selected to exhibit its *Violano-Virtuoso* as part of the United States Patent Office display. This machine was selected more because of its curiosity value than for any other reason. Other products in the exhibit such as the Ives Calorimeter and the

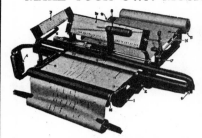
Leabarjan made a number of different music roll perforators. They ranged in size from small hand-operated machines like the one shown above to large commercial models. Music roll making was a painstaking task that required much experience. Only the most venturesome home player piano owner would attempt to cut his own rolls, especially as thousands of different music roll titles were available at local stores for 50¢ to $1 each.

Parallax Stereogram were apt to be less interesting to the average viewer. Mills never forgot this recognition. The last *Violano* to roll off of the assembly line around 1929 carried the notation, "DESIGNATED BY THE U. S. GOVERNMENT AS ONE OF THE EIGHT GREATEST INVENTIONS OF THE DECADE" . . . as did every other one of the 4,000-odd machines which preceded it!

Prohibition spread throughout America on a local option basis during World War I. In January, 1920, Prohibition was adopted nationwide, marking the end of one of the best customers of the coin-operated piano business. Saloons and bars all across the land closed their doors, at least officially. The bootleg operations and speakeasies which replaced them compensated for the loss only to a degree.

The era of large orchestrions ended, for all practical purposes, with Prohibition in 1920. The number of larger machines sold in America after that date was but a small fraction of the amount sold during the height of the market from about 1905 to World War I. Most machines in the 1920-1930 era were smaller. The cabinet and keyboard pianos and small orchestrions of Seeburg were among the most popular, as were the coin pianos of Nelson-Wiggen and Western Electric.

Sound movies, which completely revolutionized the theatre business in 1926 and 1927, took another good customer out of the market. To the scrap heap went untold hundreds of automatic pianos, orchestrions and photoplayers, to be replaced by electronic tubes, speakers and wires.

The complete end of the coin-operated piano business was signaled by the growing popularity of radios and, to a lesser extent, juke boxes in the 1920's. For some reason or other the scratchy music of the radios and record discs won favor over the honky-tonk sound of the coin pianos. The final death knell came with the great Depression of the 1930's. Most coin-pianos were junked or broken up and sold for parts. A number of orchestrions in a Tulsa, Oklahoma warehouse were sold for $5.00 each to a buyer who wanted them for the electric motors in each one. Oswald Wurdeman, owner of about 350 Western Electric coin pianos out on location in Minnesota, rounded them all up around 1930 and split each machine apart . . . because the iron piano plate in each would bring $1.75 from a scrap metal dealer.

A few firms, those which diversified into other fields, survived, but most coin-operated piano manufacturers went bankrupt. The names of Electrova, Berry-Wood, Coinola, Peerless, Cremona and countless others are remembered today only by the machines which are preserved in collections. The business of coin piano and orchestrion manufacturing disappeared forever from the American scene.

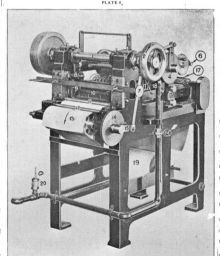

The Acme Combination Master Roll and Music Roll Perforator was intended for commercial use. Today Edward Freyer of Flemington, New Jersey uses a similar machine to recut standard "A," "G," Link and other coin piano and orchestrion rolls for collectors.

The Children's Party

"THE reason why boys and girls leave home," once said a keen observer, "is that so few homes are made interesting for young people. The natural craving for amusement very often overcomes personal attachments."

Will you admit that you cannot give your children better reason to pass their evenings with you than to seek elsewhere for an outlet for youthful spirits? If you have sought for means to make your home attractive and have failed to solve the problem, why not provide music? Then there will be a source of constant interest and enjoyment for the young people.

And there is still another important reason why you should have such an instrument—it will develop the finer instincts in minds which are most receptive to influence. It will cultivate perceptions and create and enlarge ideals which might otherwise never become matured.

You can buy a piano or a violin, but consider that it will be years before a child can play either of them well, and then only if practice has been a daily duty regularly performed. Why should you spend money for music lessons, and why should the satisfaction of enjoying the best playing of the best compositions be deferred when you can have at once, more than years of practice can give?

Look back upon your own childhood and think what it would have meant to you then if you could have had such a means of recreation. Consider how satisfying it would have been for you to learn while still young, all the fine points of musical literature? Do you know them even now?

If you had to sacrifice the advantages now available with these instruments, see that your children have them.

Page from the Mills catalogue, The Electrical Mastery of Music, illustrating the Mills Viol-Cello. The Viol-Cello incorporated a violin and cello, as the name implies. It was not successful as no way was found to mechanically finger the cello strings properly.

A Dream of a Dance

THINK of gliding through the steps of a Strauss waltz played as only masters can play it, and with all the beauty that the composer himself would put into it if he were present!

Waltz, two-step, schottische, "barn-dance," or the classic minuet are all played with perfect harmony by the magic touch of this instrument which is always ready, which never becomes fatigued, and which is never subject to "moods."

The dancing academy will find that our instruments are not only the best for use in teaching the various steps, but that their music is much more distinctive in character than that of the piano and violin as played by the usual assistants. Pupils will be interested as well as instructed, and an interested student is the one best satisfied and most easily taught.

The entire range of the best dance music is covered by the rolls we have prepared for this purpose. From the famous waltzes to the latest two-step, you can choose as many selections as you wish.

The great variety of compositions thus made available by one of these instruments gives an important advantage over "hand playing" in addition to the superior quality of the music.

Aside from their musical superiority, the "Viol instruments" present an advantage in the small floor space which they occupy.

From every point of view, therefore, we offer ideal instruments for this special use, which although secondary to other purposes is still worthy of consideration.

We invite managers of dancing academies, proprietors of summer resorts and others interested in dance music to ask for any further information desired.

The Mills Viol-Xylophone was similar to a Violano-Virtuoso but had a xylophone instead of a piano. Evidently only a few were made for they are virtually non-existent today.

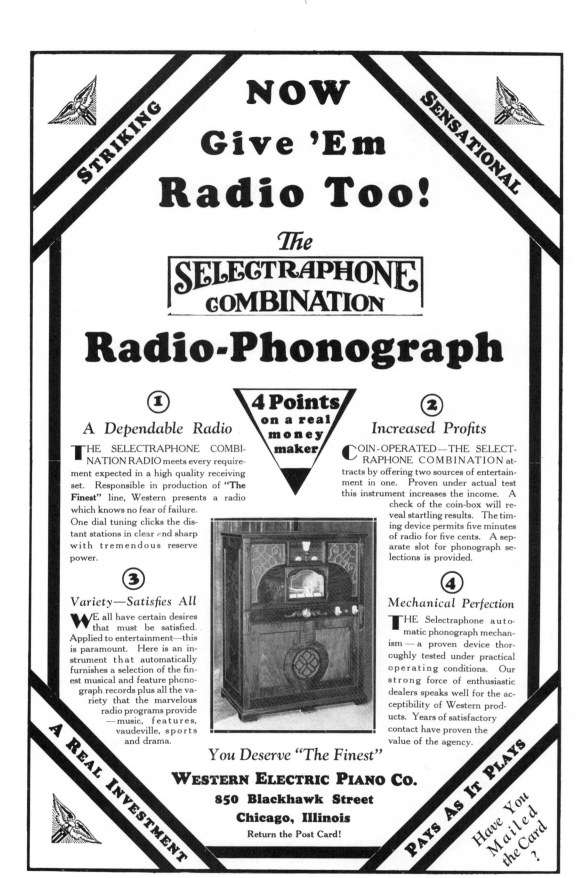

NOW Give 'Em Radio Too!

STRIKING · SENSATIONAL

The SELECTRAPHONE COMBINATION

Radio-Phonograph

4 Points on a real money maker

① A Dependable Radio

THE SELECTRAPHONE COMBINATION RADIO meets every requirement expected in a high quality receiving set. Responsible in production of **"The Finest"** line, Western presents a radio which knows no fear of failure. One dial tuning clicks the distant stations in clear and sharp with tremendous reserve power.

② Increased Profits

COIN-OPERATED—THE SELECTRAPHONE COMBINATION attracts by offering two sources of entertainment in one. Proven under actual test this instrument increases the income. A check of the coin-box will reveal startling results. The timing device permits five minutes of radio for five cents. A separate slot for phonograph selections is provided.

③ Variety—Satisfies All

WE all have certain desires that must be satisfied. Applied to entertainment—this is paramount. Here is an instrument that automatically furnishes a selection of the finest musical and feature phonograph records plus all the variety that the marvelous radio programs provide—music, features, vaudeville, sports and drama.

④ Mechanical Perfection

THE Selectraphone automatic phonograph mechanism—a proven device thoroughly tested under practical operating conditions. Our strong force of enthusiastic dealers speaks well for the acceptibility of Western products. Years of satisfactory contact have proven the value of the agency.

You Deserve "The Finest"

WESTERN ELECTRIC PIANO CO.
850 Blackhawk Street
Chicago, Illinois
Return the Post Card!

A REAL INVESTMENT · PAYS AS IT PLAYS · Have You Mailed the Card ?

The coming of the new age . . . In the 1920's and 1930's coin pianos were gradually replaced by jukeboxes such as the model shown above. Keeping in step with the times Western Electric, Seeburg, Wurlitzer, Rock-Ola and others entered the jukebox business. The Western Electric "Selectraphone Combination" combined two popular appeals . . . the jukebox and the radio.

Chapter 3

In the chronicle of coin-operated pianos and orchestrions many firms appeared, lived a brief day in the sunlight and then disappeared into the oblivion of time. Save a mention or two in the trade journals of the day little is known concerning many of these ephemeral companies.

"The Monarch Musical Instrument Company (maker of the Monarch Electric Piano), while comparatively a new concern, has made rapid progress in its line. The company was organized less than six months ago with a capital of $10,000. and it began business in a small shop in Young Street... The Capital has just been increased to $100,000.... Many of its instruments have already been placed in operation, and one has sold others, for as yet the company has begun no organized sales campaign. The merit of its product alone has been more than sufficient to sell the entire output, and as a matter of fact a number of advance orders are now on the books... ...we have no hesitation in saying that the company is destined to become one of the foremost concerns in its line within a short time..."

The above announcement, appearing in 1912, presaged a bright future for Monarch. However, fate must have intervened (or else the above-mentioned sales campaign *never* was organized!) for the firm passed into obscurity. The same tale was repeated dozens of times for dozens of others. Only a few hardy firms ever made the climb to success.

Among those who did succeed in the field of coin-operated music during the early part of this century was the Rudolph Wurlitzer Company. With its *Tonophone* Wurlitzer was the leader in the field in the late 1890's when the market was at its beginning in America. When the curtain closed three decades later some of the last coin pianos to be made bore the Wurlitzer label. From the little $500.00 *Pianino* to the gigantic $10,000.00 *Paganini Violin Orchestra* Wurlitzer had a machine for every musical need, for every musical desire.

Illustration from a Wurlitzer catalogue of World War I vintage showing the scope of the Wurlitzer musical business at that time.

The author, holding an early Wurlitzer catalogue, stands with Mr. Farny Wurlitzer during a visit to his North Tonawanda office. Above is a portrait of Rudolph Wurlitzer, founder of the firm.

Entrance to the Wurlitzer factory at North Tonawanda, New York. Photograph taken in 1964.

To a large degree the history of the Rudolph Wurlitzer Company's activities in the coin-operated piano and orchestrion field is the history of the field itself. A study of Wurlitzer, its products and the methods by which it sold them is, in a sense, a study of the entire industry. Wurlitzer's hundreds of different styles of machines, its activities in the market from the beginning in 1899 until the end during the early 1930's and the sheer volume of its sales were equalled by no other manufacturer.

During the preparation of this book Mr. Farny Wurlitzer, son of Rudolph Wurlitzer, made available to the author the historical records and catalogues of the Wurlitzer Company. Mr. Wurlitzer, who personally supervised the coin piano and orchestrion part of the business from 1909 onward, was in a unique position to contribute first-hand knowledge. This he did admirably. Many important facts concerning the Wurlitzer Company and its competitors would have otherwise been lost forever to history had it not been for Mr. Wurlitzer's interest. Photographs taken in the Wurlitzer factory, photographs of limited production and one-of-a-kind machines, original advertisements and brochures . . . these and many other things from the Wurlitzer files and records shed new light on the mechanical music industry during the early twentieth century.

During the beginning years of this century the Rudolph Wurlitzer Company was well diversified in the music field, as it is today. In addition to the coin-operated pianos and orchestrions a wide line of other products reached the marketplace. The Wurlitzer band organs for skating rinks and carousels, the mighty Wurlitzer Hope-Jones Unit Orchestra theatre pipe organ, a complete line of band

instruments, harps, pianos and even a collection and inventory of rare violins . . . all were of high quality and all achieved prominence and a large share of the market in their respective fields.

The Rudolph Wurlitzer Company, with its worldwide operations and multi-million dollar sales of today, had a humble beginning.

Rudolph Wurlitzer was born in Schoeneck, Germany on January 30, 1831, the son of a musical craftsman. At the time of Rudolph's birth the family was already steeped in nearly two centuries of musical tradition. In the 1600's his forebear, Nicholas Wurlitzer, was an honored member of the Lutemaker's Guild, a distinction conferred only upon a selected few.

Young Rudolph's formal education consisted mainly of learning in the schools of Schoeneck and Plauen. His spare time was mainly occupied with musical instrument making taught by his father, Christian Gottfried Wurlitzer.

When Rudolph finished school he was told that there was no opportunity for him in the family trade in Germany. The business was destined to go to Constantin, a favored younger brother.

This disheartening news prompted Rudolph, after some consideration, to seek his fortune in America. With no funds of his own, Rudolph approached his father for the necessary passage money. His request was flatly refused. Fortunately an uncle, Wilhelm, finally provided the $80.00 required.

In 1853 Rudolph Wurlitzer, then in his twenties, sailed across the Atlantic Ocean to America. After an uneventful journey his ship docked at Hoboken, New Jersey. (The exact location is not clear; Hoboken is the most probable.) Rudolph's first employment was with a local grocery store. With no money and with a negligible knowledge of the English language it was a difficult beginning.

Realizing that his grocery job offered little in the way of compensation or advancement potential Rudolph decided to move to Cincinnati. His route took him by way of Philadelphia, a large and bustling city which held many attractions. The young immigrant considered making his home there, but after an encounter in the street with a rude Philadelphia man he continued on to Cincinnati.

Peddling trinkets door-to-door was Rudolph Wurlitzer's first job in Cincinnati. Next came work in a department store at a salary of four dollars per week. With the future in mind Rudolph wanted to set aside twenty-five percent of his earnings as savings. He soon realized that this would be virtually impossible to do in addition to maintaining room and board. The savings program was started only when the owner of the store consented to let him sleep in a packing crate on the premises.

In 1854 Wurlitzer secured a job as a clerk with the Heidelbach & Seasongood Bank in Cincinnati. This new $8.00 per week position included the privilege of sleeping in a loft over the bank.

Only a few steps from the bank was a retail music store which Rudolph visited often. The selling prices of the instruments were very high there compared to the values with which he was familiar in Europe. The dealer, one Mr. Johnson, bought his wares from a jobber who, in turn, purchased the instruments from an importer. The importer bought from a factor who bought from a European purchasing agent. The agent bought from European manufacturers. With this seemingly interminable chain of middlemen, each one of whom took a profit, the retail music store made only a slight gain despite the high selling prices.

Sensing an opportunity, Rudolph contemplated selling musical instruments as a part-time venture. Attractive profits could be realized by eliminating the middlemen.

In 1856 he sent his savings of $700.00, earned at the bank and by extra outside work, to his father in Germany. Soon a selection of German musical instruments, mainly woodwinds, arrived in Cincinnati.

Upon receiving the shipment Rudolph Wurlitzer took the instruments to Johnson's music store and tried to sell them. His offer was refused outright.

Not knowing whether he priced them too high, whether the quality was poor, or what the problem was Rudolph asked the music merchant for a frank evaluation of what was wrong.

The storekeeper said something to the effect: "Young man, you could not sell these fine musical instruments at this low price if you had obtained them honestly."

Rudolph then requested time to think the situation over and recalculate his prices. Subsequently he revisited the store owner and told him that he had imported the instruments and had probably figured his costs incorrectly. With his newly raised prices, he made a $1500.00 profit. At the new valuations the instruments sold immediately! This incident marked the beginning of the Wurlitzer business in America.

The importation of more instruments increased Rudolph's trade to the point at which it was more than just a sideline. To provide inventory space a small upstairs room was rented at 4th and Sycamore streets in Cincinnati.

Soon his employers, Heidelbach & Seasongood, recognizing his outstanding business ability, suggested he strike out on his own. With their good wishes he left the bank and devoted full time to his music business.

Beginning in 1860 Wurlitzer sold drums to the United States Army. A small factory was set up to manufacture drums on the premises. Next came an order for military trumpets and bugles which were imported from Germany. From the very beginning of the Civil War the Union troops marched to the cadence of Wurlitzer music.

The business prospered. It did so well that one of Rudolph's brothers, Anton, came to America to assist. Shortly after his arrival Anton Wurlitzer saw limited service in the Civil War. Fighting as part of the Seventh Regiment of the Ohio Volunteers he sustained a bullet wound in his head. The bullet lodged within his skull and was never removed, causing him to have frequent headaches for the remainder of his life.

In 1865 a branch store was opened at 82 Dearborn Street in Chicago. It was the first of several dozen branches which would be opened over a period of years.

Rudolph Wurlitzer and Miss Leonie Farny exchanged marriage vows in September, 1868. In 1871 their first male child, Howard, was born.

The partnership of Wurlitzer & Brother was formed about this time; later to be dissolved with the incorporation of the Rudolph Wurlitzer Company (with Rudolph as president) in 1890.

In these early years most of Wurlitzer's efforts were concentrated on regular musical instruments. A few imported music boxes, crank-operated Automatic Pianistas which sold for $450.00 each, mechanical organs and a few similar items were carried in stock, but evidently these formed only a minor part of sales.

Beginning in the 1880's America became interested in music boxes. Cylinder-operated Swiss, German and French music boxes were imported by the thousands. Music boxes operated by metal discs grew in popularity. These were mass produced by Symphonion, Criterion, Stella, Regina, Polyphon and others.

Aware of the growing demand for music boxes Rudolph Wurlitzer secured a sales distributorship from the Regina Music Box Company of Rahway, New Jersey. Regina was the largest manufacturer of music boxes in America. The Regina machines sold well. In time the Rudolph Wurlitzer Company grew to be the largest single sales outlet for the many different Regina musical products.

In 1896 Wurlitzer persuaded Regina to equip some of its music boxes, particularly the large 27-inch diameter disc changer machines, with coin slots. These large glass-fronted *Orchestral Corona* models would play the choice of one tune from a selection of twelve for a coin (usually a nickel) deposited in the slot. The great success of these Regina machines provided Wurlitzer with an insight into the great potential for coin-operated music.

Orchestral Regina, No. 5.

LONG-RUNNING MOVEMENT. WITH COIN ATTACHMENT.

Two large Steel Combs, with 175 Tongues, tuned in chromatic scale embracing over 7 octaves.

Dimensions of Tune Sheets, 27 ins. diameter.
Case in Mahogany or Oak; dimensions, 79 x 43 x 18 inches.

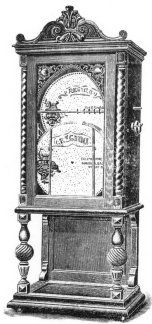

Sublima Corona, No. 38.
with Piano Sounding Board.
AUTOMATIC TUNE CHANGING DEVICE.
WITH COIN ATTACHMENT. LONG-RUNNING MOVEMENT.
Two large Combs, with 130 Tongues,
tuned in chromatic scale, embracing over 7 octaves.
Case in Oak or Mahogany.
Dimensions, 78 x 32 x 24 inches.

No. 38, Flat.—Case with flat front, like cut.
No. 38, Round.—Case with round front.

Orchestral Corona, No. 34
With Piano Sounding Board.
WITH AUTOMATIC TUNE CHANGING DEVICE.
LONG-RUNNING MOVEMENT. WITH COIN ATTACHMENT.

Two large Combs, with 175 Tongues, embracing
over 7 octaves.
Dimensions of Tune Sheets, 27 inches diameter.
Case in Oak or Mahogany, highly polished;
dimensions, 75 x 39 x 24 inches.

The Regina Music Box Company of Rahway, New Jersey was the leading manufacturer of music boxes in America. By the late 1890's the Rudolph Wurlitzer Company was the largest single sales outlet for Regina products. Regina models #38 and #34 shown above have the automatic tune changer, a rack which stored twelve discs, any one of which could be individually selected for playing. The machines could be adjusted to play the tune sheet through either once or twice upon receipt of a coin. The success of the Regina machines inspired Wurlitzer to develop further the field of coin-operated music.

The large-scale entry of Wurlitzer into the field of mechanical music traces its beginning to 1897. In that year Eugene DeKleist, a manufacturer of barrel organs, sought to expand his market for the brass trumpets he used in these machines. DeKleist journeyed to Chicago where he met with officials of Lyon & Healy, leading instrument retailers in that city.

The Lyon & Healy firm wasn't interested but directed DeKleist to the Rudolph Wurlitzer Company in Cincinnati. After hearing the proposal Wurlitzer placed a large order for the brass trumpets.

By 1897 Eugene DeKleist had been in America only a few years. A native of Dusseldorf, Germany, he made his first trip to the United States in 1892. In that year the United States government increased the import tariff on barrel organs, making it unprofitable to import them from the manufacturing centers of France and Germany. In 1893 DeKleist, long experienced in the field, started the North Tonawanda Barrel Organ Works. Encouragement

and assistance were provided by the Armitage-Herschell Company, builders of merry-go-rounds and carousels. To provide a start the machinery and woodworking equipment of the defunct Hewitt Furniture Company were purchased and moved into a newly constructed building.

Over the next few years many different types of machines were produced by DeKleist's enterprise. A North Tonawanda Barrel Organ Works catalogue of the day lists barrel organs, quatours, hurdy-gurdies, flute organs, harmonipans and military band organs of many varieties.

During DeKleist's 1897 Cincinnati visit to sell trumpets he talked with Howard Wurlitzer. Howard was Rudolph Wurlitzer's eldest son and had entered the family business in 1889. Knowing full well the sales success of the coin-operated Regina music boxes, Howard Wurlitzer encouraged De-Kleist to develop and build a coin-operated piano.

It took DeKleist two years to develop the automatic piano. For the music source he used the

An early scene in North Tonawanda, New York. Standing in front of a large military band organ are Eugene DeKleist, George Herschell (third and fourth from right), James Armitage (to the left of DeKleist, near the center of the band organ) and others. (Photo from "A Pictorial History of the Carousel," by courtesy of the author, Frederick Fried.) Band organs manufactured by DeKleist were used to provide music for Armitage-Herschell merry-go-rounds.

This barrel-operated machine manufactured by Eugene DeKleist played tubular chimes automatically. The pinned barrel is partially visible through the grillwork at the bottom of the machine.

pinned cylinders similar to the ones used in his merry-go-round organs. The results were well worth waiting for.

In 1899 the new piano was marketed under the name of the Wurlitzer *Tonophone*. The electrically-operated machine had a capacity of ten tunes and would play a melody through twice upon receipt of a nickel.

Wurlitzer's first order with DeKleist was for two hundred Tonophones at a cost of $200.00 each. The *Tonophone* was a smash success from the very instant it appeared. Once the demand started, the market for coin-operated pianos grew like wildfire. Wurlitzer made the most of the market and, as a result, so did DeKleist. The many reorders for *Tonophones* forced DeKleist to change from a leisurely workshop-type of operation to a busy production-line factory.

Within a year or two Wurlitzer became the sole agent for the sale of DeKleist's products in the United States. The success of the *Tonophone* led to the development of many other types of coin-operated machines. The little *Pianino*, the harmonious *Mandolin Quartette* and its big brother,

the *Mandolin Sextette*, and several varieties of coin pianos with keyboards poured forth from the De-Kleist factory and were marketed under the Wurlitzer label.

The lucrative business with Wurlitzer made De-Kleist wealthy. For years he had lived in a home near the factory. With his new riches DeKleist purchased a large mansion complete with a stable of fine horses. His pleasure boat, the steam launch *Nollendorf*, was one of the area's finest. The sport of speedboating captured DeKleist's fancy. Boat racing on the nearby Niagara River and in Florida occupied an increasing amount of his time. To complete the picture Eugene DeKleist entered the political scene and become mayor of North Tonawanda. To befit his mayoral duties DeKleist moved his offices from the factory to a suite in the Shelton Hotel downtown. With so many interesting things to do he had time to visit the factory only two or three times a year!

This inattention to business resulted in a sharp decline in the quality of the machines produced, bringing many complaints to Wurlitzer and its distributors.

To remedy the worsening situation Howard Wurlitzer, then the active head of the Wurlitzer business, visited North Tonawanda. DeKleist was presented

A DeKleist self-playing xylophone similar in construction to the self-playing tubular chimes.

Mammoth Military Band Organ—Style 160 (122 Keys)

Operated by Perforated Paper Music Rolls. For the Largest Rinks in existence.

Mammoth Military Band Organ

This style is truly the most wonderful self-playing musical instrument of its kind ever built. It is equal in volume to a full brass band of from twenty to twenty-five pieces, and so perfectly is the music rendered that persons on the outside of the building where it is playing could not tell it from a regular military brass band.

It is designed to fill the largest Skating Rinks in existence—and will do it to perfection.

The cost of a band of sufficient pieces to fill a Rink the size this Organ will fill, will pay for the instrument in less than one season. Owners of the very largest Rinks should investigate this marvelous instrument. It will save its cost in a very few months, and make its owners absolutely independent on the music question.

The case of the Mammoth is thoroughly in keeping with the music. It may be had either in golden or weathered finish of quarter-sawed oak. It is imposingly magnificent in appearance, with handsome fluted columns, filled out with gold-leaf. The arrangement of the drums and cymbals in the richly carved top is also highly effective.

INSTRUMENTATION:

120 Violins.	40 Piccolos.
29 Violoncellos.	50 Flutes.
29 Bass Violins.	13 Brass Trombones.
30 Clarionets.	27 Brass Trumpets.
148 Accompaniment Pipes.	

DIMENSIONS:

Height, 10 ft. 4 in., with drums. Width, 10 ft. 6 in. Depth, 4 ft. 6 in.

PRICE—Including 18 selections of music.. $5,500.00

Music Rolls contain from 1 to 3 pieces each.

Motor furnished at cost to us.

Monster Military Band Organ—Style 155 (100 Keys)

Operated by Perforated Paper Music Rolls. For Large Size Rinks.

Monster Military Band Organ

This style is known as "The Monster," and is designed to fill any but the very few extremely large Rinks. In musical results it is equal to a band of from twelve to fifteen pieces, and will give perfect satisfaction in all Rinks with floor space of from 10,000 to 20,000 square feet.

Style 155 is being used in some of the largest and best Rinks in the country, and in every case is giving excellent satisfaction.

The money that would have to be paid out for a band that would give the same results as Style 155 will pay for the instrument in a very few months.

The case is massive but simple in style, and will add fifty per cent. to the appearance of any Rink in which it is installed.

"The Monster" may be had in quarter-sawed oak, with choice of golden or weathered finish. The leaded glass panels which admit of a view of the numerous brass horns inside, in front of Organ, may be removed, if desired, this making the Organ sound much louder.

INSTRUMENTATION:

75 Violins.	36 Flutes.
25 Violoncellos.	36 Piccolos.
25 Clarionets.	10 Brass Trombones.
21 Bass Violins.	21 Brass Trumpets.

DIMENSIONS:

Height, 6 ft. 10½ in. Width, 8 ft. 8¾ in. Depth, 8 ft. 3¼ in.

PRICE—Including 18 selections of music.. $3,250.00

Music Rolls contain from 1 to 3 pieces each.

Motor furnished at cost to us.

Shipping weight, 2,200 lbs.; net weight, 1,510 lbs.

Band organs were intended primarily for use with merry-go-rounds and in skating rinks. Early models used pinned cylinders, but after about 1900 the trend was toward perforated paper rolls. The "Monster" and "Mammoth" models were two of the largest band organ styles manufactured by Eugene DeKleist's North Tonawanda Barrel Organ Works (name later changed to The DeKleist Musical Instrument Works) and marketed by the Wurlitzer organization. A 1907 catalogue stated: "The military band organ is designed for use in amusement parks, roller skating rinks, dancing pavilions and outdoor resorts of every description where a powerful organ of first-class musical qualities is required. We have only recently perfected the military band organ so as to use perforated paper rolls instead of the old-style pinned cylinders. The advantage of the paper rolls over the cylinders is so great that the results obtained produce an altogether different type of instrument. By the use of the paper rolls we get a perfect repetition and can make the tunes of any desired length, both features impossible with the band organ. The paper rolls are so much cheaper and convenient to change that the owner can afford to have a variety of selections and change them frequently. The music rendered by these new styles is very fine and effective, as is also the finish and general appearance of the cases, and there is nothing on the market that will so satisfactory answer the purposes for which they are intended. A personal inspection of this line is necessary to obtain an adequate idea of the wonderful strides that have been made in perfecting this class of musical instrument. Prices range from $575.00 up to $5500.00."

Display of The DeKleist Musical Instrument Works at the 1904 Louisiana Purchase Exposition in St. Louis. Machines on display include self-playing chimes (far left), Tonophone (large piano with oval glass front) and two large band organs with a Pianino between them. Attendance at national fairs and expositions was an important part of automatic musical instrument merchandising during the early 20th century.

with an ultimatum: sell out to Wurlitzer or else Wurlitzer would take away its business and set up facilities to manufacture band organs and coin pianos elsewhere.

In 1908 DeKleist agreed to sell, with the valuation to be made on an inventory basis. There were so many assets to be figured that it took Eugene DeKleist six months to calculate the price. In January, 1909, the deal was closed.

To effect the purchase Wurlitzer formed a new corporation, the Rudolph Wurlitzer Manufacturing Company. The capitalization was one million dollars; $600,000.00 in common stock and the balance in preferred stock.

The preferred stock paid 8% interest and was redeemable for the issue price at Wurlitzer's pleas-

ure. DeKleist was given $200,000.00 worth of preferred stock and $112,500.00 cash in full payment for his interest. Of this amount DeKleist personally retained $250,000.00 and gave $62,500.00 cash to James Thompson, a partner.

Later Wurlitzer exercised the repurchase option and retired the preferred shares. Part of the original sale agreement was the stipulation that DeKleist was to remain "president" of the North Tonawanda factory until 1911. In actuality, DeKleist put in an appearance at the factory only once during that time!

Eugene DeKleist returned to Europe with his family. In Berlin he established a luxurious residence. The last year of his life was spent in Spain. When crossing the Pyrenees on a trip from Spain to Berlin in July, 1913, DeKleist suffered a heart attack and died.

THE HOUSE OF WURLITZER
FACTORY AND WAREROOMS
ESTABLISHED, 1856

CINCINNATI WAREROOMS
117-119 & 121-
EAST 4TH ST.

THE RUDOLPH WURLITZER MFG. CO
PIANOS & AUTOMATIC MUSICAL INSTRUMENTS

FACTORY
NEW YORK

THE RUDOLPH WURLITZER CO.

THE RUDOLPH WURLITZER CO.
MUSICAL INSTRUMENTS.
THE RUDOLPH WURLITZER CO.

NEW YORK
WAREROOMS
25 & 27 W. 32 ST Bet. Bway & 5 Ave.

CHICAGO
WAREROOMS
266 & 268 WABASH AVENUE

This page from an early Wurlitzer catalogue shows the North Tonawanda factories and three Wurlitzer showrooms. The small two-story building in the foreground was the original DeKleist factory.

THE HOUSE OF WURLITZER

T̲HE HOUSE of Wurlitzer was founded at Cincinnati, by Mr. Rudolph Wurlitzer, Sr., in the fall of 1856.

Our business has grown steadily with each successive year, until today our Cincinnati buildings occupy sixteen floors, 55,000 square feet of floor space, and we operate large warerooms in six other cities, namely: Chicago, New York, Philadelphia, Cleveland and Columbus, Ohio, and St. Louis, Mo. At each point we carry a complete line of the Wurlitzer Automatic Musical Instruments and specialties.

Our factories are, by far, the most extensive in the world devoted to the manufacture of Automatic Musical Instruments. They cover 15 acres of ground and contain 125,000 square feet of floor space.

One might well marvel at the success of our business, for we sell ten times as many Automatic Musical Instruments as all other firms combined. Our record of success has been owing to our determination to send out only Instruments of the highest musical quality and durability, such as we could unhesitatingly recommend.

We have always had the future of the Automatic Musical Instrument thoroughly at heart, and have made them from first to last with the same conscientious care exercised by the makers of the highest grade Pianos. Furthermore, we always aim to give every customer an absolutely fair deal and the most liberal treatment. On these points we refer you to hundreds of satisfied customers.

Any banking firm or commercial agency will inform you on the point of our financial rating and responsibility.

We have always adhered strictly to the *one-price-and-that-price-the-right-one* policy. We do not claim to make or sell the cheapest instruments on earth, for every musical instrument worthy of the name must have musical quality, and musical quality necessarily costs something to produce. However, our prices are always fair and reasonable, and we promise not only to give you a far better instrument than could be secured elsewhere, but at a price which you will at once agree is entirely reasonable.

Should you wish further information on any point in this catalog not entirely clear, do not fail to write to us at once. We want your order, and pledge ourselves to give you the best value in the world for the money.

THE RUDOLPH WURLITZER CO.

The Automatic Musical Instrument

Its Past, Present and Future

The intending purchaser of an Automatic Musical Instrument will be interested in knowing something of their history. It has been only sixteen years since we placed the first practical self-playing Piano on the market. Sixteen years seems a remarkably short period for the perfection of our present wonderful line of Automatic Musical Instruments.

Looking back, we ourselves are filled with wonder that so much has been accomplished in so short a time. Notwithstanding, we know how every working day has been filled with the hardest and most painstaking work, performed always with enthusiastic regard for the highest ideals.

On the all-important point of musical quality, there is simply no comparison between Wurlitzer Instruments and others. Price alone is not a safe guide. If we were to offer a PianOrchestra for $100.00, manufacturers of imitation goods would probably come out with something represented as just as good for only $99.00. Our prices can be matched by small imitators only by the use of cheap materials in construction. The fact that we are the world's largest manufacturers, and produce ten Automatic Musical Instruments to one for all other firms combined, enables us to make our prices extremely low.

We offer our patrons the largest, best and only complete line of Self-Playing Musical Instruments to be found.

The line embraces fourteen distinct types of instruments, and many different styles of each type, affording the purchaser of an automatic musical instrument the opportunity of selecting one exactly suited to his purpose.

For instance, for Skating Rinks, we manufacture the perforated paper roll Military Band Organ, which is designed exclusively for this purpose, and adapts itself perfectly to the requirements of the skating rink business.

For Moving Picture Theaters, Dance Halls, Beer Gardens, Hotel Lobbies, Large Cafes, and all sorts of places where an orchestra is usually employed, we build the PianOrchestra, which takes the place of a full orchestra, and is the only perfect Orchestrion in the world.

The Pianino, the Mandolin Quartette, the Mandolin Sextette, the Wurlitzer Harp, the Violin Piano, the 65-Note Player Piano, and the Wurlitzer 88-Note Player Piano, are excellent attractions for the smaller places, such as Cafes, Restaurants, Moving Picture Theaters, Ice Cream Parlors, Drug and Cigar Stores, Saloons, etc.

Not only is our line the largest and most complete in the world, but each and every instrument bearing the name of "Wurlitzer" is acknowledged by all who have had any experience with Automatic Musical Instruments to be superior in every respect to any similar instrument on the market.

As the pioneers in the manufacture of Automatic Musical Instruments and the creators of the only complete line of Automatic Musical Instruments, we have had a world of experience that is of inestimable value to our patrons. Customers, living in any part of the United States or Canada, desiring a self-playing musical instrument for any specific purpose, will find exactly what they are looking for in this line, and they can be assured if we recommend it as suitable for their purpose, that it will give perfect satisfaction for that purpose.

WURLITZER Has Just the RIGHT Instrument For YOUR Business

T̲HE list of all the different lines of business successfully using Wurlitzer Automatic Musical Instruments to be complete would have to include nearly every kind of public and semi-public place of entertainment in existence.

Perhaps we could not cover the situation better than by saying that the Wurlitzer Instruments are successful wherever people congregate.

It is just as important that you get the right musical instrument for your business as it is that you have the right street location or the right business methods.

This is where the extensive Wurlitzer line and the Wurlitzer years of experience come in for our customers' benefit.

The following table is made up from our own records and while it is by no means complete (every day some of our branches are selling entirely new lines of business) no doubt it will help you to pick out from the catalog the one or two instruments best suited for your business.

Write us a few details, then, and we will advise you intelligently the best type and style of instrument suitable.

Amusement Parks:
Military Band
PianOrchestra
Violin-Flute Piano Style CX

Billiard Halls:
Violin Piano
Flute Piano
PianOrchestra
Violin Pianino

Beer Gardens:
PianOrchestra

Bowling Alleys:
PianOrchestra

Boats (Excursion):
PianOrchestra
Military Band Organs

Cafes:
Harp
Violin Pianino
Violin Piano
Flute Piano
Paganini Orchestra

Confectioneries:
Harp
Violin Pianino
Flute Piano
PianOrchestra

Cigar Stores:
Pianino
Violin Pianino
Violin Piano
Harp

Clubs:
PianOrchestra
Violin-Flute Piano Style CX
Flute Piano

Dance Halls:
PianOrchestra
Violin-Flute Piano Style CX
Motion Picture Orchestra

Drug Stores:
Harp
Violin Pianino
Flute Piano

Department Stores:
Flute Piano
Violin-Flute Piano Style CX
PianOrchestra

Groceries:
Violin Pianino
Style A Flute Piano
Paganini Orchestra
Concert Orchestra

Hotels:
Flute Piano
Violin-Flute Piano Style CX
Bijou Orchestra

Hotels—Continued
PianOrchestra
Paganini Violin Piano
    Orchestra

Lodges:
Flute Piano

Lunch Rooms:
Harp
Violin Pianino

Merry-Go-Rounds
Merry-Go-Round Band
    Organ

News Stands:
Harp
Violin Pianino

Post Card Studios:
Violin Pianino
Harp
Violin Piano

Railroad Depots:
Violin Pianino
Harp
Pianino

Restaurants:
Harp
Flute Piano
Violin-Flute Piano Style CX
PianOrchestra
Paganini Violin Piano

Another important feature of our instruments is that we have always aimed to make each one a *real musical instrument*, not simply a mechanical one. The mechanical construction of any self-playing musical instrument is of very great importance, because upon the simplicity of the mechanism depends the practical working of the instrument, but most important of all are its musical qualities.

In the early days of Automatic Musical Instruments, the manufacturers worked on the principle that their playing without the aid of human hands was sufficient attraction to make them popular, but we now realize that they must be good musically.

In the matter of woods and finishes, we offer our patrons the widest range of choice. Most of our instruments may be had in any of seven different finishes, including mahogany, five different oak and ash finishes.

The oak finishes are golden, light weathered, dark weathered, Flemish (which is a very beautiful dark golden oak, with a decided greenish cast), and silver gray, also silver gray ash.

The silver gray oak and ash finishes are something new and decidedly attractive. These are black dull finishes, with a white lead filler in the pores, which gives it a rich silver gray finish.

THE PROFITS

We are often asked the question: "How profitable are Automatic Musical Instruments?"

Experience has proved conclusively that there is no legitimate investment that will pay owners of all sorts of public places as well. For instance, many of our customers have taken the price of the Pianino out of its receipts in six months. Others, buying the larger and finer instruments, have done even better in proportion, and the average receipts show profits ranging anywhere from 50 per cent. to 300 per cent. on the investment.

This per cent. is based entirely on the receipts taken from the instruments where they are used with nickel-in-the-slot attachments, no account being taken of the profits made from the increased business that the music attracts to the place.

In the case of a Military Band Organ for a Skating Rink, a PianOrchestra for a Restaurant, Cafe, Nickelodeon, etc., where the instrument is used as a substitute for a human band or orchestra, it becomes far more profitable by increasing the patronage and reducing the music cost at the same time.

IN CONCLUSION

Before entering into a detailed description of the instruments included in our line, we would like to call attention to the growing popularity of Self-Playing Musical Instruments. Since they have been developed to their present high degree of perfection, the demand for them in all sorts of public places where people congregate for pleasure and amusement has grown so great, that at times, it has been a problem with us to fill our orders. Especially has this been true with the Military Band Organs for Skating Rinks, and the PianOrchestra for the larger public places where orchestras were formerly employed.

The human race loves music, the impulse to enjoy it when the opportunity is afforded is an irresistible one, and in this advanced day of civilization, no public resort, such as Hotels, Cafes, Restaurants, Nickelodeons, Beer Gardens, Dancing Pavilions, Skating Rinks, Merry-go-Rounds or Public Amusement Resorts of any description, is complete without a first-class Automatic Musical Instrument to furnish music for its patrons at any and all times.

Pages from early Wurlitzer automatic musical instrument catalogues describing the Wurlitzer firm and uses for its machines.

Wurlitzer constantly encouraged piano dealers to handle the Wurlitzer line.

This 1912 postcard announces the opening of the Kansas City branch. Over the years the Wurlitzer Company built a large force of dealers.

WURLITZER HAS GREAT DISPLAY AT SAN FRANCISCO EXPOSITION.

You have no doubt heard of the big Wurlitzer exhibit at the Panama Pacific Exposition. A special Auditorium has been built, seating several hundred people, where continuous concerts are given daily upon a No. 3 Unit.

There are also special Displays of the Wurlitzer Piano and Wurlitzer Harp.

This exhibit is located in the Demonstration Hall of The United States Steel Corporation, Palace of Mines and Metallurgy.

———

Our friend Skeer is now out upon an extended Northwestern trip, selling Theatre instruments. He has just reached Seattle, and his first letter suggests great prospects for a big business along the Coast.

Every mother's son of us wishes him well and sends him this message:

"Good luck to you, George. If there is any business out there we know that you are the Boy who can get it."

POINTERS FOR THE SALESMAN.

Before you make an approach, put yourself in your prospect's place. Try to imagine how he feels, what he is thinking, what he needs. Talk your goods over with him beforehand. Don't say one word that will bump him off the order-track. And when you've sold him in your mind, march in and sell the man himself.

Don't fly off the handle because your customer-to-be does. Be patient, even sympathetic. The most important thing in the whole day's work is to get his viewpoint, to understand what feature of your goods or your talk jars him. Knowing this, you can wipe it out and often close the order on the strength of his reaction.

You must expect them to be skeptical, prejudiced, reluctant, indifferent to what you offer them. If they were not, there would be no job for you as salesman. Your boss could hire a messenger boy to collect the orders. Don't quarrel then, with conditions that give you your opportunities and put order-takers out of the race.

Personality is the strongest single force in salesmanship. But the solicitor who depends on it alone, can't compete with the salesman who backs up his magnetism by demonstrating the selling points for his goods. Even the cobbler has hitched his wax-ends to an electric motor. Or else moved into a side-street shop.

SOME "BLACK" EXPRESSIONS.

W. O. Black, Manager of the Cincinnati Store's Piano Department, and general, all around "Tonic-Man," has an exceedingly picturesque vocabulary, which for sheer hard hitting originality has Elbert Hubbard stricken dumb and over in the corner making signs.

Here is a sample of the way Black lines it out.

"He lies like a gas meter.

He hasn't any more friends than an alarm clock.

He's so lucky that if he fell in the river he'd come out with a bran' new suit and money in his pocket.

Next month we'll stack them to the ceiling. Customers are going to come in so fast they'll have me jumping sideways.

The Piano they wanted me to take in exchange was made 10 years before Eve." etc., etc.

Black is SOME "Black" Pepper Pot.

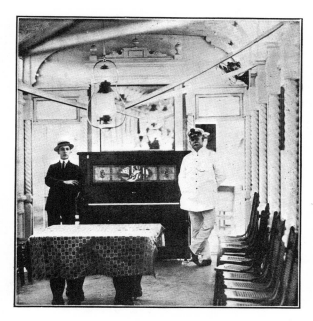

OUR FOREIGN TRADE.

We have 20 Electric Pianos, Style I, on board small steamers running from the Coast of Columbia to the interior on the Magdalena River. This picture shows a Wurlitzer Piano on board one of these vessels, with the captain and the son of our agent standing by.

We will soon have an article on "Wurlitzer Foreign Business," which will show its enormous scope, etc. Wurlitzer instruments can now be found all over the world. We have them in Japan, China, Java, Siberia, Hawaii—even in far off Constantinople.

———

The Advertising Man is preparing an elaborate Booklet upon our large Unit Orchestra installations, featuring the big $40,000 Unit at Seattle, and others of special importance.

We have also started a vigorous campaign of Theatre Orchestra advertising in the Moving Picture World, taking half a page in every issue of this paper.

———

We have received an interesting letter from Mr. Henry Von Steinert, Manager of the Automatic Department, of the W. F. Frederick Piano Co., Pittsburgh, regarding the sale of a "K".

He had the chance of selling this instrument, but there was only 12 ft. of space in front of the screen and there was on Exit door at each side. As you know, the instrument needs 15 ft. 4 in. When Mr. Von Steinert found that this was the case, he did not become discouraged and decided that he could not sell them an instrument. What he did was to place the two boxes and then place the Piano in front of them at an angle. To connect them up they had to use over 3 ft. of tubing to 31 valves, but the instrument is working splendidly. It really makes a very good appearance arranged this way and Mr. Von Steinert is very enthusiastic about this sale.

———

You know there is always more than one way of doing a thing, so when you run up against a proposition of this kind the next time, use the ingenuity that Mr. Von Steinert did and sell the instrument—and then GET IT IN some way.

———

Wurlitzer branched out to foreign countries. The above page from "The Wurlitzer Booster" shows a Wurlitzer coin-operated piano on a South American river steamer.

SECTIONAL VIEWS OF
THE MAMMOTH WURLITZER FACTORIES
WURLITZER STATION, NORTH TONAWANDA NEW YORK

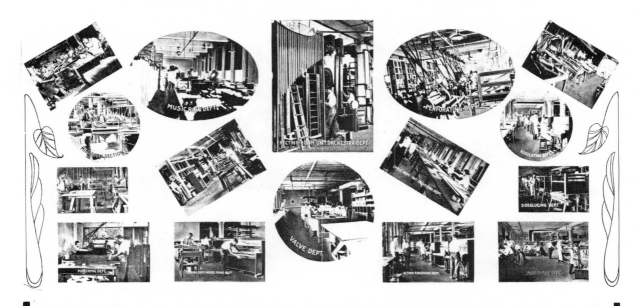

16 DISTINCT DEPARTMENTS SHOW THE MAGNITUDE OF WURLITZER PRODUCTION

Views of the Wurlitzer manufacturing facilities circa 1920.

The Wurlitzer Hope-Jones Unit Orchestra

From 1910 onward the manufacture of theatre organs was an important part of the Wurlitzer activities at North Tonawanda. We include information concerning the theatre organs (as well as photoplayers and band organs) to show the extent of the Wurlitzer mechanical musical instrument business.

Robert Hope-Jones, an English organ builder and inventor, came to America in 1903. Following brief employment with two organ builders he established the Hope-Jones Organ Company in Elmira, New York in 1907. Hope-Jones' organ building ideas and innovations were incomparable. Many improvements made in organ building methods during this period can be credited largely to his efforts. The leathered lip, the tibia family of stops, the diaphone and the double touch were all invented or improved by Hope-Jones.

In 1910 Wurlitzer acquired the Hope-Jones Organ Company and moved it from Elmira to North Tonawanda. Robert Hope-Jones was engaged to supervise the manufacture of the organs which were now known as "Wurlitzer Hope-Jones Unit Orchestras." His salary arrangement was $60.00 per week plus a percentage of sales; such percentage to be instituted if and when the organ manufacturing became profitable. However, in the first two years of operation Wurlitzer lost $200,000.00 on the organ division. Much of this deficit was due to the fact that Hope-Jones was constantly walking around the factory interfering with the production of the workers by continually making changes and revisions.

To solve this problem Hope-Jones was banned from the factory. He was told that if and when organ manufacturing became profitable he would be provided with a research laboratory where he could do experimental work to his heart's content. Faced with this news Robert Hope-Jones became disillusioned. On September 14, 1914, he committed suicide.

After some growth pains the business of organ making did become profitable. With its many unique features the Wurlitzer Hope-Jones Unit Orchestra became America's best seller for theatre use. Thousands were installed in all parts of the United States and in many foreign countries. The "Mighty Wurlitzer" achieved a fame accorded to few other products in American history. In the years after 1920 during which the market for coin-operated pianos declined the Hope-Jones Unit Orchestra was the mainstay of the Wurlitzer business.

An idea of the Wurlitzer dominance in the theatre organ field may be gained by an article, "The U.S. Organ" appearing in the April, 1931 issue of Fortune. Excerpts: "The Wurlitzers are modernists and are perhaps the only organ builders who have a thorough understanding of the modern public. A stream of unsolicited testimonials makes it clear to them that persons for whom organ music is dull and uninspiring are converted to this instrument upon hearing the colorful, at times passionate, Wurlitzer tone ... In the era of installing organs for motion picture theatres the Wurlitzer organ drove other makers (except W.W. Kimball Co.) out of the theatre business, helter-skelter; for this field, more than any other, is dominated by what the public likes. But the company's success has not been confined to America, for it has a healthy exporting business, and this is maintained against restrictive tariffs and in spite of the fact that Wurlitzer organs are expensive to begin with ... They are the most progressive builders in the world and their instruments are the most perfect mechanically ... Their gross organ business is in the neighborhood of $6,000,000.00 a year, and their business ability is such that they present to their competitors (who are for the most part less able financiers) a front that is constantly mobilized with great reserves behind it. Their factory capacity is one organ a day ..."

With its brass trumpets, tubas, clarinets, oboes, chimes, xylophone, drums, and countless other ranks and sound effects the Hope-Jones Unit Orchestra was at once awe-inspiring and majestic. Although many other makes of theatre organs appeared in their day the names "Wurlitzer" and "theatre organ" were synonymous.

Today the American Association of Theatre Organ Enthusiasts numbers several thousand members, all dedicated to the preservation of theatre organs, their sound and history ... once the enjoyment of millions.

TAE FINEST
THEATRE ORCHESTRAS
are built by
WURLITZER

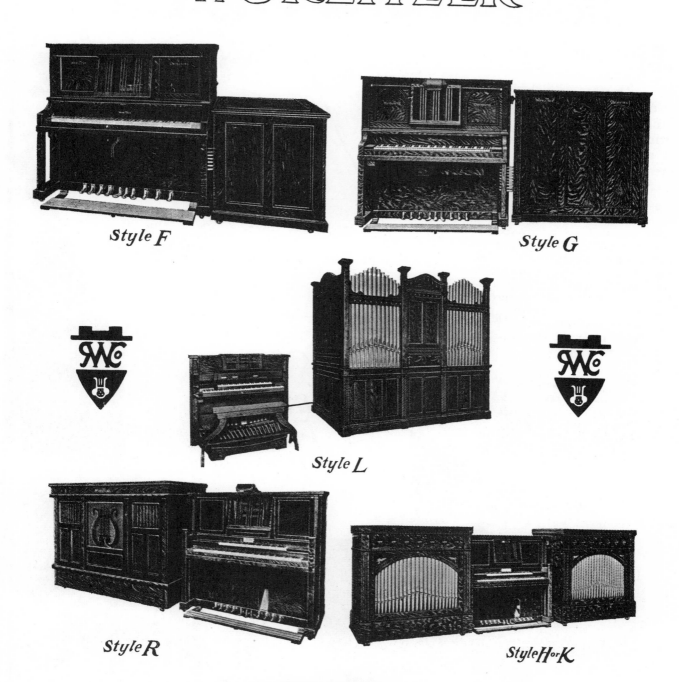

Style F

Style G

Style L

Style R

Style H or K

INSTALLED
IN A THOUSAND THEATRES

Wurlitzer photoplayers (see also p. 30) were the smallest theatre instruments built by this firm. Some, like the Style L, were really quite large. All featured a player mechanism which utilized paper rolls. Similar mechanisms were installed on a few of the larger Hope-Jones Unit Orchestras.

Above: Advertisement for the Wurlitzer Hope-Jones Unit Orchestra organ. Thousands were sold, mainly in the quarter-century from 1915 to 1940. Later installations were mostly overseas as the American market for theatre organs diminished sharply with the introduction of sound movies in the late 1920's.
On the right page: Views of theatre organ building at Wurlitzer's North Tonawanda facility in March, 1919.

UNIT ORCHESTRA
Erecting Dept.

UNIT ORCHESTRA
Cable Dept.

UNIT ORCHESTRA
Metal Pipe Dept.

UNIT ORCHESTRA
Console Dept.

UNIT ORCHESTRA
Making Reservoirs

UNIT ORCHESTRA
Flue Voicing Dept.

UNIT ORCHESTRA
Voicing Dept.

UNIT ORCHESTRA
Metal Pipe Dept.

BAND ORCHESTRA DEPT.
Testing Room

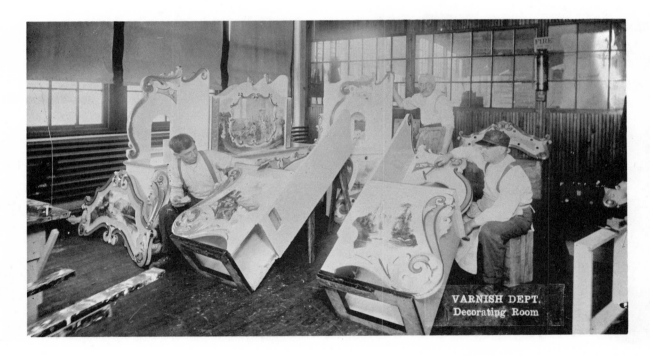

VARNISH DEPT.
Decorating Room

The above 1919 North Tonawanda scenes show Wurlitzer Style 153 band organs being made. Instrumentation of this particular model consisted of 164 pipes in several ranks, a 16-note set of orchestra bells, bass drum, snare drum and cymbal. It was especially recommended for "three-abreast carouselles and open-air dance pavilions." From the DeKleist days until the 1930's Wurlitzer sold a large variety of band organs. A 1929 catalogue lists thirteen different models ranging in size from the small Style 103 "designed especially for miniature carouselles, kiddie swings and other children's amusements — jut the size for a pit show" to the gigantic Style 180 which contained 480 pipes, bass drum, two snare drums, set of orchestra bells, two cymbals and a Chinese block. In America the business of band organ building was headquartered in North Tonawanda. In addition to DeKleist and later Wurlitzer other firms such as the North Tonawanda Musical Instrument Works, the Artizan Factories, Inc. and the Niagara Musical Instrument Works all had a share of the market. European band organs made by Gavioli, Ruth, Mortier, Marenghi, Limonaire Freres and others were widely imported. To remedy the difficulty in later years of producing music for these machines many were converted to play Wurlitzer rolls. Band organs are the only type of roll-operated Wurlitzer instrument of the "good old days" still in active use today. Photoplayers, coin-operated pianos and orchestrions and theatre organs (although most organs are not roll-operated) which play today mostly do so because hobbyists have spent many hours of loving care on them. Band organs are a different story. A large but diminishing supply still holds forth with their music on merry-go-rounds all over the country. Their operators often paint them gaudy non-original colors and usually could care less about their historical value; their main concern is that a band organ is a traditional part of a carousel, and without this attraction revenue might be lost.

After the Rudolph Wurlitzer Manufacturing was formed in North Tonawanda, Farny Wurlitzer, Rudolph's youngest son, came from Cincinnati to take charge.

Farny Reginald Wurlitzer was born in Cincinnati December 7, 1883. Before he reached school age his two older brothers, Howard E. and Rudolph H., were already active in the operation and management of the Wurlitzer musical enterprise.

Following the completion of his elementary school education Farny Wurlitzer attended the Cincinnati Technical School, a private vocationally-oriented high school, for four years.

In view of the firm's extensive trade with Europe, Rudolph Wurlitzer, Sr. suggested that his son learn to speak the German language fluently and become familiar with European manufacturing techniques.

In September, 1901, seventeen-year-old Farny Wurlitzer sailed to Europe alone.

Soon after his arrival in Germany he continued his education and learning of the German language at a commercial school in Hamburg.

In 1902 his brother Howard joined him for a visit to the Leipzig Trade Fair. There on display were huge orchestrions, a type of machine which Farny and Howard Wurlitzer had never seen before. They were both very impressed with the size and musical capabilities of orchestrions and thought that the Rudolph Wurlitzer Company should distribute them in America.

At the trade fair the Leipzig firm of Ludwig Hupfeld, A.G. dominated the exhibits. Their display featured many different models. Howard Wurlitzer approached the Hupfeld company to seek the exclusive right to market Hupfeld orchestrions under the Wurlitzer name in the United States. He also requested the privilege of having his brother, Farny, visit the Hupfeld factory and work there for several months in order to gain familiarity with the machines. Hupfeld agreed to everything in the distributorship proposal except Farny Wurlitzer's apprenticeship at the factory. Hupfeld was fearful that Wurlitzer would use the knowledge acquired to set up competing manufacturing facilities in the United States. The negotiations were stalemated on this particular point.

Not easily discouraged, Howard Wurlitzer looked elsewhere. He learned of the small firm of Philipps

Via booklets, postcards and folders cafe owners and others were constantly reminded of the need for Wurlitzer products. Wurlitzer's advertising during this period was superb. Unlike many of its contemporaries, Wurlitzer was not interested in a price competition, in fact, on a comparative basis its machines were usually more expensive than those of its competitors. Wurlitzer's competition was that of high quality . . . a feature which was stressed endlessly. If it was a Wurlitzer it was the best to be had. "On the all important point of musical quality, there is simply no comparison between Wurlitzer instruments and others" a catalogue noted. As even the beginning university student in marketing could point out quickly the Wurlitzer sales strategems were based upon sound economic theory.

& Sohne, manufacturers of automatic pianos and orchestrions. Their factory was located in Bockenheim, a suburb of Frankfort-am-Main. The Philipps line was not as extensive as Hupfeld's, but their quality was of the highest order.

After due discussion Philipps & Sohne agreed to let Farny Wurlitzer spend six months working in the factory, which he subsequently did.

Wurlitzer's first order with Philipps was for four orchestrions. Payment was made with cash in advance via a letter of credit. These machines were shipped to America and were sold as Wurlitzer *PianOrchestras*.

Foreseeing a large business with Philipps, Farny Wurlitzer requested the usual trade privilege of making subsequent purchases on an open account basis. As references the Rudolph Wurlitzer Company's impeccable banking and financial statements were presented. Philipps, however, showed no interest in even checking the references and said that business would only be done with cash in advance.

Upon learning of this attitude Rudolph Wurlitzer, Sr. made plans to personally visit Philipps in Germany. Farny Wurlitzer laid the groundwork for the arrival of his father.

No expense was spared to make Rudolph Wurlitzer's accommodations as ostentatious as possible. The finest and most lavish hotel suite was secured. An ample supply of foil wrapped 75c cigars was purchased. A fine coach and team of splendid horses were hired for transportation around town, to and from the hotel suite.

When Rudolph Wurlitzer arrived he was attended with splendor befitting a king. The Philipps people were overwhelmed by this munificent display. Without even a single financial inquiry they agreed to the suggested Wurlitzer terms of payment three months after the machines were shipped!

In 1904 Farny Wurlitzer returned to the company headquarters in Cincinnati. The next year was spent on the road. As a sales representative he called upon Wurlitzer dealers and distributors in San Francisco, New Orleans and other western and southern cities.

In 1906 Farny Wurlitzer assumed charge of the automatic musical instrument department at the Cincinnati office. Headquartered on the sixth floor this division did a lively business with the sale and repair of these machines, which were becoming an increasingly important part of Wurlitzer's total business.

The visitor to the new 121 East Fourth Street building was greeted by a magnificent array of Wurlitzer machines. Several different *PianOrchestra* styles, the automatic *Harp*, the *Mandolin Quartette* and *Sextette*, the *Pianino* and various types of band organs . . . all were there to enchant and entice the would-be-buyer.

From the automatic musical instrument department in Cincinnati Farny Wurlitzer went in 1909 to the main office of the newly-acquired North Tonawanda facilities. In the years before 1909 and in the golden years afterward thousands of coin pianos and orchestrions were to emanate from the North Tonawanda factories, which continually enlarged to meet the growing market. But this is jumping ahead . . . On the pages to follow we let the different Wurlitzer machines tell the story themselves.

Photograph of the Automatic Musical Instrument Department in Wurlitzer's Cincinnati building in 1906. Partially obscured and standing in the far corner are (from left to right) a Pianino, a Tonophone and an Automatic Harp.

Repair department for automatic musical instruments at the Wurlitzer headquarters in 1906. The photographs on this and the preceding page were taken in that year for use in a special Music Trades issue commemorating Wurlitzer's fiftieth anniversary 1856-1906. The unusually large number of Automatic Harps in the above illustration is accounted for by the fact that these particular instruments were made near Cincinnati and were probably stored in the repair department in Cincinnati pending shipment to various purchasers.

Various PianOrchestras, band organs and other automatic musical instruments filled Wurlitzer's automatic musical instrument showroom in Cincinnati. During this time Farny Wurlitzer was in charge of these operations.

Drop 5¢ in the slot for a Real Concert

THERE'S A **WURLITZER** Instrument Here

"A real concert" was promised to those who read this placard and then dropped a nickel into the coin slot of the Tonophone, Pianino, Orchestra Piano or whatever type of machine was on the premises.

Chapter 4

The Wurlitzer *Tonophone,* first marketed in 1899, was among the first coin-operated pianos to appear on the American scene. In the Wurlitzer line it was the very first of literally hundreds of different variations and types of coin-operated pianos which would be produced during the next three decades.

The Wurlitzer flair for convincing advertising was (and still is) one of the major factors contributing to that firm's success. In 1900 the *Tonophone* provided ample opportunity for Wurlitzer's copy writers. Not only did they have the *Tonophone* itself to sell, they had the whole *idea* of coin-operated music. There was no point in convincing a tavern owner that he needed a *Tonophone* if he did not basically believe that music would help his business.

In the direction of promoting the entire field of coin-operated music, and particularly Wurlitzer machines, an early advertisement read:

"Much has been said about music in cafes, hotels and other public places. We will now, however, take up the matter in all of its distinct and separate phases.

Music as a Revenue

Past experience has proven that nothing is more profitable than music in public places. The American people are very fond of music, and when the opportunity presents itself do not hesitate to loosen their purse-strings to hear their favorite march, or the latest popular song, or some sweet strain from Faust, Martha, or other well-known operas. Testimonials in this circular will show that our electric musical devices pay as high as 300%, and never less than 50%, on the investment. In what other line could you make a safe investment that would pay such profits?

Music as a Business Stimulator

Aside from the cash returns that are received from our electrical musical devices, they are also wonderful business stimulators. Music is a wonderful attraction and it is sure to attract those who would otherwise pass by; thus, the stranger enters and amid the sweet strains of music sips the sparkling wine and passes many pleasant hours. Where could music be more

$668.20 In Four Months

St. Louis, Mo., May 21, 1902.

The Rudolph Wurlitzer Co., Cincinnati, Ohio.

Gentlemen: A little over four months ago I purchased a Tonophone from you, paying $650.00 for same. Since that time it has taken in $668.20, or more than the amount I paid for it. Not only has it proved to be an income producer by itself, but it has increased my bar trade far beyond my expectations, and although it is kept pretty busy, it never gets out of order, but does its work at all times and under all conditions. I consider it the best investment I ever made, am more than pleased with it, and would hardly know how to get along without it, as it is constantly drawing people into my place that otherwise would not enter it.

Very sincerely yours,
JAMES CUNNINGHAM,
925 Olive St., "The Metropole."

October 11th, 1904.

The International Automatic Music Company,
No. 2 W. Twenty-ninth St., New York City, N. Y.

Gentlemen: I shall accept the Tonophone at the end of the period of probation. The Subway Tavern finds it a delightful adjunct to our arrangements here. We have stationed it in the restaurant and our patrons are pleasurably surprised at the quality of the musical product, many, while descending the stairs, expecting to see a virtuoso at the keys. Business men find it a gentle mollient of their troubles and many prefer to drop a nickel in the slot rather than patronize the department wherein we sell beverages. For a public house such as we are conducting, it is proving, aside from what I have said, a good business proposition.

Yours truly,
THE SUBWAY TAVERN CO.
Jos. Johnson, Jr., President.

Two early Tonophone testimonials. Introduced at the turn of the century the Tonophone quickly captured a large share of the coin piano market.

appropriate and more enjoyable? We have un-solicited testimonials to show that some of our automatic musical instruments have been the means of increasing bar trade 25%. If such is the case, why not have music?

The Charming Influence of Music

Americans who have traveled abroad enthusiastically praise the custom of having music in public places, which is universal in all large cities in Europe.

Americans, as a rule, are great admirers of music, believe in its elevating influence, and also believe it to be necessary for the full enjoyment of life. Music, however, to be cultivated among the masses should be in all public places where it will burst upon the ear uninvited. What could, therefore, be more appropriate in a public place than one of our TONO-PHONES or any other of our automatic musical instruments? The program covers the entire field of musical productivity and embraces all ages. The classically inclined can be accommodated as well as the admirer of ragtime ... Nothing is more soothing than the refined and elevating influence of music.

Music as a Modern Acquisition

No modern saloon with advanced ideas is now without music. The present advanced condition of our public places is due to the desire of the proprietor to give his patrons that enjoyment which is both refined and elevating, and certainly nothing could be more so than

THE TONOPHONE
Automatic Piano with Nickel-in-Slot Attachment.

STYLE 1 Oak or mahogany, including one cylinder, with direct current motor, **$600.00**

STYLE 2 The same equipped with alternating current motor, **$650.00**

SOLD FOR CASH OR ON MONTHLY PAYMENTS.

Extra cylinders, 10 tunes, $40.00   Cylinders exchanged for $5.00

The Tonophone was a coin-operated barrel piano. Music was provided by a ten-tune pinned cylinder.

music. The modern saloon has become the magnet for the better element of the male community. This is due to several causes:

First: To the charming influence of music, which is now a necessary acquisition to every modern saloon.

Second: To the congregation of men occupied in different callings who meet for quiet interchange of thought. Politics, literature and the arts are here discussed, and are now favorite topics in the modern saloon.

Third: To the prevalance of art (either in painting or in plastic art) with which these m a g n i f i c e n t establishments are now adorned.

Let us once more impress upon the proprietors of modern cafes and other public places, that you must have MUSIC to attract the better element, and as long as it is profitable and increases your trade, why not have it?"

What tavern owner in the early 1900's could resist the above flattery ... and appeal to the 50% to 300% profits his pocketbook might miss if he didn't install the latest in Wurlitzer music? The above, although primarily a Wurlitzer advertisement, provides an excellent rationale of the necessity and desire for coin-operated music in this era.

Via thousands of promotional leaflets and reprinted testimonials public places everywhere were introduced to the *Tonophone*.

THE KEYBOARD TONOPHONE
Automatic Piano with Nickel-In-Slot Attachment.

STYLE 3 Oak or mahogany, including one cylinder, with direct current motor, **$750.00**

STYLE 4 The same, equipped with alternating current motor, **$800.00**

SOLD FOR CASH OR ON MONTHLY PAYMENTS.

Extra cylinders, 10 tunes, $40.00   Cylinders exchanged for $5.00

The Keyboard Tonophone can be played by hand the same as any other Piano

Tonophone styles 3 and 4 had keyboards. These were less popular than the keyboardless styles, due no doubt to the $150 higher price.

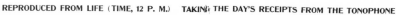

A boxful of nickels on the bar and two more boxfuls on the floor . . . the "day's receipts" of the Tonophone. The Hoeffler Mfg. Co. was a Wurlitzer distributor.

The public liked the honky-tonk sound of coin pianos. The public liked *Tonophones*. In the beginning years of the industry the *Tonophone* carved out a large niche in the market.

One disadvantage of the *Tonophone* was the fact that new cylinders cost $40.00 each, an immense sum in those days. To alleviate this situation, the cylinders could be rented for just $5.00 each, or 50c per tune.

The advantages of the *Tonophone* were extolled in advertisements. Any one of the ten tunes on the cylinder could be selected at will simply by turning the arrow on a circular dial on the outside of the case. If one's favorite melody were *Under the Anheuser Bush* one could listen to it a dozen times in succession on the *Tonophone*. On any other piano of that day one would have to listen to many unwanted tunes in the interim until the favorite reappeared in sequence.

Also, each tune played through twice for a nickel. However, this was almost a necessity as the limited amount of space available on the cylinder dictated that each tune had to be short; often with a refrain or two omitted.

The coin slot of the *Tonophone* would accept only nickels. The slug rejector assured that the owner's anticipated several dollars per day intake would not be interfered with by iron washers, tokens and other miscellaneous round objects which invariably found their way into coin-operated machines.

LIST OF MUSIC CYLINDERS FOR TONOPHONES—Continued.

No. 407

1. In the Shade of the Old Apple Tree .... Song
2. Shame on You .... Song
3. Dan-Dan-Danuel .... Song
4. Won't You Fondle Me? .... Song
5. Adlyn .... Waltz
6. Moonlight .... A Serenade
7. By the Watermelon Vine, Lindy Lou .... Song
8. He's Me Pal .... Song
9. Karama .... Japanese Romance
10. The Goo-Goo Man .... Song

No. 408

1. Shame on You .... Song
2. Princess Pokohontas, March and Two-Step
3. The Rival King .... March
4. In the Shade of the Old Apple Tree .... Song
5. The Yankee Doodle Boy .... Song
6. Heinie .... Song
7. Love in a Mango Tree .... Song
8. Gibson Girl .... Waltz
9. Just My Style .... Song
10. Nordica .... Waltz

No. 409

1. The Little Brown Man of Japan ... Song
2. Jolly Me Along .... Song
3. Moonlight .... A Serenade
4. The Rifle Range ... March and Two-Step
5. Darkey Tickle ...... Char. Dance
6. Where the Southern Roses Grow . Song
7. Helmet of Navarre .... Song
8. The Magnet ...... March and Two-Step
9. Sambo and Dinah .... Song
10. Ev'ry Little Bit Helps .... Song

No. 410

1. Lucy Linda Lady .... Song
2. Lonesome .... Song
3. In the Shade of the Old Apple
4. Just My Style .... Song
5. Ev'ry Little Bit Helps .... Song
6. On a Crocodile .... Song
7. Nordica .... Waltz
8. Oh that We Two were Maying .... Song
9. Moonlight .... A Serenade
10 What the Brass Band Played, Two-Step

No. 411

1. Dixie Belles ...... March and Two-Step
2. Fall in Line .... March
3. Zacatecas .... March
4. Southern Roses .... Char. March
5. Car-Barlick Acid .. March and Two-Step
6. Poppies .... A Japanese Serenade
7. Adlyn .... Waltz
8. Voices of the Night .... Waltz
9. Midnight Fire Alarm .. March and Galop
10. True Blue Through and Through. Song

No. 412

1. Willow Grove March.
2. Elseeta .... March and Two-Step
3. The Yazoo ... Cake Walk and Two-Step
4. A-Sa-Ma .... Char. March
5. Sleepy Hollow ..... Droll Int. Two-Step
6. My Old Wild Western Rose ...... Song
7. The American, or True Blue ..... March
8. Salute to America, March and Two-Step
9. The Bird and the Bottle, Dance from "Woodland."
10. In Society.

No. 413

1. Don't Be Cross .... Song
2. Over the Waves .... Waltz
3. Black Diamond .... March
4. In the Shade of the Old Apple Tree .... Song
5. The Blue Bells of Scotland .... Song
6. Killarney .... Song
7. A Bit o' Blarney .... Song
8. Uncle Sammy .... March
9. Miserere from "Il Trovatore."
10. High Pride ...... March and Two-Step

No 414

1. Up the Street .... Two Step
2. The Radium Dance, from Piff, Paff, Pouf
3. Tommy .... Medley Waltz
4. Farewell Mr. Abner Hemingway, Two Step
5. In the Shade of the Old Apple Tree, Song
6. Bright Eyes, Goodbye .... Song
7. Moonlight .... A Serenade
8. My Hindoo Man .... Song
9. Sylvia .... Medley Schottische
10. The Giggler ..... March and Two Step

Page from a Tonophone music cylinder catalogue. Cylinders cost $40.00 each.

Coin-operated pianos of all kinds were curiosities in the early 1900's. Regardless of the type and quality of music they played a steady stream of nickels flowed into their slots.

The novelty of coin-operated music at that time is illustrated by an extract from the *New York Sun*:

"The restaurant dearest to the men of Washington Market acquired a Tonophone (electric piano) for its main dining room the other day. The patrons patronized it liberally and there was continuous music from noon till evening, which the waiters seemed to enjoy as much as anybody.

The favorite tune of the half dozen popular airs played was *Killarney.* When that started up for the first time, a German, who had ordered sauerkraut and pig's knuckles, got corned beef and cabbage by mistake, and a dyspeptic looking man got a mug of ale and a brace of chops instead of crackers and milk."

Testimonials by the dozens poured into the offices of Wurlitzer and its distributors. Joseph Johnson, Jr., president of New York's Subway Tavern Company, liked the quality of the *Tonophone* music so

DISCONTINUED

The Tonophone

CASE DESIGN No. 2

A page from the Wurlitzer archives showing the Tonophone, case design No. 2 with an oval glass front.

"Points of Superiority" of the Tonophone.

well that he was prompted to write: "...We have stationed it in the restaurant and our patrons are pleasurably surprised at the quality of the musical product. Many, while descending the stairs, expect to see a virtuoso at the keys..."

Williams and Minckel, proprietors of the Suburban Garden, reported that, "We are much pleased at the result produced by placing the *Tonophone* in our picture parlor. With many years' experience in running resorts and places of amusement, we can truthfully say that, as a money-maker, a drawing attraction and a grand entertainer, we have never had its equal."

Tonophone sales boomed. DeKleist's North Tonawanda factory and Wurlitzer's sales department were kept busy by customers like the firm of Mark & Wagner, which wrote: "We take pleasure in stating that we have purchased six of your *Tonophones* and have placed one in each of our phonograph parlors....We shall want several more of your machines in a short while..."

To meet every musical taste hundreds of different Tonophone cylinders, each offering ten different tunes, were available. Irishmen spent a nickel to hear *The Wearing of the Green*, Scotchmen spent their money to hear the *Blue Bells of Scotland*... and still others, with different national heritages, listened to *Dolores Cubanola* or *Unter der Linden*.

The Louisiana Purchase Exposition (St. Louis, 1904) was commemorated by *Meet Me in St. Louis, Louis* and the *St. Louis Tickle*, both of which were available for a nickel in the *Tonophone* slot. *Come Take a Trip in My Air-Ship* told of the latest means of travel.

Other *Tonophone* tunes such as *Wait Till the Sun Shines, Nellie, Give My Regards to Broadway* and *Turkey in the Straw* are just as familiar today as they were then, over half a century ago.

Over a period of about ten years *Tonophones* were made in two major styles, with keyboard and without. In addition there were a number of minor variations in case designs, a choice of woods and finishes, oval glass or rectangular glass in the front of the piano case, and so on.

Tonophone and PianOrchestra
BOTH IN ONE SALOON

A Sure Indication That Music Pays in Saloons, Cafes and Other Public Places

CHAS. WEBER, San Francisco, Cal.

THE RUDOLPH WURLITZER Co., Cincinnati, O.

Gentlemen:—I wish to state that music has been the life and success of my business. About two years ago I was induced to purchase one of your Tonophones, which I did very reluctantly. I very soon, however, discovered my folly, as the Tonophone paid for itself in less than one year and increased my bar trade 15 to 20 per cent.

I have since added one of your $3,500 PianOrchestras, and must say I am highly delighted with the same. The PianOrchestra is beyond a doubt the most wonderful musical instrument in existence. Aside from being a splendid investment, it is the means of bringing the better class of people into my place of business. Wishing you the success you justly deserve, I beg to remain, yours truly,

CHAS. WEBER.

Charles Weber of San Francisco wrote an enthusiastic endorsement for the Tonophone and PianOrchestra.

This Tonophone advertisement appeared about 1905.

Tonophones were produced from 1899 to about 1908. *Tonophone* production was curtailed in favor of the Wurlitzer *65-Note Player Piano* which replaced it as the basic full-sized coin piano in the Wurlitzer line. To make the large repertoire of inexpensive ($4.00 for a roll containing five tunes) *65-Note Player Piano* roll music available to *Tonophone* owners many of the *Tonophones* were remodeled and converted to roll operation.

Tonophone cylinders were made for several years thereafter, but finally production of these was discontinued also.

Considering the technological advances which had been made in Europe by the late 1890's, the *Tonophone* with its antiquated pinned cylinder was obsolete when it was first put on the market. The Wurlitzer Company itself admitted this later (circa 1912) when it included the following as part of a catalogue for band organs: "We knew the old-fashioned pinned cylinder ... could never be adapted to the purpose, because of the harshness of the music; the lack of means of regulating the tempo; the trouble and time necessary to change the music; the impossibility of putting a complete waltz or two-step on a cylinder (the music can not be any longer than the circumference of the cylinder); and the expense of new music ..."

However, the *Tonophone* served its intended purpose well; that of introducing America to coin-operated Wurlitzer music. In 1899 there was one Wurlitzer model on the market, the Tonophone. By 1908 there were dozens of different models ranging from the small *Pianino* to the colossal *PianOrchestras*. For all of this the *Tonophone* was indeed a splendid and timely preview of things to come.

Two Tonophones at the Cliff House
The Finest Resort in the World.

CLIFF HOUSE, SAN FRANCISCO, December 25, 1902.

GENTLEMEN:

I take great pleasure in being able to express my entire satisfaction in connection with the "Tonophone."

Both instruments have run away ahead of my expectations, and a few months will see them paid for out of their own earnings.

Besides being good money-makers, they also are great "entertainers," and I can safely say to you that during my twenty years experience at the Cliff House, I have never seen or heard of anything of this description which could give such universal satisfaction.

Wishing you all the seasons compliments and a prosperous New Year.

Yours truly,

J. M. WILKINS, MANAGER.

The Cliff House satisfied its patrons with two Tonophones. Today a fine collection of automatic musical instruments is housed at Sutro's ... just a stone's throw from the present-day Cliff House.

Good Music makes the Drinks Taste better

Drop a Nickel

THERE'S A WURLITZER Instrument Here

This placard is typical of many which saloonkeepers were given to help them attract money into their instruments.

Chapter 5

First introduced about 1902, the 44-note *Pianino* was the first Wurlitzer coin piano to operate from a perforated paper roll. With their bulging keyboardless fronts the first *Pianino* models resembled abbreviated *Tonophones* more than anything else. At the time of the *Pianino's* debut the *Tonophone* was the staple instrument of the Wurlitzer line. The *Pianino* was intended for those who wanted a smaller or less expensive machine.

As a distinct coin-piano type the 44-note machines were most popular in the 1900 to 1910 decade. Numerous brands were marketed by various manufacturers. Among the most popular 44-note pianos were the *Pianolin* (made by the North Tonawanda Musical Instrument Works . . . a firm formed by previous DeKleist employees), the *Electrova* (sold by the Electrova Company division of Jacob Doll & Sons, Inc.), the Mills *Automatic Pianova* (distributed by the Mills Novelty Company), several

Peerless styles (Engelhardt & Sons) and the Wurlitzer *Pianino*.

At the time of its introduction the *Pianino* claimed several points of superiority:

"The *Pianino* is the product of many years' experience in building Automatic Electric Pianos, and is presented to the public as the acme of perfection. The *Pianino* is the only Electric Piano playing from perforated music rolls which is an absolute success. The music is played with such accuracy and expression that it is almost impossible to believe that the instrument is played mechanically and not by expert hands.

The *Pianino* is the only Electric Piano fitted with an automatic rewinding device, which, when the end of the roll is reached, automatically rewinds itself in thirty seconds. The *Pianino* therefore requires no attention, which

THE PIANINO

Nickel-in-Slot Electric Piano, with 44 Notes
In a Handsome Oak or Mahogany Case

THE PIANINO is the product of many years experience in building Automatic Electric Pianos, and is presented to the public as the acme of perfection. The Pianino is the only Electric Piano playing from perforated music rolls which is an absolute success. The music is played with such accuracy and expression that it is almost impossible to believe that the instrument is played mechanically and not by expert human hands.

The Pianino is the only Electric Piano fitted with an automatic rewinding device, which, when the end of the roll is reached, automatically rewinds itself in thirty seconds. The Pianino therefore requires no attention, which makes it valuable for all public places of amusement.

Another important feature not found on any other automatic piano is the regulating device, whereby the time can be changed to any desired tempo. The perforated paper music rolls are only 5½ inches wide; contain six pieces each, and play from 15 to 20 minutes. As a money-maker the Pianino bids fair to head the list.

STYLE 1 Including one roll of music, upon which there are six pieces, with **direct current motor** **$500.00**

STYLE 2 Including one roll of music, upon which there are six pieces, with **alternating current motor** **$550.00**

Sold for Cash or on the Easy Payment Plan.

Extra Music Rolls of 6 Tunes, Each $4.50

LIST OF MUSIC UPON APPLICATION

THE PIANINO IS NEAT AND COMPACT, OCCUPYING A VERY SMALL SPACE

The early Pianino resembled the Tonophone — compare this Pianino with the Tonophone illustrated on page 96. Like the Tonophone the Pianino was an instant success. Pianinos continued to be good sellers for nearly three decades . . . a record in the coin-operated piano industry.

Another early Pianino case design.

makes it valuable for all public places of amusement.

Another important feature not found on any other automatic piano is the regulating device, whereby the time can be changed to any desired tempo. The perforated paper music rolls are only 5½ inches wide; contain six pieces each, and play from 15 to 20 minutes. As a money maker the *Pianino* bids fair to head the list."

One thing becomes clear as one reads contemporary catalogues and printed material issued by the Wurlitzer Company: modesty was not an attribute of the Wurlitzer advertising department. Every advantage or point of excellence, no matter how small, of a Wurlitzer machine was exploited to the fullest extent. Likewise, subtle and not-so-subtle comparisons were made between Wurlitzer machines and those of its competitors. For instance, the 44-note *Pianolin* made by the competing North Tonawanda Musical Instrument Works operated from an endless paper roll. A Wurlitzer sketch of the times shows the owner of an endless-roll type of machine being strangled in entangling loops of an endless paper roll, much like in the tentacles of an octopus!

Wurlitzer Pianino

The standard 44-note Electric Piano with Mandolin attachment and without keyboard. *Equal in tone to that of any full scale Piano*; a feature that makes it remarkable.

Height, 5 feet. Width, 3 ft. 4 in. Depth, 1 ft., 10½ in. Shipping weight, 625 lbs.

"Equal in tone to that of any full scale piano" read this Pianino catalogue description of about 1916.

WURLITZER Pianino

The standard 44-note Electric Piano with Mandolin attachment and without keyboard. Equal in tone to that of any full scale Piano. This instrument is equipped with the long-tune roll frame playing a 6 or 12 tune roll; a feature that makes it remarkable.

Height, 4 ft. 5 in. Width, 2 ft. 10½ in. Depth, 2 ft. 7¾ in. Shipping weight, 500 lbs.

This page from a 1922 Wurlitzer catalogue shows one of the later Pianino case designs.

However, modesty rarely contributes to success— particularly in a highly competitive market . . . and the coin piano market was hotly competitive at that time. Part of the Wurlitzer success story can undoubtedly be laid to superb advertising and sales promotion campaigns. If Wurlitzer developed a new process or technique every prospective coin piano buyer was sure to learn of it quickly.

The first *Pianinos* were sold for $500.00 each, including one six-tune roll of music. If desired the *Pianino* could be obtained with an alternating current motor (instead of the standard direct current) for $50.00 extra. Additional rolls were available for $4.50 each.

The source of motive energy was no small problem in the early 1900's. It seems that the installers of coin operated pianos were prepared to meet every need. Some manufacturers offered the buyer his choice of machines powered by electricity, a gasoline engine, a spring-wound clockwork system or by water power (using a compact water turbine). Others (like Wurlitzer) offered two main power sources; motors driven by direct current and motors driven by alternating current.

The purchaser of a *Pianino* had his choice of

Program card for the Pianino.

The Pianino

44-Note Electric Piano.

The Pianino is so far superior to any other 44-Note Player that there is really no comparison. In construction, it is simplicity itself, while the tone and expression are truly wonderful.

The materials used in the construction of the Pianino are the best money can buy. The case, which is of very attractive design, may be had in beautiful figured mahogany or quartersawed oak. The oak cases come in golden, Flemish, light and dark weathered, and silver gray finishes.

The top panel of the case has a beveled plate glass panel. The interior lights up while playing, giving the instrument an exceedingly attractive appearance.

The important features of the Pianino, which are covered by patents and cannot be had in any other 44-Note Electric Piano, are as follows:

The Automatic Music Roll Rewinding Device, which keeps the small music roll (only 5½ inches wide) always wound on the two spools, thus preventing the paper from expanding or shrinking and getting out of shape, as it does in all endless roll instruments, where the paper lies loosely in folds in a box. This device is further illustrated and explained on pages 6 and 7, and is so important that no one, having had experience, would for one moment consider an instrument without it.

The Direct Drive Gear eliminates the old-fashioned belts and pulleys. (See pages 8 and 9 for illustration and description).

The Magazine Coin Detector Slot is a recent invention, that will hold nickels enough at one time to run the roll through, and at the same time prevent the working of the instrument with spurious coins.

The advantage of the slot in holding a number of nickels at one time, is that it often means doubling and trebling the receipts, as it results in many customers putting a quarter's worth of nickels in at a time, who otherwise might put in only one. The device is illustrated and explained on pages 8 and 9.

The Mandolin Attachment is another splendid feature of the Pianino which provides a beautiful variation in the music. The attachment may be thrown off or on in a second's time.

The Pianino also has a metal tracker bar and tracker frame. All metal parts are nickelplated.

A glass opening in the front opposite the tracker board shows the music roll in operation; each tune on the roll is numbered. Corresponding numbers with the name of the tune appear on the program in the upper panel, enabling customers to know what tune they will hear next.

Any number of our nickel-in-the-slot boxes can be used in connection with the Pianino, so that it may be played from any part of the house.

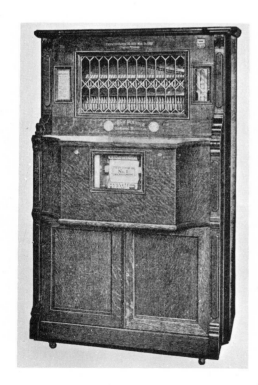

Height, 4 ft. 8 in.   Width, 3 ft.   Depth, 1 ft. 9 in.

PRICE—Complete, with Electric Motor and 1 Roll of Music, containing 6 selections.....$500.00
Extra Music Rolls, containing 6 selections each.......................... 3.00

Shipping Weight, 625 pounds.
Net Weight, 430 pounds.

This Pianino design was popular from about 1906 to 1913. The clear glass allowed patrons to watch the piano hammers in action.

mahogany or quarter-sawed oak woods. To suit various decors the machines were available in a number of different finishes including golden, Flemish, light and dark weathered and silver gray styles.

The *Pianino* was a best-seller for Wurlitzer. Production continued well into the 1920's. Along the way many improvements and refinements were made.

The automatic music roll rewinding device was one of the *Pianino's* main selling points. This mechanism prevented "the paper's expanding or shrinking and getting out of shape, as it does in all endless-roll instruments where the paper lies loosely in folds in a box." This was a pointed reference to the aforementioned music-handling system used by the North Tonawanda Musical Instrument Works' competing *Pianolin*. Of course, there are two sides to every story. Probably the builders of the *Pianolin* would point out the thirty seconds of wasted and non-money-making silence when the Pianino rewound at the end of the sixth tune. With the endless-type roll the music played continuously.

Wurlitzer was quick to point out that the music roll rewinding device permitted a roll to be changed in just a few seconds. They were one up on the *Pianolin* with this point . . . as any one who has spent time with the clumsy endless rolls knows well. Changing the roll of a *Pianolin* was a five to ten minute task . . . if no errors were made.

Another feature of the *Pianino* was the *direct drive gear*. This was "a remarkable new invention that does away entirely with troublesome, old-fashioned belts, pulleys and countershafts." Evidently the person who wrote the advertisements for the *Pianino* was not familiar with the large

The Pianolin, a competitor of the Pianino manufactured by the North Tonawanda Musical Instrument Works, used the endless-roll system. Wurlitzer Pianino ads pointed out the difficulties of this system.

Wurlitzer *PianOrchestras* being marketed at the same time. Or, perhaps *PianOrchestra* buyers were not shown *Pianino* literature, for the huge *PianOrchestras* employed the same troublesome belts and pulleys that the *Pianino* eliminated.

The magazine coin detector slot was another *Pianino* innovation. With this device the *Pianino* could take in several nickels at a time, resulting in larger receipts. A customer could now change a quarter at the bar and drop all five nickels, one-by-one, into the slot. Further profits could be made by deploying cast-iron wall boxes at various booths in a restaurant or other public place. The $10.00 to $15.00 cost per wall box was usually paid for quickly by the added business which resulted.

To provide a variation in the sound of the *Pianino* each machine was equipped with a *mandolin attachment*. This device, a small slotted curtain containing a row of metal buttons, would produce a tinkly mandolin-like effect when lowered between the piano hammers and the strings.

The various *Pianino* improvements — the roll rewinding device, the direct drive gear, etc. — although introduced via the *Pianino* were employed on most of Wurlitzer's other types of coin-operated music machines.

Two leading contenders in the 44-note piano field — the Pianino and the Pianolin, here shown side-by-side.

The anatomy of a Pianino. In the bottom of the case is the vacuum pump with the reservoir or equalizer on top of it. Above the reservoir is the electric motor which drives the pump by means of cranks and drives the roll mechanism by shafts and friction discs. Behind the roll mechanism is the pneumatic stack which is encased in a wood housing. The individual pneumatics in the stack when collapsed on signal from the roll sound the piano notes via wood push-rods. This particular machine was restored to perfection by Steve Lanick of Pittsburgh, Penna.

Automatic Music Roll Rewinding Device

(See description on opposite page.)

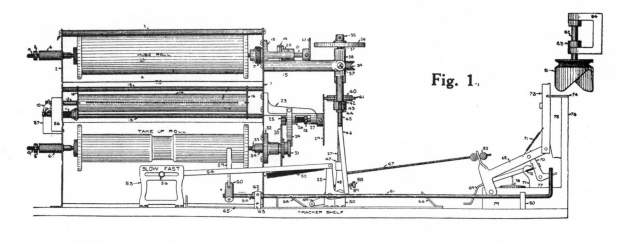

Fig. 1.

Changing Music Roll on Pianino

Changing Music Roll on Mandolin Quartette

These two pictures are taken from life and show how simply and quickly the music rolls can be changed on all our instruments.

Automatic Music Roll Rewinding Device

(See Fig. 1.)

A patented device found in all Wurlitzer Automatic Musical Instruments and in no other; one of the most important advances ever made in the mechanism of self-playing musical instruments.

The music roll is driven by the newly-patented Wurlitzer system of friction discs and pulleys. All troublesome chains, sprockets and cog wheels are done away with, and with them the source of three-fourths of all operating troubles.

The Wurlitzer Friction Discs and Pulleys secure direct transmission of operating power, and are infallible in action, causing the instrument to play smoothly, noiselessly and in perfect time. It is practically impossible for the friction disc system to get out of order. Nothing like it is to be found in any self-playing musical instrument except a Wurlitzer.

It automatically rewinds the music when it is played through, besides keeping it always wound on the music roll and take-up roll. This prevents the paper's expanding or shrinking and getting out of shape, as it does in all endless-roll instruments where the paper lies loosely in folds in a box.

Another advantage of this device is that the music roll may be changed in a few seconds, without stopping the operation of the instrument. By shifting lever 65 to the right the music is stopped, while the operation of the instrument continues. This is an advantage when quiet is desired temporarily for answering telephone calls, etc.

Thus, customers are furnished with frequent changes of music while they are in a mood to continue playing the instrument, if they can have a change to suit them.

A glance at the photographic reproductions at the bottom of the opposite page, will show the ease with which the music is changed on Wurlitzer instruments.

It is variety and constant change of music that brings in the nickels. The Automatic Music Roll Rewinding Device makes a change of program practically as easy as continuing the same one over and over. Is it any wonder Wurlitzer's Automatic Musical Instruments, equipped with this device, are in a class by themselves as money-makers?

The operation is very simple. In starting the instrument up, the perforated paper music roll is slipped into position at the top, and the loose end drawn over the tracker bar and fastened to the take-up roll at the bottom.

As the roll is played, it unwinds from the top, winding onto the take-up roll. When it is played through, an opening in the paper roll near the end, causes the rewind bellows to collapse, opening the rewind valve (78). The valve is connected with the shift rod (67), which moves, causing the leather-bound friction pulleys (41 and 36) on the right to reverse and rewind the paper onto the music roll at the top.

When the music is entirely rewound, the small trigger (59) falls into a notch in the take-up roll. This releases the rewind valve (78), which, in closing, returns the gears to their proper position.

The take-up roll then draws the paper over the tracker bar until the first hole in the paper is reached, when it stops, and the nickel used in playing the previous selection is dropped into the cash box.

Left-hand page: The Automatic Music Roll Rewinding Device and the ease of changing music rolls — from a 1912 Wurlitzer catalogue.

This page: Explanation of salient Wurlitzer features, the Automatic Music Roll Rewinding Device, the Direct Drive Gear and the Coin Detector Slot. These features were not unique to the Pianino but were found in other Wurlitzer instruments of this era (circa 1912). Wurlitzer issued many different catalogues of automatic musical instruments over the years. The typical format consisted of a few pages concerning the history and operations of the Wurlitzer Company followed by descriptions of Wurlitzer mechanisms (such as the ones described on this page). Then came a list of automatic instruments for sale ranging from the Automatic Harp, Pianino and Mandolin Quartette to the 65-note instruments and, finally, the large PianOrchestras and Paganini Violin Pianos. In some instances a few pages at the back of the catalogue were devoted to the Wurlitzer line of band organs and theatre photoplayers. All in all they made very interesting reading and did an effective job of selling in their day.

DIRECT DRIVE GEAR

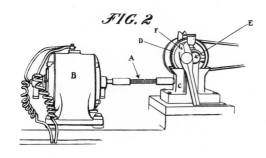

COIN DETECTOR SLOT

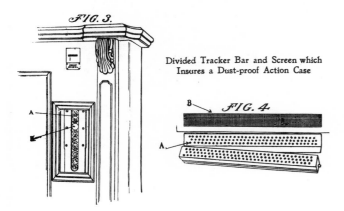

Divided Tracker Bar and Screen which Insures a Dust-proof Action Case

DIRECT DRIVE GEAR

(See Fig. 2.)

A remarkable new invention that does away entirely with troublesome, old-fashioned belts, pulleys and countershafts. The Direct Drive gear marks the greatest advance ever made toward the simplification of the mechanism.

It consists of a steel worm and fibre gear connected with the motor by a spring shaft. This works the entire mechanism of the instrument, is as simple and practical as A, B, C, and cannot give trouble.

A flexible steel shaft (A) connects the motor (B) and the standard (C), which supports the gear (D).

The movement of the crank-shaft (E) causes the pump stick (F) to move up and down. This works the feeder bellows creating the suction, which operates the pneumatics of the instrument.

This is all there is to the Direct Drive Gear. To anyone at all familiar with the working of ordinary automatic musical instruments, the illustration on the opposite page and the above explanation convey a world of meaning.

In place of this simple and perfect working mechanism, the ordinary instrument would have a small pulley on the motor carrying a belt, from 4 to 6 feet long, connecting with a large pulley on a counter-shaft. Then another belt, from 6 to 8 feet long, running from a small pulley on the counter-shaft to a large pulley on the crank-shaft.

Did you ever try to repair a loose or broken belt?

Not only does the old style arrangement in other makes of instruments mean endless trouble from slipping, breaking belts and pulleys, but it means also a great waste of power, because of friction resulting from the complicated and noisy mechanism.

In other words, it takes more electric current to run one of them, and consequently the operating expense is far greater.

The Wurlitzer Direct Drive Gear is incorporated in all Wurlitzer Automatic Musical Instruments. It eliminates trouble and repairs and reduces the cost of electric current to a minimum.

COIN DETECTOR SLOT

(See Fig. 3.)

A most ingenious feature, that prevents our instruments being played with anything except a U. S. 5-cent piece (nickel).

The slot (A) and every coin dropped into it are exposed in plain view in the front of the instrument, so that an attendant can see its contents at a glance.

We have made exhaustive experiments with every form of magnetic, balance, and other coin detectors, and find that the open magazine which exposes its contents is the only practical and successful one.

Around 1910 to 1915 the 44-note pianos generally went out of style. Although Wurlitzer continued the manufacture of its *Pianino* most others in the industry dropped this type of machine. Seeburg, Coinola, Western Electric and others marketed larger 65-note pianos taking a style "A" roll. Lest a prospective buyer think that these machines were better than a *Pianino* the catalogue descriptions of the *Pianino* were changed to read: *Equal in tone to that of any full-scale (88 note) piano; a feature that makes it remarkable.*

The Rudolph Wurlitzer Company had the foresight and business acumen to think its projects out thoroughly from the very beginning. As a result many economies were effected by the interchangability of parts between different machines. However, Wurlitzer's forethought is no more evident than in their system of roll styles.

A comparison will point this out. Nearly every time that Engelhardt & Sons produced a new type of machine they produced a distinct style of roll which would fit that particular type and no other. As a result the logistics were staggering. Inventories had to be kept and brought up to date on nearly *two dozen* different types of *Peerless* rolls!

Wurlitzer provided a sharp contrast. About a dozen different types of rolls were all that were necessary to provide the latest music for well over a hundred different machine styles.

Thus the *Pianino* roll was versatile. Rolls for the *Pianino* could be used on the *Violin Pianino* and the *Bijou Orchestra* as well. In addition to providing perforations for the playing notes, shutoff, rewind and sustaining pedal the *Pianino* roll had provisions for turning on and off violin and flute pipes, xylophone and mandolin attachment as well as playing a snare drum.

The first *Violin Pianinos* were elaborate affairs. Standing between five and six feet high the cases were ornamented with wood inlays, carvings, scrollwork and art glass. In addition to the piano/mandolin sound of the *Pianino* these machines featured twenty-one violin pipes and twenty-one flute pipes which provided a pleasant accompaniment. Although the prices of all Wurlitzer machines varied over the years, in general the *Violin Pianino* sold for about $200.00 more than the regular *Pianino*. Thus, in March, 1920, a *Pianino* sold for $575.00 and a *Violin Pianino* sold for $750.00. In June, 1920, the prices were $600.00 and $800.00 respectively.

After the first few years of production the *Violin Pianino* was more or less standardized (there continued to be minor variations in casework and art glass) to the model with a height of 4' 8", a width

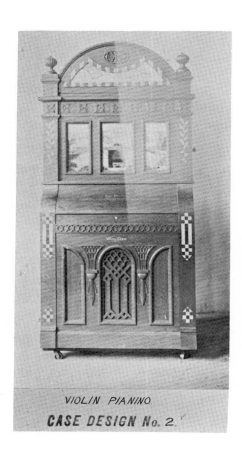

VIOLIN PIANINO.
CASE DESIGN No. 2.

VIOLIN PIANINO.
CASE DESIGN No. 3

These early Violin Pianinos boasted particularly elaborate case designs. Instrumentation of these machines consisted of a piano, mandolin attachment, twenty-one violin pipes and twenty-one flute pipes.

Wurlitzer Violin Pianino

The regular Pianino (44 note Electric Piano with Mandolin attachment and without keyboard) combined with 21 Violin Pipes and 21 Flute Pipes.

The different case finishes are illustrated in natural colors on page 5.

Height, 4 ft. 8 in.   Width, 3 ft.   Depth, 1 ft. 9 in.

Shipping weight, 625 lbs.

Exterior and interior views of the Violin Pianino. Beginning in the mid-1920's Violin Pianinos were manufactured with xylophones as standard equipment. The xylophone was in a horizontal position behind the curved wood panel just above the pipes.

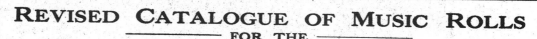

REVISED CATALOGUE OF MUSIC ROLLS
FOR THE

WURLITZER
=PIANINO=

VIOLIN PIANINO

AND BIJOU ORCHESTRA

THE RUDOLPH WURLITZER COMPANY

NEW YORK   **CINCINNATI**   **CHICAGO**

Cover of a Pianino music roll catalogue.

Wurlitzer Bijou Orchestra

Designed to meet the demand for a small automatic orchestra suitable for any but very large public places.

The "Wonder Lamp" at top in center is very attractive. It constantly revolves and changes colors when playing. The art glass designs vary somewhat.

Instrumentation:—A 44-note Piano with Mandolin attachment, 21 Violin Pipes, 21 Flute Pipes, Xylophone and Snare drum. The violins, mandolin, xylophone and drum may be cut off individually or all together.

Height, 8 ft. 7½ in. Width, 5 ft. 7½ in. Depth, 1 ft. 11½ in. Shipping weight, 1200 lbs.

The Wurlitzer Bijou Orchestra was made in several different case designs. The one illustrated above features a "wonder lamp" at the top — a feature also widely used on larger Wurlitzer orchestrions. Instrumentation consists of piano, mandolin attachment, twenty-one violin pipes, twenty-one flute pipes, xylophone and snare drum. Bijou Orchestras utilized the Wurlitzer automatic roll changer, allowing a large variety of tunes to be on the machine at one time.

of 3', and a depth of 1' 9". In the late 1920's *Violin Pianinos* had xylophones added as standard equipment.

The granddaddies of the machines operated from the *Pianino* rolls were the large *Bijou Orchestras.* These were orchestrions and evidently were intended for the motion picture trade.

The *Bijou Orchestra* featured a 44-note piano with mandolin attachment, 21 violin pipes, 21 flute pipes, a xylophone and a snare drum. Judging from the rarity of these machines today (few collectors have ever seen one) production was limited. Probably most buyers preferred the Wurlitzer orchestrions operating from the 65-note *Automatic Player Piano* roll. Although these latter orchestrions cost a little more than the *Bijou Orchestra* the larger 65-note roll allowed more notes and orchestral effects to be played.

The *Bijou Orchestras* featured the *Wurlitzer automatic roll changer,* a complicated device which permitted six music rolls to be stored on the machine at one time. As most *Pianino* rolls contained six selections this gave the Bijou Orchestra a repertoire of thirty-six different tunes.

The roll changer gave the *Bijou Orchestra* (and the many other machines in the Wurlitzer line which incorporated this feature) great musical versatility as one roll could be all marches, another all classical music, another all ragtime, and so on.

As *Pianinos* were manufactured over a long span of years many hundreds of different music rolls were cut for them.

Almost any popular tune of the 1900 to 1928 era can be found on a *Pianino* roll. A *Pianino* roll catalogue issued in the early 1920's featured selections in the following categories, as indexed in the inside back cover: blues and rag rolls, Bohemian rolls, Cuban rolls, Greek rolls, Hawaiian rolls, Hungarian rolls, Irish rolls, Italian rolls, march and patriotic rolls, Mexican rolls, operatic rolls, Polish rolls, Russian rolls, sacred rolls, Scotch rolls, Spanish rolls, Swedish rolls and waltz rolls.

Tunes such as the following mirrored events of the times: *The Liberty Loan March, We Don't Want the Bacon (What We Want is a Piece of the Rhine), One-Step, Rudolph Valentino Blues* and *Ray and His Little Chevrolet.*

Other tunes such as the *Rat Proof Rag, Whose Izzy Is He?, The Rag With No Name* and *She Gypped Egypt* were undoubtedly novelty numbers.

There was no better way to keep up to date with new tune releases than by dropping nickels into a *Pianino* slot.

Exterior and interior views of the Wurlitzer Bijou Orchestra. This machine is in the collection of Terry Hathaway of Santa Fe Springs, California. It was obtained from the Raney collection ... a group of about seventy-five coin pianos and orchestrions that was dispersed in the 1950's. Note that the side "wings" of the Bijou Orchestra are more decorative than functional. Nearly all of the apparatus is contained in the center section.

Wurlitzer Bijou Orchestra

With Wurlitzer Automatic Roll Changer

Designed to meet the demand for a small automatic orchestra suitable for any but very large public places.

The finish illustrated above is green weathered oak. Other finishes are shown in natural colors on page 5.

Instrumentation:

A 44-note Piano with Mandolin attachment, 21 Violin Pipes, Xylophone and Snare Drum. The violins, mandolin, xylophone and drum may be cut off individually or all together.

Height, (including statue) 8 ft. 7½ in. Width, 5 ft. 7½ in. Depth, 1 ft. 11½ in.

Shipping weight, 1200 lbs.

Original catalogue description of the Bijou Orchestra. This machine is similar in case design to the Hathaway instrument shown on the preceding page.

Chapter 6

In 1908 the first *Wurlitzer 65-Note Player Piano* was introduced. Roll-operated, this machine replaced the *Tonophone* as the standard large coin-operated piano. In the words of a Wurlitzer catalogue of the day:

"THE NEW WURLITZER 65-NOTE PLAYER PIANO is one of our latest triumphs in the perfection of our Electric Pianos. A number of recent and most important improvements make this instrument so nearly perfect mechanically, that all chance of its ever getting out or order is practically eliminated. Besides, important parts are now made of metal instead of wood, so that the instrument, with proper care, will last a lifetime.

The tracker box, which is the frame holding the music roll, is made of metal, and is absolutely true, insuring the perfect tracking of the music roll.

The take-up roll, on which the perforated paper music roll winds as it is fed off its spool has adjustable metal flanges on the end to admit of the spool's being made any width. This prevents the edges of the music from turning up.

The *65-Note Player Piano* also has all the valuable improved features of our automatic instruments, including the Music Roll Rewinding Device, the Direct Drive Gear, the Magazine Coin Detector Slot, Mandolin Attachment, and Electric Lights for lighting up the interior when playing. It also has a full keyboard of 88 notes for hand playing, and in this connection the front may be tilted to act as a music rest, just as with the regular home piano.

These cases are of chaste, simple design, with plain mouldings and very little carving,

CATALOGUE OF MUSIC FOR THE
WURLITZER
65 NOTE
PLAYER PIANO
ALSO ALPHABETICAL LIST OF ALL THE SELECTIONS

PRICE OF ROLLS, $4.00 EACH

THE RUDOLPH WURLITZER CO
CINCINNATI   CHICAGO
117-121 E. FOURTH ST.   266-268 WABASH AVE

LIST OF MUSIC ROLLS FOR THE
WURLITZER
65 NOTE
PLAYER PIANO
These Music Rolls are also used on the 65-Note Violin Piano and the Remodeled Tonophone.

ROLL No. 1.
Florida Rag—Characteristic.................Geo. L. Lowry
Whistle—Intermezzo ....Leon Copeland
Waving Palms—Waltz ....B. H. Starks
Ragtime Nightmare—March and Two-Step.......T. Turpin
Bachelor Maids—March and Two-Step........Floyd St. Clair

ROLL No. 2.
Hearts and Flowers—Flower Song.........Theo. M. Tobani
Beautiful Blue Danube—Waltz.............Johann Strauss
Flower Song ....Gustave Lange
Wedding o' the Winds—Waltz...............John T. Hall
Traumerei—Reverie ....R. Schumann

ROLL No. 3.
Harum Scarum—March and Two-Step........L. W. Young
Carpet Rags—Char. Two-Step ....R. W. Conner
Coleville Coon Cadets—March.............Harry Freeman
At a Ragtime Reception—Rag Medley.......Ben M. Jerome
Colored Aristocracy—Cakewalk ....G. W. Bernard

ROLL No. 4.
The Bos'n Rag—Cakewalk..................Fred. S. Stone
Topsy Turvy—Two-Step....................L. V. Gustin
Queen of the Ragtime—Two-Step...........Jas. H. Davis
A Cakeless Cakewalk—Cakewalk............C. J. Wolcott
Original Rags—Char ....Chas. N. Daniels

MUSIC ROLLS FOR THE WURLITZER 65-NOTE PLAYER PIANO.

ROLL No. 5.
Swipsey—Cakewalk ....Joplin & Marshall
Ragtime Skedaddle—Cakewalk.................Geo. Rosey
Alabama Dream—Cakewalk ....Geo. D. Barnard
Society Swells—Cakewalk ....J. L. Ritchie
Raz Mataz—Cakewalk ....Wm. Smith

ROLL No. 6.
Loveland Waltzes ....Abe Holtzmann
Popularity—March and Two-Step...........Geo. M. Cohan
Dream of Heaven—Waltzes ....A. W. Bauer
Havana—Intermezzo ....Theo. F. Morse
Southern Dream—Waltzes.................Harry J. Lincoln

ROLL No. 7.
Bunch of Blackberries—Cakewalk and Two-Step, A. Holtzmann
Tipperary—March ....James M. Fulton
Symphia—Waltzes ....A. Holtzmann
Bit o' Blarncy—Two-Step ....J. F. Helf
Palmah House—Schuffle ....Libbie Erickson

ROLL No. 8.
The Diplomat—March and Two-Step......John Phillip Sousa
Love's Dream After the Ball—Waltz..............Czibulka
Dixie Blossoms—March and Two-Step........Percy Wenrich
Happy Birds—Waltz ....Edw. Holst
American Girl—Two-Step ....Victor Herbert

ROLL No. 9.
Silence and Fun—Ragtime Essence ....Chas. S. Mullen
Peter Piper—Two-Step ....S. R. Henry
Sleepy Lou—Raggy Two-Step ....Irene Giblin
Moon Winks—Three-Step ....Geo. Stevens
Maple Leaf Rag ....Scott Joplin

The first Wurlitzer 65-Note Player Piano roll catalogue, circa 1908. Note that the rolls were also suitable for use on the 65-Note Violin Piano and the remodeled Tonophone. In later years the 65-Note Player Piano roll (with its name changed to "Automatic Player Piano") was used on a multitude of different styles.

The Wurlitzer 65-Note Player Piano

Height, 4 ft. 10 in.   Width, 5 ft. 2 in.   Depth, 2 ft. 3 in.

PRICE—Complete, with Electric Motor and 1 Roll of Music, containing 5 selections.....$700.00

Extra Music Rolls, 5 selections each....................................   4.00

Shipping Weight, 1,025 pounds.
Net Weight, 755 pounds.

Like other Wurlitzer machines of the pre-1910 period this early style of the 65-Note Player Piano did not have art glass but had clear glass panels which revealed the interior of the machine. George Messig, who worked for Wurlitzer in the New York City branch about this time, wrote us that: "Wurlitzer started a store on West 32nd Street, New York City, which displayed and sold orchestrions and coin-operated pianos. They also put these instruments in various places with a commission to the location owner of 25% of the nickels in the coin box. A different roll of music was put on each week. Some places took in $18.00 or more per week. If the receipts were below $2.00 per week the machine was taken out. Sometimes people would devise ways of cheating the piano by tying a string on a nickel so that it would not drop in the coin box. Iron washers with holes would not work but they would prevent further nickels from going in because a little trigger would go in the hole."

The Wurlitzer 65-Note Player Piano

THE NEW WURLITZER 65-NOTE PLAYER PIANO is one of our latest triumphs in the perfection of our Electric Pianos. A number of recent and most important improvements make this instrument so nearly perfect mechanically, that all chance of its ever getting out of order is practically eliminated. Besides, the important parts are now made of metal instead of wood, so that the instrument, with proper care, will last a lifetime.

The tracker box, which is the frame holding the music roll, is made of metal, and is absolutely true, insuring the perfect tracking of the music roll.

The take-up roll, on which the perforated paper music roll winds as it is fed off its spool has adjustable metal flanges on the end to admit of the spool's being made any width. This prevents the edges of the music from turning up.

The 65-Note Player Piano also has all the valuable improved features of our automatic instruments, including the Music Roll Rewinding Device, the Direct Drive Gear, the Magazine Coin Detector Slot, Mandolin Attachment, and Electric Lights for lighting up the interior when playing. It also has a full keyboard of 88 notes for hand playing, and in this connection the front may be tilted to act as a music rest, just as with the regular home piano.

The cases are of chaste, simple design, with plain mouldings and very little carving, and are very solid and substantial in construction. In the top panel are two plate glass openings on either side of the tracker box opening, through which the electric-lit interior is seen. The cases come in beautifully figured quarter-sawed oak, in golden, light and dark weathered, Flemish and Silver Gray finishes; also silver gray ash and mahogany.

Any number of our nickel-in-the-slot boxes can be used in connection with the 65-Note Player Piano, as with the Pian-Orchestra, so that it may be played from any part of the house.

Complete catalog of music mailed upon request.

In the above description Wurlitzer notes that the 65-Note Player Piano "with proper care will last a lifetime."

Interior of Wurlitzer 65-Note Player Piano

The mechanisms of the 88-Note Player Piano, Pianino, Mandolin Quartette and Mandolin Sextette, are practically the same.

A—Slot approach.
B—Magazine for coins.
C—Action case.
D—Music roll.
E—Tracker bar.
F—Take-up roll.
G—Tempo Regulator.
H—Music roll friction disc.
J—Music roll friction pulley.
L—Take-up roll friction disc.
M—Take-up roll friction pulley.
N—Mandolin attachment.
O—Rewind device.
P—Suction tube to action case.
Q—Regulating valve.
R—Feeder bellows.
S—Pump sticks.
T—Standard for shaft gear.
U—Flexible shaft.
W—Motor.
X—Money drawer.

and are very solid and substantial in construction. In the top panel are two plate glass openings on either side of the tracker box opening, through which the electric-lit interior is seen. The cases come in beautifully figured quarter-sawed oak, in golden, light and dark weathered, Flemish and silver gray finishes; also silver gray ash and mahogany.

Any number of our nickel-in-the-slot boxes can be used in connection with the *65-Note Player Piano,* as with the *PianOrchestra,* so that it may be played from any part of the house."

The statement that the cases were of "simple design, with plain mouldings and very little carving" did not remain accurate for very long. Soon the 65-note machines were being produced in a wide varieties of styles, some of them with elaborate ornamentation and frillwork that would make a Chinese temple builder envious.

All in all several hundred different styles and minor varieties of the *65-Note Player Piano* were produced. Many were one-of-a-kind items produced on special order. Certain others were made only in small quantities. No style remained absolutely constant for very long. Variety, the spice of life, was also the spice of Wurlitzer pianos. On these pages are shown just a few of the many case designs produced.

Also introduced about 1908 was the Wurlitzer *Violin Piano.* Taking the *65-Note Player Piano* roll, the *Violin Piano* essentially was a regular 65-note piano with a set of thirty-eight violin pipes placed behind the sounding board. In contrast with the *Solo Violin Piano* of later years (which strived to imitate a violin rather than just provide a violin-like effect) the *Violin Piano* of 1908 played the same notes at the same time the piano hammers did. The violin pipes did not play continuously, but only when turned on by a control perforation in the roll.

The *65-Note Player Piano* roll was the Wurlitzer standard . . . much the same as the "A" roll and "G" roll were the Seeburg standards. More Wurlitzer machine styles used this type of roll than any other. The perforations in the 65-note roll provided for piano, mandolin effect, control pedals, orchestra bells or chimes, two ranks of pipes (in practice, usually one rank of violin pipes and one rank of flute pipes) and various traps. Some machines used only a part of the roll's capabilities . . . the piano and mandolin, for instance. Others used all of the orchestral potential.

The Wurlitzer *Violin Piano,* with its mellow harmony, sold very well. Soon models were being produced with drums and a triangle added. These orchestrions were first sold as Wurlitzer *Violin-Flute Pianos.* Later the name was changed to the Wurlitzer *Orchestra Piano.*

The Violin Piano—Style A

Back view illustrating the Violin Pipes. The front is the same as that of the 65-Note Player Piano. See page 22.

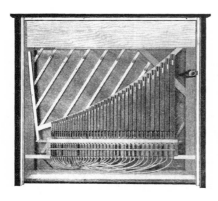

Height, 4 ft. 10 in. Width, 5 ft. 2 in. Depth, 2 ft. 9 in.

PRICE—Complete, with Electric Motor and 1 Roll of Music, containing 5 selections.....$975.00
Extra Music Rolls, 5 selections each... 4.00

Shipping Weight, 1,150 pounds.
Net Weight, 875 pounds.

The Violin Piano—Style A

THE VIOLIN PIANO is the latest addition to our line of self-playing musical specialties. In its class it is about the most attractive entertainer from a musical standpoint we have ever put on the market.

The Violin Piano is our regular 65-Note Player Piano, with the addition of a full set of fine violin pipes placed in the back behind the soundboard. Its appearance in front is the same. These pipes play in unison with the notes of the piano, giving the effect of a violinist accompanied by a piano. The musical effect is very charming and totally different from that of any other instrument on the market.

The mechanism of the Violin Piano is identically the same as the 65-Note Player-Piano, with the exception of an extra pumping bellows and set of valves to operate the pipes. It has our Direct Drive Gear, Magazine Coin Detector Slot, Automatic Music Roll Rewinding Device, Metal Tracker Bar and Frame (metal parts handsomely nickel-plated), Tracker Bar Adjusting Screw, Adjustable Music Roll Flange, Tempo Regulator, Mandolin Attachment, and all the other modern improvements embodied in our up-to-date instruments.

The cases are beautifully figured mahogany, and selected quarter-sawed oak in five different finishes—golden, light and dark weathered, Flemish and the new Silver Gray Oak and Silver Gray Ash, with plate glass openings in the top panel through which the electric-lit interior is seen. Handsome mouldings and carvings embellish the cases, and give the instrument a highly artistic appearance, entirely in harmony with its musical effects.

The same music rolls used on our 65-Note Player Piano are used on the Violin Piano. They contain five selections each and can be changed in five seconds, without even stopping the operation of the instrument.

A stop controls the pipes, so that the violin pipe section may be cut out and the piano played alone. The back of the instrument is adjustable, and can be opened to make the tone loud, or closed to make it soft. The instrument has the full regulation piano keyboard of 88 notes, and can be played by hand in the usual way, if desired.

Any number of our nickel-in-the-slot boxes can be used in connection with the Violin Piano, so that it may be played from any part of the house.

The Violin Piano bids fair to become one of our most popular entertainers. For any one looking for the latest novelty in an automatic music maker, it is the "one best bet."

The Flute Piano—Style A

The Flute Piano is the same as the Violin Piano, described above, except that it is equipped with Flute pipes instead of Violin. The music has the typical soft flute quality and is wonderfully attractive.

PRICE—... $975.00

Complete catalog of music mailed upon request.

The Violin Piano was a modified 65-Note Player Piano with a set of wood violin pipes added behind the sounding board.

Labels from 65-Note Wurlitzer rolls. The large label at the left is from a ten-tune long-frame type roll. The labels at the right are from the shorter roll-changer rolls.

The above list of prospects omits two of the main users of coin-operated pianos — houses of prostitution and speakeasies. The above illustration is from a flyer that was sent to various coin piano dealers and operators to encourage them to handle the Wurlitzer line. The Style IX piano was evidently one of the more popular models for many Wurlitzer pianos still in existence today are of this type. Six of the eight numbered spaces on the front of this and certain other Wurlitzer pianos contained tune cards similar to the small labels shown on the facing page. The other two spaces contained information for operating the roll changer and other data.

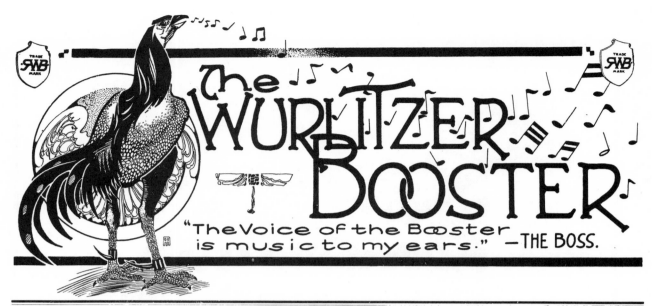

The WURLITZER BOOSTER

"The Voice of the Booster is music to my ears." —THE BOSS.

VOL. I   SEPTEMBER, 1913   No. 9

New Style "S" Price $550.00

THIS New Style is cheap in price only. Its owing to its simple construction that we are able to sell at this low figure. You will find a market for it often. Has long time frame, chain driven roll mechanism, three adjustments for speed—small 1-10th horse power on sliding base—strong spring keeps motor back and insures uniform belt tension— magazine switch and iron box. The soft stop and mandolin stop can be controlled from outside.

The Wurlitzer Booster, a monthly house organ, gave information concerning new models, sales experiences and techniques and other useful suggestions to help with dealers' sales of coin pianos, orchestrions, photoplayers and pipe organs. The issue above highlights the new Style S, which was one of the few Wurlitzer pianos which had the roll mechanism under the keyboard. Other S series machines such as the SA and SS also had this feature.

THE WAY WINTER DOES IT.

Sam Winter, Chicago Office.

Mr. Jones has a saloon in a fair neighborhood, and he could not see where he could improve his business by buying an electric piano. I called on him ninety-seven times within the last six months, and all I could get out of him was "nothing doing."

Finally, I made up my mind to either sell him or know the reasons why. I was going to get an argument out of him if I had to lick him in order to do so. We finally got to talking pianos, and he makes a break to me that if I can show him where an electric piano will boost his business he might consider letting me put one in on commission. That's just the start I wanted.

"You know that a good many of my neighbors object to music, and I am apt to lose their trade." "Yes, and you will also admit that there are a good many of your neighbors that have no use for a saloon or a saloonkeeper, and nothing would please them better than to put you out of business." "That is so, but that don't show me where any electric piano is going to increase my trade."

"Isn't it a fact that among all your customers you don't average three new customers a day? You have people going by your place all day, and still you tell me that you depend on your neighbors for your business. You are not getting the transient trade, that you will admit is the best—and why not? Simply because you haven't backbone to go after their trade."

"Well, that's true to a certain extent, but will you guarantee that if I put in one of your pianos I will increase my business?"

"I will not only guarantee that you will increase your trade at least 75 per cent, but possibly double it, and am willing to wager a $5 hat to boot."

"Well, how much commission will you pay me?"

"Commission, did you ask? Why, we will do even better than commission—we will give you the receipts of the machine and make you a present of the piano within two years."

"How's that?"

"This new sixty-five-note piano that you see illustrated here sells for $700, the terms are $70 down and $7 a week. Now, if your instrument takes in $10 a week you keep $3 and pay our collector $7, which is credited to your account, not figuring your additional profit in sales."

"Well, I would sooner get 25 per cent of the receipts and have nothing on my mind?"

"Do you mean to tell me that you are willing to pay $1,000 license, $75 a month rent, $75 a month to your bartender, and figuring $25 incidental expenses, and still you are willing to give away to operators 75 cents of every dollar taken in?"

"Certainly not."

"Well, that's exactly what you are trying to do. You want to give away 75 cents of every dollar taken in. If you can find operators to give you 25 per cent, even 50 per cent, buy their own instruments, take care of them on the commission basis, it surely ought to be a better proposition to buy your own instrument and get all the receipts."

"Well, suppose my instrument only takes in $4 a week, I would have to make up $3 each week."

"That's true, and if you furnish free music all day and had to pay $7 a week, you would be more than satisfied to pay it if it doubled your business, wouldn't you?"

"Certainly."

"Furthermore, these pianos that we are selling for $700, you must admit that they are worth the price, aren't they?"

"Well, I don't know about that."

"If I were to sell you this machine now for $270, you would buy it right at this minute, wouldn't you?"

"Certainly."

"I am going to prove to you, that if your piano should happen to run $4 a week, you would not pay more than $270 for this $700 instrument. You are going to give me

now $70, which will leave a balance of $630. You have 90 weeks in which to pay the balance. Taking your own figures, $4 a week, in 90 weeks it will have earned $360, which leaves a balance of $270. You are willing to buy this instrument for $270, aren't you?"

"Yes, but your piano is not worth more than $500. I have had a number of different salesmen from different concerns call on me, and judging by the illustration, your piano is not worth any more than that. In fact, some of the cases are far more beautiful than yours."

"Do you judge a woman by her clothes?"

"No, not always."

"You shouldn't judge a piano by its case, either. A piano should be judged by its tone, the construction, material used and the firm building it. Let me tell you about the company I represent:

"In 1856 Rudolph Wurlitzer started in the music business in Cincinnati, and today we have branches in every principal city in the United States, and a large factory, which employs thousands of people.

"It is not only unwise but unsafe for a customer to buy a piano produced by firms that are either weak financially or not firmly entrenched in the automatic business. The promises I make to you are assured by financial strength, long manufacturing experience and a fine product. Disappointment and failure are inevitable if the buying of an electric piano is based on the impractical promises, commissions and other alleged inducements which are always a part of frail enterprises. You have a right to expect high intrinsic value and the utmost co-operation of the company maintaining constant service.

"In many cases this service is mythical, and you should satisfy yourself that the company selling you an electric piano has the facilities to render efficient service; and in the electric piano business, like many others, it is easy to be misled.

"Our pianos have received boundless praise. It is a serious evil, the lack of discrimination in buying pianos.

"Certain evils are almost inseparable from the ever-growing enterprise, and favored by the fact that most any piano will render service for a brief period.

"A number of ill-equipped manufacturers have succeeded in selling a few pianos. The result, of course, has been disastrous. Picture the plight of yourself buying an electric piano from a manufacturer who goes into the hands of a receiver. You can neither get service nor parts, and the demise of the maker means that you might as well have no piano. Because of these circumstances, the man who contemplates the purchase of an electric piano should be possessed of certain facts before buying a piano.

"You will realize that the piano built with the utmost care, best possible material used, sold on a legitimate basis by a firm that has an interest in his product, is the piano that you should buy. You will appreciate the fact that an electric piano, like any other piece of machinery from which music is expected, must have, first of all, practical quality; back of it there must be a good reputation, financial responsibility and the assurance of continued service. Such a company is the Wurlitzer Company."

"You change rolls every week, don't you?"

"No, you don't want us to change rolls."

"Why not?"

"Well, in the first place you have no choice. You are just as apt to get a Chinese roll as a Swedish roll. The results you can imagine. A lot of Germans come in, one drops a nickel and 'The Wearing of the Green' commences to play. How long could you hold that crowd?

"Changing rolls for you, you will be unable to please your customers. You would have to be satisfied with the rolls that are six months to a year old, and the result would be a loss of trade, not a gain."

"How much are your rolls?"

"They are 30 cents a selection, and they will easily bring you in twenty times the amount."

"Let me see your contract."

Salesmanship fifty years ago . . . selling a Wurlitzer 65-note piano in 1913.

The Wurlitzer Automatic Music Roll Changer

This invention means as much to the production of automatic music as the multiple printing press means to newspaper printing

What the Wurlitzer Music Roll Changer Is

A mechanical device built on the principle of the original Ferris Wheel of the Chicago World's Fair.

The wheel is loaded with six music rolls. The illustration shows one of the rolls being played. After it is played through entirely, or partly, as preferred, it is automatically rewound and the magazine wheel revolves to the next roll that it is desired to play.

Advantages of the Wurlitzer Music Roll Changer

A capacity of 6 music rolls; that is, 25 to 30 different selections, since each roll contains 5 to 6 pieces.

The entire set of rolls may be played through, one after the other, without any attention whatsoever. This means a musical program of an hour and a half to three hours duration without repetition and without any bother.

This device has been pronounced a marvel of mechanical ingenuity and effectiveness. We have been at work on it for many years, knowing that when perfected, it would revolutionize the automatic musical instrument business, and place the Wurlitzer Instruments so far beyond other makes that all comparison would cease.

There is nothing to compare with the Wurlitzer Music Roll Changer. There can be nothing at all like it for every feature and part is fully covered by patents that have been taken out in the United States and foreign countries.

Although a number of European machines featured roll-changing mechanisms Wurlitzer instruments were the only American-made coin pianos to have them.

STYLE 'I' No. 4
SPECIAL DESIGN

This unusual photograph from the Wurlitzer archives shows a special design with THREE wonder lights! Each one revolved as the music played. This particular machine was made to order for a customer in Puerto Rico.

All orchestrions operating from the 65-note roll had keyboards which permitted manual playing of the piano part.

The Wurlitzer keyboard orchestrions were made in a wonderful array of styles, including models with the "wonder light," a feature also used on the *Bijou Orchestra* and on several styles of the *PianOrchestra*. The rotating jeweled bulb of the wonder light was an attention-getter. Most Wurlitzer orchestrions manufactured after 1921 had this feature as standard equipment.

The *Wurlitzer Roll Changer*, originally available only on the imported *PianOrchestras* (for $200.00 extra), was an optional "extra" on most other Wurlitzer machines beginning shortly after 1909 when patent rights were purchased from Verstraelen and Alter of New York City. By 1920 most Wurlitzer coin-operated pianos and orchestrions were incorporating the changer as standard equipment.

For catalogue purposes the letter "X" was added to the description of a machine when it featured the changer. Thus a Wurlitzer style L *Orchestra Piano* would be a machine with a long roll frame type of mechanism and a style LX would be the same machine, but with a roll changing mechanism.

With typical flair Wurlitzer had this to say about the roll changer:

"The *Wurlitzer Automatic Roll Changer* has been pronounced a marvel of mechanical ingenuity and effectiveness. We have been at work on it for many years, knowing that when perfected it would revolutionize the automatic musical instrument business and place the Wurlitzer instruments so far beyond other makes that all comparisons would cease..."

The *65-Note Player Piano* rolls and most other Wurlitzer rolls were perforated at the Wurlitzer factory in North Tonawanda. Only the very early *PianOrchestra* rolls which were made by Philipps in Germany and Wurlitzer *Harp* rolls which were made in Rising Sun, Indiana, were exceptions.

The music rolls were made from a master roll. The master was prepared by musicians using a scale stick on which were marked the various notes and positions of the control perforations for operating the pedals, pipes, drums and other effects.

After the lines were marked by the musicians a team of girls cut out the required perforations on the heavy master paper. After checking for errors the master was placed on the perforating machine. Up to ten rolls could be made in a single cutting by one perforating machine. The long row of perforating machines at the North Tonawanda factory had a tremendous combined output.

Four different models of Wurlitzer pianos which used the 65-Note Player Piano roll. Literally hundreds of different case and art glass variations were produced.

From memory Mr. Farny Wurlitzer furnished us with this description of the roll cutting process:

"As you probably know, a music roll gets larger in diameter as it winds up. It also gradually plays the music faster. Our perforating machines were automatically adjusted to allow for this. As a result the tempo remained the same on our music rolls throughout the playing. This was absolutely necessary as we made rolls with 5, 10, 15 and 20 selections and, of course, those with twenty selections were very long and the music really couldn't have been playable otherwise; it would have gone too fast.

In addition to this, in connection with the making of the rolls for our organs (referring to the Wurlitzer Hope-Jones Unit Orchestra theatre pipe organs made at the North Tonawanda factory — ed.) we had a perforating machine that we built here that perforated the

Above left: Style I, case design No. 22.
Above right: Style SA, a piano with a rank of flute pipes. Note the roll mechanism is of the long-frame type and is below the keyboard — a rare feature.

MUSIC ROLL DEPT.
Perforating Room

A long row of roll perforating machines at Wurlitzer's North Tonawanda plant. Most rolls for Wurlitzer pianos, orchestrions, band organs and theatre instruments were produced right on the premises. In later years most of the equipment was junked.

This Kansas City man will tell it to you straight

When it comes to putting up to you the proposition of Music, we believe that it will sound very much more sincere and convincing if we have an ACTUAL USER of a Wurlitzer Instrument tell you what it has positively proven to him in his own daily experience.

Let us introduce to you

A. J. SCHMIDT
1301 Grand Ave.
KANSAS CITY, MO.

It is an exceptional endorsement when Mr. Schmidt stops short in a crowded day to go to the trouble of posing for photographs and writing testimonials— when he gets nothing for it. It is he who says that Wurlitzer Music has made money for him, and not Wurlitzer. He talks "sense" because he has had the real experience.

MR. SCHMIDT WRITES--(See his Original Letter on the back)

"I bought a Wurlitzer Automatic Piano 16 months ago, and am very much pleased with same. It is a money maker and I would not be without one."

Just because you are interested in ANYTHING that will give you a bigger patronage, you should go into this Music proposition further.

Write for the big, new, handsomely illustrated free Wurlitzer Catalogue, showing many styles of fine Automatic Musical Instruments. All sold on the "EASY PAYMENT" Plan.

Without obligation, fill in and return the enclosed card TODAY.

The Rudolph WURLITZER Company

KANSAS CITY, MO.: 1016 Walnut Street

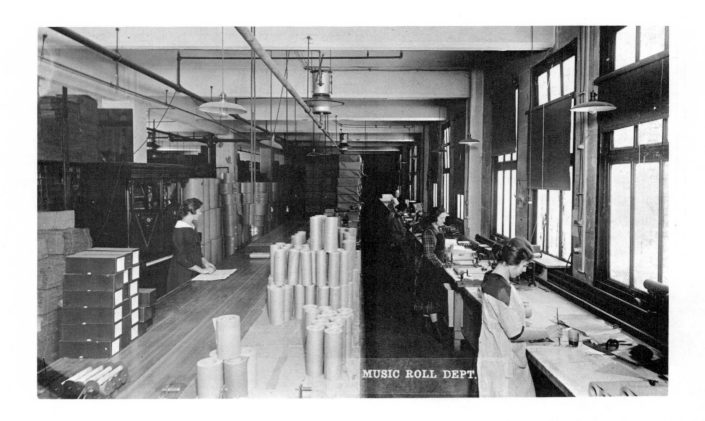

A scene from the Music Roll Department at Wurlitzer's North Tonawanda factory in March, 1919. The orchestrion behind the lady on the left is either a Style C or CX and was probably used to maintain a quality check on the rolls produced.

This Wurlitzer coin piano is unusual in that it has art glass both above and below the keyboard.

We completely discontinued our Music Roll Department in 1934. We then sold the machines that were used for making the merry-go-round organ rolls to the T.R.T. Manufacturing Company. The other machines were destroyed. The demand for rolls had practically ceased."

In the 1920's Wurlitzer issued monthly catalogues of new roll releases. Each listing featured new popular tunes plus melodies from the past which were favorites.

music roll as the organist played. A minute after he finished playing we could replay what he had just played. In those days there weren't any tape recorders and artists were often quite astonished to hear their own playing. I recall that one of them said, 'Tear that up, I am going to do it over again.' There were always some errors because if a musician touched a key slightly the perforating machine would perforate that note. These errors, of course, could easily be corrected . . .

STYLE 'X' & 'XX'
CASE DESIGN No. 5.

Another one of the many case designs used for the 65-Note Automatic Player Piano.

Sometimes special prices were given to move out-of-date rolls. A 1925 offer read:

"Owing to the fact that the popular music does not remain in demand for a period longer than six months, we have accumulated a stock of the various styles of rolls with music cut previous to six months ago, and in order to dispose of these we are offering them at half price. Our customers should bear in mind that only a limited supply of these rolls is available and that first come will be first served."

Introduced at a price of $4.00 for a *five-tune* roll in 1908, the price dropped to the point at which $4.00 could buy a *ten-tune 65-Note Player Piano* roll in 1925.

In 1925 Wurlitzer roll prices were as follows:
65-Note Player Piano:

Five-tune rolls for roll-changer: $2.00 without metal spool; $3.00 with spool.

Five-tune rolls for long roll frame instruments: $2.25 each.

Ten-tune rolls for long roll frame instruments: $4.00 each.

Fifteen-tune rolls for long roll frame instruments: $6.00 each.

Twenty-tune rolls for long roll frame instruments: $8:00 each

Wurlitzer Violin-Flute Piano—Style C

One of our biggest sellers. It combines a Piano with Mandolin attachment, 38 Violin Pipes, 38 Flute Pipes, Bass and Snare Drums and Cymbals. The different musical divisions can be disconnected at will. The art glass designs vary somewhat.

This instrument is equipped with long tune frame which will play 1, 5, 10, 15 or 20-tune roll. The different case finishes are illustrated in natural colors on page 5.

Height, 7 ft. 4 in. Width, 5 ft. 4 in. Depth, 2 ft. 8 in.

Wurlitzer Violin Piano—Style B   **Wurlitzer Flute Piano**—Style B

Same as above, except that it does not have Flute Pipes.   Same as Violin Flute Piano—Style C—except that it does not have Violin Pipes.

Shipping weight, 1500 lbs.

Violin-Flute Piano, Style C. The catalogue designations did not remain constant. For instance, many different-appearing machines were made all having the catalogue description of style C or CX (with roll-changer). The various Wurlitzer keyboard orchestrions were best sellers. More Wurlitzer keyboard orchestrions survive today than do those of all other manufacturers combined.

Wurlitzer Electric Piano—Style X

With Wurlitzer Automatic Roll Changer

In every way the handsomest and most desirable electric piano on the market. It is entirely gear driven—no belts nor pulleys. The Music Roll Changer provides a repertoire of 25 to 30 different pieces of music and causes the receipts to far eclipse those of any straight piano ever known.

The different case finishes are illustrated in natural colors on page 5.

Height, 4 ft. 10 in. Width, 5 ft. 2 in. Depth, 2 ft. 3 in. Shipping weight, 1050 lbs.

TELEPHONE 7099 MAIN

CHAS. J. SANDOW'S
CAFE AND RESTAURANT
11 ATLANTIC AVENUE
BROOKLYN, N. Y.,   September 20th   1913

The Rudolph Wurlitzer Company,
32nd Street, bet. 5th & 6th Aves.
New York City.

Dear Sirs:—

I thought I would let you know just how much receipts the Violin-Flute Piano I purchased from you about a year ago is taking in. This instrument has taken in every week since I have it from $20. to $40. per week. You may think this unusual but it is a fact.

The instrument is not only more than paying for itself but it is a big attraction in my place and has increased my business 50%. No cafe or restaurant should be without one today.

Yours very truly,

Chas J Sandow

Wurlitzer Violin-Flute Piano—Style DX

With Wurlitzer Automatic Roll Changer

A new style instrument that is far ahead of any now on the market. It has all the exclusive Wurlitzer mechanical improvements, which make it practically trouble-proof, and for beauty of design and tonal quality it is unexcelled. The art glass designs vary somewhat.

The various musical sections can be cut off at will.

Instrumentation:

Piano with Mandolin attachment, 38 Violin Pipes (21 First Violin and 17 Viola), 38 Flute Pipes.

Height, 4 ft. 11 in. Width, 5 ft. 3 in. Depth, 3 ft. Shipping weight, 1250 lbs.

Wurlitzer Violin-Flute Piano—Style D

Same as above, except equipped with long tune frame instead of roll-changer—playing 1, 5, 10, 15 and 20-tune roll.

The Style X Electric Piano was one of the first to feature the Wurlitzer Automatic Roll Changer. The device caught on rapidly. By the 1920's most Wurlitzer pianos and orchestrions had roll changers as standard equipment. The DX had the changer located behind a glass panel in the center of the machine above the keyboard — the customary location for this mechanism.

Pianino:	Five-tune rolls $2.00; with spool and end wire (for the *Bijou Orchestra* which used the roll changer) $3.00. Ten-tune rolls: $4.00.
Concert PianOrchestra:	Five-tune rolls $4.25. Metal spool, $1.25 extra.
Mandolin PianOrchestra:	Five-tune rolls $4.25. Metal spool, $1.25 extra.
Solo Violin Piano:	Four-tune rolls, 6.75. Metal spool, $1.25 extra.
Autograph Reproducing Piano:	Five-tune rolls $3.75. Metal spool, $1.25 extra.
Paganini:	Five-tune rolls, $6.75. Metal spool, $1.25 extra.

From the above listing you will note that seven different types of rolls for coin-operated instruments were being sold in 1925. Over the years several additional Wurlitzer roll types were manufactured.

The following listing includes most, if not all, different basic types of rolls manufactured for use on coin-operated Wurlitzer pianos and orchestrions:

Pianino rolls. These were used on the *Pianino,* the *Violin Pianino,* and on the *Bijou Orchestra.*

Harp rolls. These were used only on the Wurlitzer *Harp.*

Violin Piano—Style C

CASE DESIGN No. 1.

The Style C Violin-Flute Piano was one of the earliest keyboard orchestrions made by Wurlitzer. In later years machines of this type were known as Orchestra Pianos. Instrumentation consisted of piano, mandolin attachment, two ranks of pipes, bass drum and snare drum. Later models included a cymbal and triangle and (occasionally) a small set of orchestra bells.

The Wurlitzer Violin-Flute Piano—Style C

No new type of Automatic Musical instrument ever introduced has made any quicker or more favorable impression than the Violin-Flute Piano.

We had long worked on the problem of an automatic musical instrument that would satisfactorily feature the delightful combination of Piano, Violin and Flute, and the sensational success of the new Violin-Flute Piano is, therefore, doubly gratifying to us.

This instrument combines a high-grade Piano, with special violin attachment and an up-to-date orchestrion. The instrumentation of the orchestrion section consists of 38 Flute pipes, 21 Violins and 17 Violas, also a Bass Drum and Orchestra Snare Drum. It plays from the same inexpensive perforated paper music rolls used by the 65-Note Player Piano.

A distinct advantage is the ability to disconnect the different musical sections at will and play the piano, which has a full keyboard, by hand, as a regular piano. The piano may also be played automatically, independently of the pipes. This makes the Violin-Flute Piano a wonderfully versatile entertainer.

Every modern improved feature of the Wurlitzer Automatic Musical Instruments is embodied in the mechanism, especially those of our 65-Note Player Piano, such as the metal tracker bar and tracker bar adjusting screw, which insures perfect tracking of the music roll. (See page 23 for full description of these and other valuable features).

The case may be had in any of our numerous finishes of quarter-sawed oak, including Golden, Flemish, Mission, Weathered, Antwerp and the popular new Silver Gray, also Silver Gray Ash and Mahogany.

The case design is modern-school Gothic, and as the picture indicates, the numerous arch shaped panels make an exceedingly harmonious and pleasing exterior, those in front being formed of a fine quality of green art glass.

As in the case of the PianOrchestras, the Violin-Flute Piano may be operated from any section of the house, by means of coin slot boxes, or push buttons. It is proving a sensational success with smaller hotels, cafes, restaurants, dance halls, pavilions, ice cream parlors, penny arcades, etc., where its absolute novelty and wonderful music are fully appreciated.

For dancing it is ideal, as the bass drum marks the correct dance tempo perfectly.

Complete catalog of music mailed upon request.

Height, 7 ft. 4 in.   Width, 5 ft. 4 in.   Depth, 2 ft. 8 in.

PRICE—Complete, with Electric Motor and 1 Roll of Music, containing 5 selections . . .$1,350.00
Extra Music Rolls, 5 selections, each 4.00

VIOLIN PIANO—Style B.   The same as Violin-Flute Piano—Style C, except that it does not have the set of flute pipes.
PRICE— $1,150.00

FLUTE PIANO—Style B.   The same as Violin-Flute Piano—Style B, except that it does not have the set of violin pipes.
PRICE— $1,150.00

Description of the Wurlitzer Violin-Flute Piano circa 1912. The case is almost plain-looking compared to the ornate later orchestrion models.

Mandolin Quartette rolls. This roll type was used on the *Mandolin Quartette* and *Mandolin Sextette.* It featured a special solo section for playing the mandolin part, the upper range of the note scale.

65-Note Player Piano rolls. (later known as *Automatic Player Piano* rolls) This was the standard type of Wurlitzer roll and was used on most keyboard-type coin pianos and orchestrions. These rolls exist with a number of variants in labeling (such as "Hand Played 65-Note Player Piano roll," "Solo 65-Note Player Piano roll," etc.) but all have the same basic arrangement and tracker-bar layout. In addition to being used on coin pianos and orchestrions these rolls were used on many of the Wurlitzer theatre photoplayers (as were *PianOrchestra* rolls).

88-Note Player Piano rolls: This roll was used on the *88-Note Player Piano,* a short-lived type which was introduced circa 1906 and was discontinued once the *65-Note Player Piano* became the sales leader.

Solo Violin Piano rolls. This roll type was used on the *Solo Violin Piano.* Essentially this roll was two rolls in one. Its exceptional width provided space for one set of perforations to play the violin pipes (as solo) and another set for the piano notes (as accompaniment).

WURLITZER Orchestra Piano—Style BX
With Either Violin or Flute Pipes

It combines a Piano with Mandolin attachment and Violin or Flute Pipes, Bass and Snare Drums and Triangle. The different musical divisions can be disconnected at will. Art glass designs vary.

Height, 8 feet. Width, 5 ft. 4 in. Depth, 2 ft. 4½ in. Shipping weight, 1,500 lbs.

The Wurlitzer BX was one of the first Wurlitzer keyboard orchestrions with the "wonder light" feature on top. Used earlier on the Wurlitzer PianOrchestras and on machines of various German makes the wonder light was a popular and eye-catching addition.

The gentleman in the foreground is mounting the piano action in a Style I (or IX) piano. Partially visible at the far left is a Wurlitzer Automatic Harp which is in the factory for reconditioning. Harps were not originally manufactured at the North Tonawanda facility.

Cover of promotional leaflet describing Wurlitzer machines.

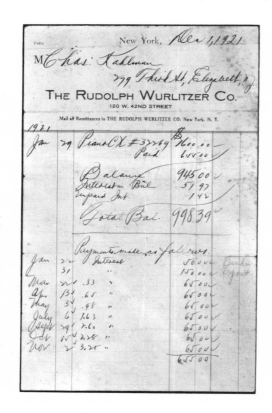

Wurlitzer Orchestra Piano—Styles C and CX

This instrument combines a Piano with Mandolin attachment, 38 Violin Pipes (21 First Violin and 17 Viola), 38 Flute Pipes, Bass and Snare Drums and Triangle. The different musical sections can be cut off at will. The art glass designs vary somewhat.

Height, 7 ft. 9 in.   Width, 5 ft. 4 in.   Depth, 2 ft. 3 in.   Shipping weight, 1,500 lbs.

Original Wurlitzer invoice for CX orchestrion. As Mr. Kahlman was a dealer in coin-operated musical machines he paid only $1600.00, a $500.00 discount from the list price at that time.

This CX case style was one of the most popular. The roll changer was located above the center of the keyboard behind the panel with the lyre design. The program cards were directly below.

128

Wurlitzer Violin-Flute Piano—Style CX

With Wurlitzer Automatic Roll Changer

This instrument combines a Piano with Mandolin attachment, 38 Violin Pipes (21 1st Violin and 17 Viola), 38 Flute Pipes, Bass and Snare Drums and Cymbal. The different musical sections can be cut off at will. The art glass designs vary somewhat.

The finish illustrated above is weathered oak. Other finishes are shown in natural colors on page 5.

Height, (including lamps) 8 ft.   Width, 5 ft. 4 in.   Depth, 2 ft. 8 in.   Shipping weight, 1500 lbs.

Wurlitzer Violin Piano—Style BX   Wurlitzer Flute Piano—Style BX

Same as above only without Flute Pipes.   Same as Style CX only without Violin Pipes.

The above case design is one of the scarcer CX styles. A machine in the author's collection has a spread-winged American eagle in the center of the top art glass panel.

Wurlitzer Symphony Piano—Style S S

Another one of the striking "S" series with Violin or Flute effects, Snare Drum
Bass Drum and Triangle.

Equipped with long roll frame which plays either 1, 5, 10, 15 or 20 tune rolls.

Height, 6 ft. 4½ in. Width, 5 ft. 2 in. Depth, 2 ft. 5 in. Shipping weight, 1,350 lbs.

The Wurlitzer Symphony Piano was one of the most compact Wurlitzer orchestrions. It employed the long roll frame mechanism which was located below the keyboard, as was the case with other machines in the S series.

*Autograph Reproducing Piano rolls. These were used on the Wurlitzer *Autograph Reproducing Piano* and featured the recorded playing of well-known pianists.

*Paganini Violin Piano rolls. This type was used on the *Paganini Violin Piano* and *Paganini Violin Orchestra*. The exceptional width of this roll (130 perforations wide) accommodated the most elaborate orchestral effects found on any type of Wurlitzer roll. Variants include "Special Hand-Played Piano Music for the Paganini Violin Piano" . . . a roll which played just the piano part of the *Paganini*, much in the manner of a reproducing piano.

*Mandolin PianOrchestra rolls. The smaller types of *PianOrchestras*, the *Mandolin* and *Xylophone PianOrchestra* styles generally used this roll.

*Concert PianOrchestra rolls. The very largest *PianOrchestras*, the *Concert* styles, with many ranks of pipes and orchestral instruments used this type of roll. Note: It is evident that a number of specialized *PianOrchestra* rolls were made . . . probably for certain early (circa 1903-1910) models. A *Style 17 PianOrchestra* roll we located was not suitable for use on either of the later

standard *Mandolin* and *Concert* types. There may be other similar examples.

The earliest Wurlitzer rolls were made of red paper which was imported from Germany. Later it was discovered that a paper manufacturer in Erie, Pennsylvania, could supply a green-colored paper which was more durable. This green paper was used for most of the later Wurlitzer rolls.

One fault with the paper used was its sensitivity to moisture changes. It would expand and contract in proportion to the humidity. Occasionally the atmosphere in Wurlitzer's North Tonawanda plant became too dry or too damp and roll production had to be stopped. Although moisture could be added to dry air in the winter by means of a spraying system there was no way to control the excess dampness in the summer.

In later years the music roll paper was paraffined. This coating was applied by the manufacturer of the paper and helped alleviate the shrinking and expanding problem.

It is probably accurate to say that more different tunes were cut on Wurlitzer *65-Note Player Piano* rolls over the years than were cut on any other single type of coin piano roll issued by any manufacturer. Literally thousands of different melodies — popular, religious, operatic, patriotic, movie themes or whatever — were available on these Wurlitzer rolls. A Wurlitzer roll catalogue issued about 1923 listed *two thousand tunes that were carried in stock at that time*. The only other type of coin piano roll which even approached this record was the widely-used style "A" roll issued for Seeburg, Western Electric and other machines.

CASE DESIGN No. 8.

Above is shown a page from a notebook in the Wurlitzer archives. The "wonder light" at the top was a peacock with a revolving brilliantly-lighted tail. The same peacock device was used on several PianOrchestra styles. The above machine probably gets the prize for being the most ornate keyboard-type orchestrion ever produced by Wurlitzer.

No records survive stating exactly how many coin pianos and orchestrions using the *65-Note Player Piano* roll were manufactured. Over the twenty-year span of their production, from about 1908 to 1928, the quantities were in the tens of thousands ... if not far more.

The ravages of time are tremendous. At the height of the coin piano and orchestrion market well over one hundred thousand machines of various makes were in active service. And yet only a thousand or two survive today. It is a matter of record that three thousand, perhaps four thousand, Wurlitzer automatic *Harps* were produced. Fewer than two dozen exist today. Of the one thousand or more Wurlitzer *PianOrchestras* made in about one hundred different styles only a very few machines have survived the intervening years. Many of the machines made by Wurlitzer and other manufacturers and illustrated in this book have achieved the ultimate in rarity today — not a single example remains ... they are known only by their pictures or catalogue descriptions.

What has happened to them all? Obsolence took most. When their usefulness ended, either when they wore out or when they were replaced by juke-boxes or sound systems, they were junked. Others, too big to be moved (like the *PianOrchestra* formerly in Los Angeles' Banner Theater) were simply

Wurlitzer orchestrion with peacock-type wonder light.

CASE DESIGN NO. 9

Wurlitzer orchestrion with the standard wonder light at the top.

boarded up or walled in by lath and plaster. Devastating floods such as those which inundated the eastern part of the United States in 1936 and 1938 claimed many others. Fires, termites, vandals ... virtually every known hazard has wrested its share of coin pianos from their storage places.

However, some *did* manage to survive. One Johnson City, New York, restaurant owner moved his *Violano-Virtuoso* into his home dining room after it ceased to pay dividends in his place of business. A Springfield, Massachusetts, snack bar owner moved his obsolete *Seeburg E* piano into his living room so that it could be used for his children's piano lessons. The Great Bend, Pennsylvania, Civic Association let their Link flute-piano fall into disrepair. A few days before its resting place, the local fire hall, was being torn down an alert collector rescued the piano from oblivion. In Chicago a tavern owner had four different coin pianos during the 'twenties. Each time a new one was acquired the former one was relegated to storage in a back room. In 1964 the tavern was razed to make way for a new highway. Luckily a collector was contacted when the owner learned that coin pianos were no longer junk but were sought-after items. A few long distance telephone calls later and the machines were in the collection of Otto Carlsen in Monrovia, California.

For several years Harvey Roehl, owner of the Vestal Press and author of *Player Piano Treasury,* had heard recurrent rumors of a barn filled with coin-operated pianos in Providence, Rhode Island. Finally the rumor was tracked to its source ... and a hoard of forty-five coin pianos was the result. Included were many *Pianinos, Pianolins,* early *Peerless* and *Electrova* models and other machines from the era 1910-1920.

Sometimes more than patience is needed to track down a coin piano or orchestrion ... for it has been the case more than once that the owner himself did not know what he had! A classic example of this is the experience of Larry Givens, a Wexford, Pennsylvania collector.

Upon hearing recurrent rumors that a large Wurlitzer *PianOrchestra* was located in Skaneateles Falls, a small upstate New York crossroads, Larry Givens decided to visit the locality. Arriving in town he made inquiries at a number of places and was told by several old-timers that such a machine used to be in the local hotel.

CASE DESIGN No. 12

Wurlitzer orchestrion Case Design No. 12. The large knob protruding from the case at the left side was used to advance the roll changer to whatever roll was desired.

Style 6 and 6X

Case Design No. 10

Another Wurlitzer orchestrion case design. Note that with the exception of the glass panels and the wonder light moulding this machine has the same basic design as the one at the upper right.

In due time he talked with the manager of the hotel in question and described the *PianOrchestra,* its instrumentation and imposing dimensions. He was then assured that no such machine was in the hotel, nor could the manager recall ever having seen such an item.

"Mind if I look around the hotel, anyway?" asked Mr. Givens.

"No, go right ahead," replied the manager.

Finally, after much searching, there it was ... The large *PianOrchestra* was located in plain view on one side of the grand ballroom on the second floor! The manager of the hotel was then called to the scene.

"So that's what that big old thing is," he said. "I never looked inside of the cabinet and always wondered what it was."

A deal to buy it was consummated on the spot.

Such are the joys of collecting. Every coin piano surviving today has a story, sometimes an adventure, to go with it.

WURLITZER Orchestra Piano—Style LX

This instrument combines a Piano with Mandolin attachment, 38 Violin Pipes (21 First Violin and 17 Viola), 38 Flute Pipes, Set of Orchestra Bells, Bass and Snare Drums and Triangle. The different musical sections can be cut off at will. The art glass designs vary somewhat. Equipped with WURLITZER Patented Automatic Roll-Changer playing six five-tune rolls.

Height, 7 ft. 9 in. Width, 5 ft. 4 in. Depth, 2 ft. 5 in. Shipping weight, 1,500 lbs.

First introduced about 1921 the LX was the standard Wurlitzer orchestrion case design used during the mid-1920's. This machine was also available without the changer, if desired. An LX in the collection of Otto Carlsen has a xylophone in addition to the other instruments — an original feature which must have been specially ordered by the first owner.

The beautiful LX shown above is now on display at Clark's Trading Post, North Woodstock, New Hampshire where it delights anyone caring to drop a coin in its slot. When the Clarks acquired it the LX had to be dismantled into many pieces (see inset at lower right) in order to remove it from its storage place. The above photograph was taken after hundreds of hours had been spent carefully reassembling and restoring it to mint condition.

STYLE·I.
CASE DESIGN No. 5.

Egyptian case — special Wurlitzer 65-Note Piano design.

Chapter 7

If the Rudolph Wurlitzer Company had been responsible for selecting the Seven Wonders of the World the chances are good that its *PianOrchestra* would have been included, probably first on the list.

The *PianOrchestra* was "The Most Wonderful Musical Instrument the World Has Ever Known" as well as "The Greatest Musical Wonder of the Age." The *PianOrchestra* was to America what the large Welte and Hupfeld orchestrions were to Europe . . . the pinnacle of perfection in mechanical orchestra music.

The first Wurlitzer *PianOrchestras*, a shipment of four machines, were obtained from Philipps of Bockenheim, Germany, in 1903. In that same year two brothers, Orville and Wilbur Wright, were experimenting with their crude airplane on the Carolina sand dunes. In the same year Henry Ford had not yet thought of the Model T, electric lights were a novelty more than anything else and the skyscraper was the latest marvel in American technology. In 1903 it was not surprising that the *PianOrchestra* was considered a wonder . . . just the dropping of a nickel would produce the authentic playing of a piano, mandolin, bass drum, snare drum, kettle drum, xylophone, orchestra bells, saxophone, oboe, bassoon and heaven knows what else.

Style 20. Price, $2,600, Including 6 Rolls of Music and One Slot Box (3 Automatic Figures.)
Style 20A. Same, with Plain Panels Instead of Automatic Figures, $2,300.

CASE DESIGN No. 1.

An early PianOrchestra style featuring mechanical figures which moved as the music played.

WURLITZER PianOrchestra in Bijou Moving Picture Theatre, San Francisco, Cal.

The instrument stands in the vestibule to the left of the ticket office.

From about 1903 to 1920 *PianOrchestras* were made in dozens of styles and in hundreds of minor variations. In fact the Wurlitzer catalogues stated that no *two were exactly alike;* there was always a minor variation in the art glass, scrollwork or other ornamentation.

PianOrchestra cases were beautifully elaborate. Catalogue descriptions varied from the "plain" cases (style 21): "...this case is void of all figures, art glass and other fancy embellishments, the beautiful and rich carvings make it by far the handsomest and richest production ever put on the market" to the ultimate in gadgetry, Style 47, which had the following description: "A strikingly unique animated scene is shown in the center of the instrument. Two Kaleidoscopic wonderlamps give forth a myriad of colored lights, simultaneously with which, lightning flashes as though a storm were brewing. Then a little steamboat is seen moving slowly across the front; and in the center appears a Zeppelin airship, immediately followed by an aeroplane — all of which is extremely interesting and never fails to get applause." The description of this particular machine went on to say: "Even *without its musical feature* the Wurlitzer PianOrchestra in itself is a great attraction."

From 1903 to 1914 all of the Wurlitzer *Pian-Orchestras* were imported from Philipps in Germany. During this time Wurlitzer purchases from Philipps

PianOrchestra No. 21

PianOrchestra Style 21 which sold for $4000.00 in 1905 was un-usual in that it featured a keyboard which extended from the front of the machine.

averaged about $250,000.00 per year which, translated into machines at their wholesale value probably represented about 150 to 250 *PianOrchestras* and *Paganinis* (these were imported also) each year. During the period of these transactions the *retail* prices of *PianOrchestras* ranged from about $1200.00 to $7500.00 or more, with the bulk of the sales being with the lower-priced machines.

Germany went to war in Europe in 1914. No machines were imported from Philipps after that time. From that time onward *PianOrchestras*, usually of designs similar to those previously imported from Philipps, were made at the Wurlitzer factory in North Tonawanda, New York.

It is not definitely known when the production of *PianOrchestras* ceased. It was probably about 1920 when Prohibition destroyed most of the market for these large orchestrions. Wurlitzer *PianOrchestras* were shown in price lists in the early 1920's, but these listings probably represent unsold machines on hand from earlier years.

As a type the *PianOrchestras* manufactured by Wurlitzer from 1914 to 1920 represent the largest and most elaborate orchestrions ever manufactured on a production-line basis in the United States.

DISCONTINUED

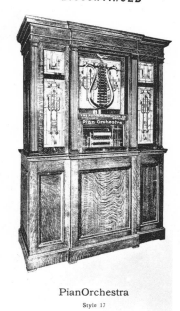

PianOrchestra
Style 17

CASE DESIGN No. 1.

At the left: PianOrchestra advertisement circa 1905. These machines, like other early PianOrchestras, were imported from Philipps of Germany.
Above: Style 17 PianOrchestra.

Präsident Taft besichtigt ein
—— PHILIPPS ——
Pianella Orchester-Werk

—— PHILIPPS ——
Pianella Orchester-Werk
in einem Rollschuh-Palast

Pianella Orchester-Werk
Modell No. 17.

AUSSTATTUNG:
Vornehm wirkendes, stilvolles Barock-gehäuse in hell Eiche mit von Seiden-stoff hinterlegten Messinggittern, echten Ölbildern und reichen Hand-schnitzereien. Besonders gut für Kon-zert und Tanzmusik geeignet.

BESETZUNG:
Grosses, kreuzsaitiges Klavier mit Man-dolinenvorrichtung, Xylophon, Glocken-spiel, Gamba-, Gambabässe-, Violino-, Violinbass-, Cello-, Bratschen-, Flöten-, Piccolo- und Klarinetten-Register. Pro-gausen, Hornpfeifen, grosse und kleine Trommel, Pauken, chinesischen Becken, Triangel, Tamburin und Kastagnetten. Antrieb der Noten durch Windmotor.

MASSE:
Höhe 3,45 m, Breite 2,20 m, Tiefe 1,27 m.
Nettogewicht ca. 1130 kg.
—— Kleine Aenderungen vorbehalten. ——

Spielt mit „PM" Notenrollen.

Pianella Orchester-Werk
Modell No. 9.

Pianella Orchester-Werk
Modell No. 15.

Pianella Orchester-Werk
Modell No. 7.

Pianella Orchester-Werk
Modell No. 11.

Pianella Orchester-Werk
Modell No. 13.

Pianella Orchester-Werk
Modell No. 6.

Pianella Orchester-Werk
Modell No. 5.

Pianella Orchester-Werk
Modell No. 16.

Pianella Orchester-Werk
Modell No. 3.

The illustrations on these two facing pages are from a sales catalogue issued by J.D. Philipps & Sohne of Bockenheim, Germany. Many of these styles were imported by Wurlitzer and marketed as PianOrchestras. Below are shown two styles of roll-changers used on the PianOrchestras. The one at the left holds six rolls; the one at the right, twelve rolls. Most machines were equipped with the six-roll changer. Note that the revolving magazine for the PianOrchestra roll changer was located below the take-up spool. The standard roll-changer used in Wurlitzer's American-made machines had the magazine above the take-up spool (see page 120).

REVOLVER-MECHANIK
oder selbsttätiger Notenwechsel. D. R. Patent.

6 teiliger Revolvermechanismus.

12 teiliger Revolvermechanismus

Dieser **sinnreiche und vielfach patentierte Apparat** ermöglicht das gleichzeitige Einlegen von 5, 6, 12 und mehr Notenrollen, welche nach dem Notenverzeichnis für das Instrument ausgewählt werden. Wenn nun diese Notenrollen **durch die einfachste Handhabung** in den Apparat eingelegt sind, so wird infolge der patentierten Mechanik jede einzelne Notenrolle **ohne irgend eine weitere persönliche Bedienung** vollständig selbsttätig eingeschaltet, nach dem Geldeinwurf gespielt, nach Ableistung des Musikvortrages zurückgerollt, umgeschaltet, und die nächstfolgende Rolle legt sich spielfertig von selbst wieder ein. Dieser Vorgang vollzieht sich bei allen Rollen, sodass ein selbständiges Repertoire bis zu 60 Stücken, alle in verschiedenem Charakter, als ununterbrochener Vortrag geboten ist.

Es kann aber auch nach Belieben **jede einzelne Notenrolle** aus der **eingelegten Reihenfolge heraus** zur selbsttätigen Einschaltung (auch für Fernschaltung) herangezogen werden, um diese speziell zu hören. **Ein einziger Fingerdruck** genügt und jede der Rollen steht einzeln nach Wunsch zur Verfügung. **Welcher unvergleichliche Vorteil** den vielbeschäftigten Herren Hôtelbesitzern, Restaurateuren, Saalbesitzern, Gastwirten und den verwandten Geschäftszweigen erwächst, ihren Gästen **ohne jede Bedienung des Instrumentes** stets eine abwechslungsreiche Konzert-Unterhaltung, Ball- oder Tanzmusik zu bieten, bedarf wohl kaum noch besonderer Hervorhebung.

WURLITZER PianOrchestra—Style 12
With WURLITZER Automatic Roll Changer

Instrumentation:

Orchestration of 37 Violin and Violoncello Pipes, Piano, Bells.
Bass and Tenor Drums, Cymbals and Mandolin Attachment.

Height, 8 ft. 6 in.   Width, 5 ft. 6 in.   Depth, 3 ft.   Shipping weight, 1500 lbs.

This Style 12 (also known as 12-A) Mandolin PianOrchestra featured a peacock with a brilliantly colored tail which revolved as the music played. The volume of the sound was controlled by a set of louvered swell shutters in the top of the machine, thus giving a degree of expression to the music. This particular model was manufactured at the Wurlitzer factory in North Tonawanda. The list price in 1920 was $2200.00.

The earliest *PianOrchestras* imported from Philipps were very ornate, usually with a large quota of "gingerbread" and carvings and often with moving mechanical figures. Due to the lack of surviving machines the only facts known about them are those in the contemporary catalogue descriptions and illustrations, many of which are shown on these pages. Little is known about the rolls which these machines used. Evidently some machines used rolls which would play on that particular type and on no other.

By 1912 the *PianOrchestras* had been standardized into two main groups; the *Mandolin PianOrchestras* and the *Concert PianOrchestras*.

Orchestrions using the *Mandolin PianOrchestra* rolls usually had a mandolin attachment on the piano. Some machines featured a xylophone as the main instrument. Located just inside the case at the front of the machine the xylophone would carry the melody, often alternating with the piano in solo arrangements. More often than not, the xylophone would be accompanied by one or more ranks of pipes. Some of these machines (there seems to have been no consistency in this regard) had *Xylophone PianOrchestra* lettered on the front, but most had *Mandolin PianOrchestra* or simply *PianOrchestra*. Other *Mandolin* styles had no xylophone at all and relied entirely on the piano and pipes.

Orchestrions using the *Concert PianOrchestra* roll generally had from about 200 to close to 400 pipes, depending on the particular style. The most popular number of pipes seems to have been 314, divided into ten or more ranks. Using metal and wood pipes the sounds of the piccolo, violin, bass violin, flute, saxophone, clarinet and several other wind instruments were imitated. The *Concert PianOrchestra* roll mainly differs from the Mandolin PianOrchestra inasmuch as the former has more control perforations to turn the larger number of pipe ranks on and off.

Like many Wurlitzer machines the catalogue numbers did not remain constant. For instance, a *Style 17 PianOrchestra* illustrated in the 1907 catalogue was entirely different in external appearance from the *Style 17* listed in the 1912 catalogue. The prices changed also. In keeping with inflationary times prices increased 50% to 75% from 1903 to 1920.

An early catalogue stated that the *PianOrchestra* was ideally suited for use in the following establishments: amusement parks, billiard halls, beer gardens, bowling alleys, excursion boats, cafes, confectioneries, clubs, dance halls, department stores, groceries, hotels and restaurants. In actuality they were used just about everywhere. The *PianOrchestras* in the author's collection were from such diverse original locations as a mining town saloon in Colorado, a theatre, a ballroom and an ice-cream factory in California!

When the first *PianOrchestras* were obtained from Philipps music rolls for them were imported also. Difficulties developed when patrons demanded the latest in American tunes, not the latest in German tunes. A few years later roll production for these was shifted to North Tonawanda to remedy this problem. By the mid 1920's the production of *PianOrchestra* rolls had diminished to the point that only one or two rolls were being released each month. At the same time dozens of new *65-Note Player Piano* rolls were being issued.

In the years since the Roaring Twenties the *PianOrchestras* have met the various fates which befell other types of coin pianos and orchestrions. However, *PianOrchestras* had one more stroke against them: their size. Due to their sheer size and weight they could not be conveniently stored in a corner once their usefulness ended. In fact, they could hardly be moved at all. To preserve a PianOrchestra meant many patient hours of careful disassembly, to say nothing of finding a place in which to store it afterwards. It was far simpler to tear it apart and haul it away for junk, and this is what was done in most instances.

In man's haste for progress the triumphs of one age are often discarded by the next generation. Whether these triumphs be masterpieces of architecture, important documents, first editions . . . or coin-operated automatic musical instruments, their value is often only realized in later years, by which time most have been long since destroyed.

Ornamentation of this machine consisted of beveled mirrors and wood scrollwork.

The PianOrchestra

"King of Automatic Musical Instruments."

THE PIANORCHESTRA is, without question, the most wonderful self-playing musical instrument ever built. It is a combination of all the different instruments used in a full symphony orchestra, assembled in a single magnificent case, and arranged to play in solo and concert work, exactly the same as a human orchestra.

It is next to impossible to convey an idea of the PianOrchestra's magnificence with printer's ink. The many handsome styles must be seen and heard to obtain a fair conception of their appearance and musical possibilities. However, a faint idea of their musical possibilities may be had from the following list of instruments they contain: Piano; Bass, Tenor and Kettle Drums; Triangle, Cymbals, Xylophones, Chimes, Castanets, Tambourine, First and Second Violin Pipes, Viola and 'Cello Pipes, Double Bass Pipes, Flutes and Clarionets, Mandolins, Saxophones, Trombones, Flageolets, French Horns, Oboes, Piccolos and Bassoons.

Some styles have a mandolin attachment, with the piano, using the flute as a solo accompaniment. These are called Mandolin PianOrchestras, and use the same music rolls. The Concert PianOrchestra is a different type, and is played by a different music roll.

All these different instruments are perfectly regulated and brought into play by automatic stops which control their playing in the same manner in which an orchestra leader controls his players by the wave of his baton.

For Hotels, the Larger Cafes, Beer Gardens, Dancing Pavilions, Ice Cream Parlors, Penny Arcades, Five-Cent Theaters and similar Amusement Resorts, there is nothing to equal the PianOrchestra as an attraction and money-maker. In large public resorts, where a number of slot boxes can be distributed about the place, connecting with the instrument, so that it may be played from any part of the house by dropping a 5-cent piece, the PianOrchestra will take in its cost in nickels within a year or so, besides doubling the volume of business.

CONSTRUCTION OF THE PIANORCHESTRA

The PianOrchestra is operated by electricity, a small electric motor being placed inside the case, and plays from perforated paper music rolls. The music rolls contain from one to six selections each, and are operated by our Automatic Music Roll Rewinding Device. The rolls can be changed in a few seconds.

All the parts of the mechanism are made of the very best materials that money can buy, and are so accurately adjusted that the PianOrchestra gives no trouble whatever. In fact, they are built throughout to stand hard wear and tear, and to last a lifetime.

The cases are of the most elaborate designs, in handsomely carved, carefully chosen woods, with rich decorations of gold-leaf and solid brass, and art glass fronts. They are indeed magnificent specimens of the cabinet-maker's art, and will greatly enhance the appearance of any place they occupy. Special cases are made to order at short notice.

Description of the PianOrchestra from a Wurlitzer catalogue. Note that "special cases are made to order at short notice." Dozens of different major designs and hundreds of minor variations were produced. Many superlatives were used to describe the PianOrchestra. In the above description it is called the "King of Automatic Musical Instruments."

Wurlitzer PianOrchestra—Style 12
With Wurlitzer Automatic Roll Changer
Instrumentation:

Piano	Orchestration of 37 Violin and Violoncello Pipes
Chimes	Bass and Tenor Drums, Cymbals and Mandolin Attachment.

Height, 8 ft. 6 in. Width, 5 ft. 6 in. Depth, 3 ft. Shipping weight, 1500 lbs.

WURLITZER

PIANORCHESTRAS

Style	Catalogue Page No.	Price
12	23	$2200.00
18	24	2950.00
29C	25	3500.00
33	26	4050.00
30A	27	3800.00
47	28	4050 00
34A	29	5250.00
32A	30	5750.00
3 Paganini	33	4250.00
2 "		3700.00
1 "		3500.00
Coin-Slot Boxes	31	15.00 each

F. O B. Factory

Wurlitzer Mandolin PianOrchestra—Style 16
With Wurlitzer Automatic Roll Changer
The art glass designs vary somewhat.

Instrumentation:

Piano	Orchestration of 42 Violin and Violoncello Pipes
Chimes	Bass, Snare and Kettle Drums
Xylophone	Triangle Tambourine Castanets

Height over all, 8 ft. 8 in. Height without Globes, 7 ft. 10 in. Width, 5 ft. 10½ in. Depth, 2 ft. 11 in.
Shipping weight, 1600 lbs.

WURLITZER PianOrchestra—Style 18
Instrumentation:

30 Violin Pipes	Bells	Cymbal	Triangle
30 Flute Pipes	Xylophone	Kettle Drum	Tambourine
24 Violoncello Pipes	Bass Drum	Snare Drum	Castanets
Piano			Mandolin attachment
	2 Automatic Stops for Pipes		

Height over all, 9 ft. 3⅜ in. Width, 5 ft 6¾ in. Depth, 3 ft. 5¼ in. Shipping weight 1600 lbs.

The PianOrchestras on this page used the Mandolin PianOrchestra roll. These designs are of World War 1 vintage. The price list at the upper right was issued on May 15, 1920. The first seven listings (Style 12 through Style 34-A) are Mandolin PianOrchestras. The 32-A is a Concert style. Many, if not all, of these were production-line items at Wurlitzer's North Tonawanda factory. The Paganini instruments in the listing were not being manufactured in 1920 but represented unsold machines on hand from pre-World War 1 days.

Wurlitzer Mandolin PianOrchestra—Style 15

With Wurlitzer Automatic Roll Changer

The art glass designs vary somewhat.

Instrumentation:

Piano	Orchestration of 37 Violin and Violoncello Pipes
Chimes	Bass, Snare and Kettle Drums
Xylophone	Triangle Tambourine Castanets

Height, 8 ft. 3 in.   Width, 5 ft. 9 in.   Depth, 3 ft. 2 in.   Shipping weight, 1500 lbs.

MANDOLIN PIANORCHESTRA.
STYLE -18-

CASE DESIGN No. 1.

At the top left is a catalogue illustration of Mandolin PianOrchestra Style 15; to the right of it is a case design variation of the same style. The Style 18 at the left boasted a particularly ornate case. The Mandolin PianOrchestra roll label above lists popular marches. Most Mandolin PianOrchestra rolls were of five-tune length and had a wide metal rod at the end for use on the Wurlitzer roll changer. However, there were variations as on all other Wurlitzer roll types. Some rolls contained only one selection, a classical number such as the William Tell Overture, for instance. Rolls such as this with uninterrupted music were used for background music in locations such as private lodges, movie theatres, etc.

Height, 7 ft. 10 in.   Width, 5 ft. 9 in.   Depth, 2 ft. 10 in.

PRICE—Including Automatic Roll Changing Device, 6 Rolls of Music and 1 Slot Box..$1,450.00
This style may also be had without the Roll Changing Device. Price........ 1,250.00

This is a very popular style, owing to its moderate price and wonderful volume of music. The cases are made of beautifully figured quarter-sawed oak, in golden, weathered, Flemish, Mission, and the new Silver Gray finishes; also in Silver Gray ash and mahogany.

The front of the case is finished with handsome mouldings and fluted pilasters. In the center is a leaded art glass panel; on either side are handsome leaded art glass doors. The design and finish of the case are exceedingly handsome, and make it an ornament in any surroundings.

Style 17 is operated by an electric motor, and plays from perforated paper music rolls, containing from two to seven selections each. The rolls are automatically rewound at the end of the last selection, and are ready to instantly repeat the program .

Any number of nickel-in-the-slot boxes can be connected with the instrument, so that it may be operated from any part of the house by dropping a nickel. Or it may be arranged to play by a push-button, where it is desired to operate it as a free attraction.

The tempo of the music is perfectly and instantaneously regulated by a small speed lever attached to the music winding shaft.

Special Dance Rolls, arranged in dance time, and playing about three minutes, with a minute and a half encore, are cut for this style. This dance music is different from the regular music, in that there is only one selection on a roll, and the drums mark time all the way through, making the most perfect music that can be had for dancing.

This style is built with the Automatic Roll Changing Device, but can be had without it, if desired.

By means of this wonderful device, six rolls of music, containing from 20 to 35 selections, are placed on the instrument at one time, and automatically interchange; thus affording a continuous program, without repetitions, lasting from one-and-a-half to three hours.

INSTRUMENTATION :

Piano, with automatic loud and soft pedal.   Orchestrion, 37 violin and violoncello pipes.
Chimes, 13 bars.   Two drums—bass and tenor, and cymbal.

A circa 1912 description of the Style 17 Mandolin PianOrchestra. Note that the purchaser is given the option of buying the machine with or without the roll changer. In later years no choice was given — the changer was standard equipment.

Clock Attachment for PianOrchestras

For playing PianOrchestras and other Wurlitzer Automatic Musical Instruments at regular time intervals.

A high-grade, non-magnetic, electric clock, that is connected with the instrument and plays it at intervals of 7½, 10, 15, 20, 30 or 60 minutes, as desired. The clock is an eight-day, a perfect timekeeper; comes in walnut or nickel-plated metal case, and can be put on the wall any distance from the instrument, or concealed within its case.

The clock connection does not interfere with the instruments being played by nickel-in-the-slot. The clock may be set to play at any interval desired, and may be disconnected at will. It makes a splendid feature where it is desired to provide patrons free music at frequent intervals, without any attention whatever to the instrument.

A favorite plan with many PianOrchestra owners is to set the clock to play the instrument every few minutes during luncheon and dinner hours, and have it operated by nickel-in-the-slot at other times.

Dimensions: Height, 10¾ in. Width, 10¾ in. Face, 8 in. across.   **PRICE**.....$15,00

In 1912 this was the ultimate in automation ... Wurlitzer instruments could be timed to play automatically at preselected intervals.

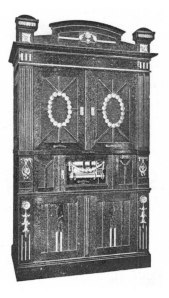

Mandolin PianOrchestra—Style 27 B

A new style of MANDOLIN PIANORCHESTRA, recently perfected, that has met with great favor. It is constructed upon a different principle from the other styles, being the only one without pipes.

Style 27 B contains a Piano, with Mandolin Attachment, Xylophone, Chimes, Cymbals, Bass and Snare Drums. These different instruments play both in concert and solo, and are automatically controlled by five expression stops, which in turn are operated by perforations in the paper music roll.

The case is quarter-sawed oak, in the elegant silver gray finish, and presents a winning appearance.

The music of this style is very diversified, ranging from Piano and Xylophone solos, accompanied by the Drums and Chimes, to a full concert performance by all the instruments mentioned. The great variety of musical effects makes it very attractive for all sorts of public places.

Any number of nickel-in-the-slot boxes may be connected with it so that it can be played from all parts of the house.

Style 27 B is operated by a small electric motor placed inside the instrument. Owing to its having no pipes, the bellows are smaller than in other styles, and for that reason a motor of very light power is used.

The perforated paper music rolls contain from one to six selections each, and are operated by our Automatic Music Roll Rewinding Device, which rewinds the roll in a few seconds after the last tune is played.

This style is so simple in construction that it is next to impossible to get out of order, and as it has no pipes, it requires no tuning, except the Piano, and once or twice a year is sufficient for that.

This style is built with the Automatic Roll Changing Device, but may be had without it, if desired.

By means of this wonderful device, six rolls of music, containing from twenty to thirty-five selections, are placed on the instrument at one time and automatically changed as each roll is played through. (See complete description of Automatic Roll Changer on page 33).

INSTRUMENTATION:

A High Grade Piano, with Mandolin Attachment.

Chimes, 13 Bars.	Five Automatic Expression Stops.
Xylophone, 30 Bars.	Drums—Bass and Snare and Cymbals.

Height, 9 ft. 1 in. Width, 4 ft. 11 in. Depth, 2 ft. 6 in.

PRICE—Including Automatic Roll Changing Device, 6 Rolls of Music and 1 Slot Box. .$1,400.00
This style may also be had without Roll Changing Device. Price. $1,200.00

Mandolin PianOrchestra Style 27-B was unusual in that it had no pipes. With a basic list price of just $1200.00 it was one of the most inexpensive PianOrchestra models. Note that the machine is "next to impossible to get out of order"—a statement which would certainly be disputed by any modern day coin piano collector who has undertaken to rebuild one of these early machines.

Mandolin PianOrchestra—Style 28

This is a splendid style of the popular-priced PianOrchestras, and makes an exceptionally fine attraction, because of the beautiful variations in its music. The Mandolin arrangement, which is brought into play with the piano solo work, makes a very charming effect.

The case of Style 28 is a very attractive and handsome design of quarter-sawed oak in the new silver gray finish. This is a dark mission, having the pores and grain of the wood emphasized by the use of a lustrous silver gray filler. It is handsomely decorated with gold-leaf mouldings and fluted panels.

The upper doors are set with stained art glass in heavy panels. The lower doors, opening to the music roll and tempo regulator, are set with beveled French plate mirrors. Colored electric lights, set in the rosettes at the top, show off the handsome exterior to the best possible advantage.

INSTRUMENTATION:

A High Grade Piano, with Mandolin Attachment.

37 Violins.	Bass Drum and Cymbals.
18 Violoncellos.	Snare Drum.

Five automatic stops control the different pipes and instruments in the same manner in which an orchestra leader controls his players by the wave of his baton.

It is operated by an electric motor and perforated paper music rolls. The music rolls contain from two to six selections each, and are automatically rewound after the last selection is played, by our Automatic Music Roll Rewinding Device.

As many nickel-in-the-slot boxes as desired may be connected with this instrument, so that it may be played from any part of the house by the dropping of a nickel in any one of the slot boxes.

Style 28 makes a splendid trade-attracter and money-getter in all sorts of public places where good music is appreciated. Installed in Cafes, Restaurants, Hotels, and similar public resorts, it will easily take in its price in nickels within a year or two at the most, and the increased business attracted to a place having music of this kind should amount to a good deal more than the receipts taken in by the instrument itself.

This style is built with the Automatic Roll Changing Device, but may be had without it, if desired.

The Automatic Roll Changing Device holds six rolls of music at one time, thus affording a program of twenty to thirty-five selections without the necessity of changing the rolls or giving the instrument any attention whatever. This wonderful device is the greatest improvement ever made in self-playing musical instruments operated by perforated paper music rolls. The advantage of a lengthy program without the bother of changing music rolls is perfectly obvious.

Height, 9 ft. 1 in. Width, 4 ft. 11 in. Depth, 2 ft. 6 in.

PRICE—Including Automatic Roll Changing Device, 6 Rolls of Music and 1 Slot Box. .$1,700.00
This style may also be had without Roll Changing Device. Price. $1,500.00

Style 28 Mandolin PianOrchestra. The copy stresses that a machine of this type should pay for itself in a year or two with the nickels it takes in.

1913 testimonial from a cafe owner who has purchased three dif-
ferent Wurlitzer machines in his time and is about to purchase
another.

Wurlitzer Mandolin PianOrchestra—Style 28

With Wurlitzer Automatic Roll Changer

Instrumentation:

Piano with Mandolin attachment

37 Violins	Bass Drum and Cymbals
18 Violoncellos	Snare Drum

Height, 9 ft. 1 in.   Width, 4 ft. 11 in.   Depth, 2 ft. 6 in.

Shipping weight, 1550 lbs.

Case design variation of Style 28.

Style 28.   Price $1,600, Including 4 Rolls of Music and One Slot Box.

Style 28.

Mandolin PianOrchestra.

PRICE $1,600.00

DESCRIPTION.

THIS style differs from the styles described on the preceeding pages in having a Mandolin Accompaniment with the piano; this accompaniment with the flute and violin pipes produces a beautiful musical effect, very odd and charming to the American ear.

The case of Style 28, while not so elaborate as some of the more expensive styles, is built of the best materials and workmanship; the panels in the front are beautiful colored art glass of a flower design, and the whole presents a very neat and attractive appearance.

On account of the music of the Mandolin PianOrchestra being entirely different from that used on the regular styles, the music rolls are cut especially for the Mandolin types, and cannot be used on the regular styles.

The Mandolin PianOrchestra has proven a great success. For Concert Halls, Cafes, Ice Cream Parlors and other like places it is one of our most popular styles.

Piano, 56 notes, Mandolin attachment, with loud and soft pedal.
Orchestrion, 74 pipes { 37 flutes, 37 violin and violoncellos.
Bass drum, snare drum and symbals.
Drums and cymbals have special arrangement to give loud and soft strokes.

Paper rolls are 9 inches wide, on steel spools, metal ends, automatic rewinding device. The rolls vary in price from $3.75 up, according to length of roll, and contain from 1 to 10 selections each. The more expensive rolls play about 20 minutes. They are so arranged that the music may be stopped at the end of each piece, or played continuously, playing one piece after another to the end; at the end of the last selection the roll automatically rewinds and starts repeating the program. In this manner the Mandolin PianOrchestra may be played for hours without any attention. The tempo can be quickly changed by means of a lever attached to the music-winding shaft.

Description of an early Style 28 Mandolin PianOrchestra from a 1907 Wurlitzer catalogue. This was before the introduction of the roll changer.

Height, 9 ft. 1 in.   Width, 4 ft. 11 in.   Depth, 2 ft. 6 in.

PRICE—Including Automatic Roll Changing Device, 6 Rolls of Music and 1 Slot Box..$5,900.00
This style may also be had without Roll Changing Device. Price...........$,700.00

Mandolin PianOrchestra—Style 28 A

Style 28 A is the same as Style 28, described on page 39, except that it contains the Xylophone in addition to all the other instruments of that style.

The added feature of a full-sized Xylophone playing in solo with varied accompaniments, provides a most beautiful and unique musical entertainment. It is something entirely new, and has attracted more attention than any musical feature ever added to the PianOrchestra.

The case of Style 28 is a very attractive and handsome design of quarter-sawed oak in the new silver gray finish. It is handsomely decorated with gold-leaf mouldings and fluted panels. The upper doors are set with stained art glass in heavy panels. The lower doors, opening to the music roll and tempo regulator, are set with beveled French plate mirrors. Colored electric lights, set in the rosettes at the top, show off the handsome exterior to the very best advantage.

Any number of slot boxes can be connected with Style 28 A, the same as with the other styles. This makes it possible to play the instrument from any table of a cafe or restaurant.

This style is built with the Automatic Roll Changing Device, but may be had without it, if desired.

By means of the Automatic Roll Changing Device, six rolls of music are put on the instrument at one time, and these rolls automatically interchange, affording a program of from twenty to thirty-five selections, without the necessity of changing the rolls or giving the instrument any attention whatever.

This feature, the most important improvement ever made in self-playing musical instruments, is patented, and can be had only on the PianOrchestra. The advantage of a lengthy program without the trouble of changing the music rolls is too obvious to need explanation.

INSTRUMENTATION :

A High Grade Piano, with Mandolin Attachment.

Orchestrion, 55 Pipes—37 Violin, 18 Cello.	*Drums—Bass and Snare and Cymbals.*
Xylophone, 30 Bars.	*Five Automatic Expression Stops.*

This Style 28-A is basically the same as the Style 28 illustrated at the bottom of page 148 but with a xylophone added. The xylophone was turned on and off at intervals by special control perforations in the roll. The xylophone rendered beautiful counter melodies and solo effects. Note that it is visible through the clear glass in the front of the machine.

The Automatic Roll Changing Device

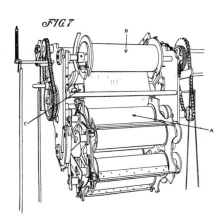

One of the most important improvements made in the PianOrchestra in late years, is the Automatic Roll Changing Device, which is patented, and cannot be found in any other instrument. By means of this wonderful device, six different music rolls are put on an instrument at one time, and are automatically changed from one to the other, as each roll is played through and automatically rewound on its spool.

Thus, from 30 to 40 selections may be placed on the instrument at one time, and played through one after the other, without any attention whatsoever.

The advantage of such a large and varied program of music, without the necessity of changing the rolls, is almost incalculable. It means that the owner of a PianOrchestra, equipped with this new device, can give his patrons an entertainment of an hour and a half to three hours' duration, with a continuous change of music, and without changing his music rolls or bothering with the instrument in any way whatever.

This wonderful device, whose mechanism is entirely of steel, is built on the same principle as the famous original Ferris Wheel, which was seen at the Chicago and St. Louis World's Fairs. The six music rolls in the wheel are carried around to their proper positions with regard to the Tracker Bar (C) in the same manner as the cars in the Ferris Wheel were operated. It works as smoothly as a fine watch movement.

For instance, the music roll (A) is shown in position to be played by passing over the Tracker Bar (C). After it is played through, it is automatically rewound by means of our Automatic Rewinding Device, and the Magazine Wheel revolves far enough to carry it out of the way and bring the succeeding roll into its place. This one is immediately taken up by the take-up roll (B), and the music continued. This operation is repeated at the end of each roll, and is continued without the slightest attention as long as the instrument is kept running.

The Automatic Roll Changing Device contains our special Tempo Regulator, described on page 10, and an Automatic Action Case Protector, which is incorporated in the Tracker Bar, and prevents dust and other foreign matters entering the action case.

The roll changing device used in the PianOrchestras. The same device is illustrated on page 141. This particular style of roll changer was used in the PianOrchestras and the Paganinis.

Wurlitzer Mandolin PianOrchestra—Style 28 B

With Automatic Roll Changer

The finish illustrated above is silver gray oak.

Instrumentation :

Piano with Mandolin attachment

37 Violins	Bass Drum and Cymbals
18 Violoncellos	Snare Drum

Height, 9 ft. 2 in.   Depth, 2 ft. 8 in.   Width, 5 ft. 4 in.   Shipping weight, 1600 lbs.

Like a number of other PianOrchestra styles this 28-B displayed an oil painting in the center of the front. Some of these paintings featured waterfalls, volcanoes and other scenes which were animated by lights illuminated in an alternating succession behind the panel.

Mandolin PianOrchestra—Style 29 C

Height, 10 ft. Width, 6 ft. 8 in. Depth, 3 ft. 4 in.

PRICE—Including Automatic Roll Changing Device, 6 Rolls of Music and 1 Slot Box..$2,600.00

This style may also be had without Roll Changing Device. Price...........2,400.00

1912 catalogue description of Style 29-C Mandolin PianOrchestra.

Mandolin PianOrchestra—Style 29 C

One of the greatest values in our entire line—a truly superb type of the perfected automatic orchestra.

Musically, Style 29 C will fit in ideally in the finest restaurants, cafes and other resorts that have had the services of capable professional orchestras.

The range and variations in the music made possible by the powerful instrumentation are almost beyond belief. There are 114 separate and distinct musical pipes in addition to an upright grand piano, with mandolin attachment, Xylophone, Chimes, Bass and Snare Drums, Kettle Drums and Cymbals, Tambourine, etc. As all of these separate instruments are perfectly reproduced, some idea may be formed of the music produced by the instrument in concert.

Like other styles of the PianOrchestra, this one is played by simple and inexpensive perforated paper music rolls, and is operated by a noiseless electric motor, which is concealed inside the case. Every up-to-date improved feature of the Wurlitzer Automatic Musical Instrument is embodied, besides it contains our new patented friction disc speed regulator and electric start and rewind button.

By simply touching this electric button, which is on the left side of the roll changing device, you can stop the music in the middle of a roll and cause it to rewind.

The Music Roll Changing Device is an invaluable feature, as in other types of PianOrchestras. As previously explained, this device holds six rolls of music, containing from 20 to 35 selections, and automatically changes the rolls as they are played through and rewound, thus affording a program of an hour and a half to three hours without repetition.

The case is indeed a picture to the eye, made of selected quarter-sawed oak, in the handsome silver gray finish, with numerous bronze decorations and trimmings.

On each side are a couple of tasty Corinthian columns, and the center space is given over to one of our brilliant oil paintings, arranged for the novel and eye-catching motion picture effect. The scene depicted is that of a forest stream winding its way through the meadows, and plunging over an idyllic waterfall. When the instrument plays, the interior lights and special mechanism convert the scene into a vivid motion picture of the most absorbing interest.

This instrument may be played from any part of the house by means of our coin slot boxes or by push buttons.

INSTRUMENTATION:

A High Grade Piano, with Mandolin Attachment.

30 Violins.	30 Violas.
24 Violoncellos.	18 Flutes.
12 Piccolos.	Xylophone, 30 Bars.
Chimes, 13 Bars.	Bass and Snare Drums.
Kettle Drum and Cymbals.	Tambourine and Castanets.

Wurlitzer Mandolin PianOrchestra—Style 29 C

With Wurlitzer Automatic Roll Changer

The finish illustrated is brown oak. Other finishes are shown in natural colors on page 5.

Instrumentation:

Piano with Mandolin attachment

30 Violins	30 Violas	12 Piccolos	Kettle Drum and Cymbals
24 Violoncellos	18 Flutes	Chimes	Bass and Snare Drums
	Xylophone		Tambourine

Height, 10 ft. Width, 6 ft. 8 in. Depth, 3 ft. 4 in. Shipping weight, 2200 lbs.

These two PianOrchestras were also designated as 29-C. Wurlitzer catalogue designations were not standardized. Often catalogue numbers were not changed when new case designs were introduced — as the machines on this page illustrate.

Mandolin PianOrchestra—Style 30 A

One of the finest types of the new MANDOLIN-PIANORCHESTRA. The artistic design of the case and splendid musical qualities harmonize perfectly and make it a high-class attraction for the very best class of public resorts.

The case is of quarter-sawed oak, in the new silver gray finish, which is a blue-black mission color, with the grain filled in silver gray, making a very handsome background for the solid brass trimmings, and the gold-leaf mouldings and rosettes.

On either side are two heavy circular columns, extending from top to bottom, encircled with solid brass collars. The doors are set with stained art glass in brass pipings. The little rosettes at the top of the case are set with colored electric lights, showing off the richness of the design to the very best possible advantage. The entire case is a splendid specimen of the combined artistry of the skilled designer and cabinet-maker.

In keeping with the beautiful exterior, the volume, technic and expression of the music is equally rich and charming.

Style 30 A contains 146 music pipes, representing as many instruments. These play in solo and accompaniment with the Xylophone, Chimes, Mandolin, Piano, Triangle, Castanets, Cymbals, Drums, etc. Some conception of the beautiful musical effects may be derived from the great number of pipes and variety of instruments it reproduces.

INSTRUMENTATION:

A High Grade Piano, with Mandolin Attachment.

30 Piccolos.	*30 Violins.*
19 Violas.	*37 Flutes.*
30 Violoncellos.	*Xylophone, 30 Bars.*
Bass and Snare Drums.	*Kettle Drum and Cymbals.*
Chimes, 13 Bars.	*Triangle, Castanets and Tambourine.*

This splendid instrument can be operated by nickel-in-the-slot boxes, the same as other styles of the PianOrchestra; but is especially adapted to the better-class places, that employ orchestras, and prefer to give their patrons first-class musical entertainment free. Proprietors find that with this Automatic Orchestra, their patronage increases rapidly, while their expense for music is practically nothing, although they can have it when they want it and as long as they want it.

Style 30 A is about equal in volume to a fifteen-piece orchestra. It is operated by an electric motor and perforated paper music rolls. The music rolls contain from two to six selections each, and automatically rewind at the end of the last selection, ready to repeat the program or be changed, as desired.

This style is built with the Automatic Roll Changing Device, but may be had without it, if desired.

By means of this wonderful device a program running from an hour and a half to two hours may be given without the necessity of changing the music rolls or giving the instrument any attention whatever.

MANDOLIN PIANORCHESTRA
STYLE - 30 A.

CASE DESIGN No. 2.

Height, 10 ft. 1 in. Width, 6 ft. 6 in.
Depth, 3 ft. 2 in.

PRICE—Including Automatic Roll Changing Device, 6 Rolls of Music and 1 Slot Box..$3,000.00
This style may also be had without Roll Changing Device. Price..........2,800.00

The Style 30-A was one of the most popular if not THE most popular Mandolin PianOrchestra style. In 1912 the 30-A sold for $3000.00. By 1920 the price had climbed to $3800.00.

The Wurlitzer PianOrchestra (automatic orchestra) in this hotel is one of its most attractive features. They have good music at their command any moment—day or night—at minimum cost.

Wm. E. Brill Jr.,
PROPRIETOR.

Brill's Hotel,
111 South 10th St.,
Philadelphia, Pa.

CAFE OF BRILL'S HOTEL, 111 SOUTH 10th STREET, PHILADELPHIA.

Brill's Hotel in Philadelphia provided its patrons with music from a Style 30-A.

The beautiful SILVER PALACE Theatre, San Francisco, which has a magnificent Wurlitzer PianOrchestra above the box office.

A massive and magnificent type of PianOrchestra, possessing superb instrumentation and exquisite decorative features.

The case is of selected quarter-sawed oak, in the handsome and original silver gray finish, with artistic panels and gold-leaf embellishments.

In the front is one of our newly devised translucent oil paintings, which is converted into a vivid motion picture when the instrument plays and the interior lights shine through. The scene depicted is that of a volcano in action by the side of a placid Italian lake.

The picture takes up a large part of the upper half of the instrument and is the largest as well as the most striking and impressive of our new moving picture arrangements.

The lurid glow of fire and lava issuing from the mountain top and the brilliant coloring of the cloud of smoke overhanging the mountain top make a life-picture that rivets the attention from first to last.

The painting is bordered by an attractive urn-shaped frame having bas relief figures of cherubs at the upper corners, and French bevel plate mirrors on either side.

Below the painting a plate glass door admits a view of the wonderful Music Roll Changing Device in operation.

There are also a number of handsomely carved bas relief figures on the front of the instrument, and the entire front is, as the description indicates, brilliantly illuminated when playng. So much for the decorative end of this elegant instrument.

Musically considered, it is even better than it looks. It combines all the possibilities of both the Mandolin and Xylophone styles of PianOrchestra, and the musical effects it produces are far superior to anything within the range of any but the foremost human orchestras found in the largest metropolitan centers.

The 121 wood and metal music pipes are so evenly distributed and perfectly balanced that their response to the action of the marvelous automatic stops can only be compared to the intelligent action of the best orchestra players, working under a skilled director.

INSTRUMENTATION:

A High Grade Piano, with Mandolin Attachment.

37 Violins.	20 Saxophones.	Triangle.
12 Violoncellos.	22 Violas.	Castanets.
15 Piccolos.	Xylophone, 30 Bars.	Bass and Snare Drums.
15 Flutes.	Chimes, 13 Bars.	Kettle Drum and Cymbals.
	Tambourine.	

This instrument is suitable for the largest cafes and public places, as its volume is sufficient to reach the farthest corner of any hall or series of connecting rooms, balconies etc. It is operated by a noiseless electric motor placed inside. Any number of nickel-in-the-slot boxes or push buttons can be connected for playing from any part of the house.

The instrument also plays from special long-playing dance rolls, and contains all our modern improvements, including the famous Automatic Roll Changing Device. This remarkable device holds six rolls of music, containing from 20 to 35 selections, and automatically changes the rolls as they are played through and rewound, thus affording a program without repetition lasting from an hour and a half to three hours.

Mandolin Pian Orchestra—Style 30 B

Height, 10 ft. 8 in. Width, 6 ft. 5 in. Depth, 3 ft. 10 in.
PRICE—Including Automatic Roll Changing Device, 6 Rolls of Music and 1 Slot Box..$3,300.00
This style may also be had without Roll Changing Device. Price.......... 3,100.00

The Style 30-B had a scene of a volcano in action on the front. The 30-B shown at the top of the page lured patrons to the Silver Palace Theatre box office.

Style 30. Price, $2,750, Including Four Rolls of Music and One Slot Box.

Style 30. Mandolin PianOrchestra.

PRICE $2,750.00.

DESCRIPTION.

THIS handsome and unique style is the very latest idea in the PianOrchestra line. In addition to all the different instruments used in the other styles it has the Mandolin Accompaniment.

This style embodies all of the orchestral instruments which, with the addition of the Mandolin Accompaniment, produces a distinctly Oriental effect very different from the ordinary style of music. So perfect is the music of this wonderful new instrument that in the rendition of Carmen and other Spanish selections one might easily imagine they could see the dancers as they dance with their cymbals and tambourines. The effect is splendid and cannot fail to charm and fascinate the music lover.

The style of the case is the splendid Art Noveau; the front is of leaded art glass in colors with plain panels, and presents a rich and elegant appearance that will be an ornament to the very finest places. It will prove especially popular in Concert Halls, Cafes, Saloons, Restaurants and kindred resorts, because of its beautiful and unique musical effects.

The music rolls for the Mandolin styles are cut specially for these instruments, and cannot be used on the regular styles.

OAK OR WALNUT CASE.

Size, Height, 10 feet,
    Depth, 2 feet 11 inches,
    Width, 6 feet 3 inches.
Piano, 61 notes, Mandolin Attachment, loud and soft pedals.
Orchestrion, 123 pipes:
    37 flutes,
    37 violin pipes,
    37 cello pipes,
    12 bass pipes.
The pipes are of special type with extra fine tone quality.
Chimes, 13 bars.
Castanets.
Cymbals.
Triangle.
Tambourine.
Bass, snare and kettle drums.
The drums, cymbal and tambourine are arranged to play loud or soft,
    according to the expression of the selection being played. This
    arrangement is a new idea that gives wonderful effect to the
    music.

In the roof of the instrument is a shutter arrangement which automatically opens and closes producing a fine graduation in the swell from the softest pianissimo to the thundering crash of the fortissimo.

Paper rolls are 9 inches wide, on steel spools, metal ends, automatic rewinding device. The rolls range in price from $3.75 up, according to length of roll, and have from 1 to 10 pieces of music on each roll. The more expensive rolls play 20 minutes. They are so arranged that the music can be stopped at the end of each piece, or the roll can be played continuously, playing one piece after another to the end; when the end is reached the roll automatically rewinds itself and starts over again. In this manner the Mandolin PianOrchestra can be played for hours without any attention. The tempo is quickly changed by means of a small lever on the music-winding shaft.

Style 30 Mandolin PianOrchestra as described in a 1907 catalogue.

A Mandolin PianOrchestra under construction at the Wurlitzer plant in North Tonawanda, March, 1919. This particular machine utilized the rare 12-roll style of changer (see p. 141). Many of the PianOrchestras manufactured in the United States were close copies of the styles which were imported from Philipps before World War I. Mostly concealed in the background (to the right of and slightly below the bass drum in the photograph) is a Style 47 Mandolin PianOrchestra (see pp. 160, 161).

Adjusting the piano action in a Style 12 Wurlitzer Mandolin PianOrchestra in the author's collection. The piano part of the various PianOrchestras could be easily removed from the back of the machine to facilitate tuning and repairs.

—————————1913

Gentlemen:

I do not wish to obligate myself in any way—but would like to know how to get Good Music at the least cost. Tell me how Wurlitzer Instruments pay for themselves and a profit besides.

Name————————————

St. and No.————————

City—————State————

P. S.—Am interested particularly in PianOrchestra Styles ____

Reply postcard sent in 1913 with a PianOrchestra catalogue.

TELEPHONE 2406 / 2407 COLUMBUS

The Edgemont Cafe

1936 BROADWAY

S. E. COR. 65TH STREET

BRANCH: S. E. COR 125TH ST. & PARK AVE.
TELEPHONE 977 HARLEM

New York   September 23,   1913

The Rudolph Wurlitzer Co.,
25-27 West 32d Street,
New York City.

Gentlemen:-

I have made such a success with your automatic musical instruments that it gives me pleasure to relate my experience.

The first instrument I purchased of you about four years ago, was one of your $700 Player Pianos, which earned a little over $2100 in about two years. I then traded this in for one of your Roll Changer Flute Pianos, receiving a fair allowance for my original piano. This new piano earned almost double the receipts of the first piano, because of the automatic roll changer, which gives a greater variety of music. Recently, I traded the second piano for a $2000 Pian-Orchestra. The Pian-Orchestra is earning still more money than either of the other instruments, and crowding my dining room nightly. It is not only the earnings I have received from these instruments, but they have been the means of doubling my business.

The fact that I have invested $3900.00 with you in three different instruments, getting a better one each time, in the last four years, is the best evidence of my success.

If you have any prospective customers who doubt the value of your instruments in the Cafe business, I will take pleasure in showing them the results I have received.

Wishing you the success you deserve, I remain

Yours very truly,

D. Niemeyer

One of the countless testimonials which played a prominent part in Wurlitzer advertising.

Wurlitzer Mandolin PianOrchestra—Style 33

With Wurlitzer Automatic Roll Changer

Instrumentation:

Piano with Mandolin attachment

49 Violins	Xylophone	Kettle Drum and Cymbals
30 Violoncellos	Chimes	Triangle
30 Piccolos	Bass and Snare Drums	Castanets and Tambourine

Height: 9 ft. 10 in.   Width, 8 ft. 2 in.   Depth, 2 ft. 9 in.   Shipping weight, 2600 lbs.

Style 33 featured a revolving "wonder lamp" near the top center. The list price of this style in 1920 was $4050.00.

Wurlitzer Mandolin PianOrchestra—Style 40 A

With Wurlitzer Automatic Roll Changer

The art glass designs, of course, vary somewhat, as we have artists constantly at work on the latest fads and fashions

INSTRUMENTATION:

Piano with Mandolin attachment

30 Violins	Chimes	Snare Drum
12 Violoncellos	Bass Drum	Tambourine
Xylophone	Kettle Drum and Cymbals	

Height, 9 ft.   Width, 4 ft. 3 in.   Depth, 3 ft. 4 in.   Shipping weight, 2,000 lbs.

Price $2,400.00 F. O. B. Factory

Including Electric Motor, 6 Music Rolls and 1 Coin Slot Box

Style 40-A had a zeppelin which moved on a small trolley wire. Similar devices were widely used on machines made by Welte, Hupfeld and other German manufacturers.

Wurlitzer Mandolin PianOrchestra—Style 33 A
With Wurlitzer Automatic Roll Changer

Instrumentation:
Piano with Mandolin attachment

49 Violins	30 Piccolos	Chimes	Kettle Drum and Cymbals
30 Violoncellos	Xylophone	Bass and Snare Drums	Triangle and Tambourine
			Castanets

Height, 10 ft. 6 in.   Width, 6 ft. 6 in.   Depth, 3 ft. 10 in.

Shipping weight, 2600 lbs.

Style 33-A had a bird cage surrounded by mirrors as an eye-catching attraction. As the music played small mechanical birds moved about.

Wurlitzer PianOrchestra—Style 34A
With Wurlitzer Automatic Roll Changer

Instrumentation:
Piano with Mandolin Attachment

49 Violins	30 Clarinets	Bass and Snare Drums
19 Violoncellos	30 Piccolos	Kettle Drum and Cymbals
30 Violas	Xylophone	Triangle
30 Flutes	Chimes	Tambourine
		Castanets

Height, 10 ft. 10 in.   Width, 9 ft. 6 in.   Depth, 4 ft. 3 in.   Shipping weight, 3000 lbs.

With 188 pipes the Style 34-A was one of the largest of the Mandolin styles. This machine was also known as Philipps Model No. 11 (see p. 140).

Height, 10 ft. 10 in.   Width, 9 ft. 6 in.   Depth, 4 ft. 3 in.

PRICE—Including Automatic Roll Changing Device, 6 Rolls of Music and 1 Slot Box..$3,500.00
This style may also be had without Roll Changing Device.   Price...........3,300.00

Mandolin PianOrchestra—Style 34

The finest regular style of the MANDOLIN PIANORCHESTRA built. It is a magnificent musical instrument, fit, both from an architectural and musical standpoint, to grace the finest public resort in the land.

The design of the case is the new Renaissance, the wood, quarter-sawed oak, in the popular silver gray finish (dark mission with the grain of the wood emphasized by the use of a lustrous silver gray filler), with solid brass trimmings and gold-leaf mouldings and carvings.

Frosted electric lights mark the rosettes and points of the mouldings, shedding a soft, mellow light over the front, and causing the handsome exterior to look handsomer still. In the center is a niche, in which stands a handsome bronze statue, also lit up by electric lights. The stained art glass in the top is paneled off with solid brass bars, and that in the wings is set in brass pipings.

The whole ensemble of this splendid style presents an appearance of refined elegance that at once attracts the eye and compels admiration. It is almost superfluous to say the musical excellence of an instrument with such an artistic case is thoroughly in keeping with its architectural features.

Some idea of its musical qualities may be had from an enumeration of the instruments it contains, and the fact that the music is arranged by the leader of one of the finest orchestras in the world.

INSTRUMENTATION:

A High Grade Piano, with Mandolin Attachment.

30 Clarionets.	Xylophone, 30 Bars.
49 Violins.	Chimes, 13 Bars.
30 Piccolos.	Bass and Snare Drums.
30 Violas.	Kettle Drum and Cymbals.
30 Flutes.	Triangle.
19 Violoncellos.	Tambourine.
	Castanets.

In addition to the splendor of its architectural beauties and its charming musical qualities, Style 34 has the Automatic Music Roll Changing Device, the wonderful improvement for holding six rolls of music, containing from twenty to thirty-five selections at one time. This device automatically changes the rolls as they are played through. A program lasting from one and a half to three hours, without any repetitions, can thus be rendered without changing a roll or giving the instrument any attention whatever.

This style may either be operated with nickel-in-the-slot boxes or played at the pleasure of the owner by a switch or electric push-button.

This magnificent instrument in a Hotel, Cafe, Restaurant, Summer Resort, or similar place, will supplant the average orchestra, and aside from the great saving in expense for music, will prove far more attractive to patrons who admire good music.

The Style 34, one of the largest Mandolin PianOrchestras, was imported from Philipps. It was a best seller in the 1908-1914 years.

Mandolin PianOrchestra—Style 38

One of our recent and most notable triumphs in producing a PianOrchestra of the highest grade of excellence at moderate cost.

The case design is chaste and elegant, closely resembling that of much more expensive styles. It is fine enough for the most select surroundings, while the music cannot possibly be equalled by any but the most skilled human orchestras.

The illustration on the opposite page does not begin to do justice to the remarkably beautiful appearance of Style 38. The beautiful coloring of the glass panels and the strips of fancy inlaid wood beggar description.

The entire front is a series of attractive panels. The upper part is topped with a strip of showy inlaid wood, beneath which is a most attractive triple-panel arrangement of stained glass, in rough finish and French plate mirrors.

A glass door opens to the Music Roll Changing Device, which can be seen in operation. This is flanked on either side with mirrors containing original cut center-pieces. Under this extends a strip of unique colored inlaid wood, similar to the one across the top.

The interior of the instrument lights up while playing, when the whole effect is one of rare brilliance.

The case is of imported Italian olive wood, and presents a winning appearance. Its showy light finish at once impresses one as being something new and altogether different from the conventional.

Style 38 includes every new and up-to-date improvement of the Wurlitzer Automatic Musical Instruments, including the matchless Music Roll Changing Device, which provides for an unlimited variety of music without interruption or bother for changing the music roll.

As much as can be justly said in praise of the prepossessing appearance of this instrument, it must be admitted that musically it is even "better than it looks."

We have succeeded to our entire personal satisfaction in securing a perfectly balanced instrumentation. The Mandolin, Violin and Xylophone sections are featured with due prominence, and in the playing of any concert selection a finer effect is obtained than was ever before possible from an equal number of music pipes.

INSTRUMENTATION:

A High Grade Piano, with Mandolin Attachment.

25 Violins.	Xylophone, 30 Bars.
10 Violas.	Bass and Snare Drums, and Cymbals.
7 Violoncellos.	5 Expression Stops.

1912 description of the Style 38 Mandolin PianOrchestra.

Wurlitzer Mandolin PianOrchestra—Style 38 B

With Wurlitzer Automatic Roll Changer

The art glass designs vary somewhat.

Instrumentation:

Piano with Mandolin attachment

25 Violins	10 Violas	Bass Drum and Cymbals
7 Violoncellos	Xylophone	Snare Drum

Height, 8 ft. 6½ in. Width, 4 ft. 10 in. Depth, 2 ft. 6 in. Shipping weight, 1500 lbs.

Style 38-B. Like all PianOrchestras of the 1903-1914 years this style was imported from Philipps of Bockenheim, Germany.

Cover of a circa 1916 Wurlitzer Automatic Musical Instrument catalogue showing a Style 30-A Mandolin PianOrchestra in a restaurant.

Mandolin PianOrchestra—Style 39

The newest model of MANDOLIN PIANORCHESTRA, in quartered oak, with "Teak" finish, is a picture to the eye and a delight to the ear.

Just glance at the arrangement and finish of the front. Could anything more attractive for a center-piece in a Restaurant or Cafe be thought of?

The case is handsome quarter-sawed oak, in the new silver gray finish—a dark shade of mission oak—having the pores of the wood emphasized by the use of a lustrous silver gray filler. The illustration does not begin to do it justice.

The art panel in the center consists of a magnificent oil painting, faced with glass. The water of the fountain is translucent, and when the instrument plays, the picture is illuminated by electric lights in the interior in such a way as to give the fountain the appearance of actually spouting water and overflowing from the bowl to the lake beneath.

This marvelous motion picture effect perfectly reproduces the various natural shades as well as the movement of the water as it gushes upward and falls sparkling as if touched by the sun's rays.

This is a most wonderful and picturesque novelty, and is causing a sensation wherever the instrument is exhibited.

Musically, this instrument is above criticism. It will give perfect satisfaction in the best Restaurants, Cafes and other resorts that have used first-class orchestras for the entertainment of guests.

It has all of our new patented features, including the Automatic Roll Changing Device, which holds six music rolls, containing from two to six selections each, and automatically changes these rolls as they are played through and rewound. This furnishes a continuous program of from twenty to thirty-five selections, without the necessity of changing the music rolls or giving the instrument any attention whatever—in a word, an unlimited variety of music without interruption or bother of changing the music rolls.

Style 39 may be had without Roll Changing Device, if desired.

Any number of Magazine Slot Boxes may be connected with the instrument so that it may be operated from any part of the house.

The instrumentation is evenly distributed and perfectly balanced, and represents the final result of the years of careful study we have given to this all-important feature.

INSTRUMENTATION :

A High Grade Piano, with Mandolin Attachment.

30 Violins.	*Bass and Snare Drums.*
12 Violoncellos.	*Kettle Drum and Cymbals.*
Xylophone, 30 Bars.	*Tambourine.*

Height, 9 ft. 6 in. Width, 5 ft. 3 in. Depth, 2 ft. 10 in.

PRICE—Including Automatic Roll Changing Device, 6 Rolls of Music and 1 Slot Box . .$2,000.00
This style may also be had without Roll Changing Device, if desired. Price. . 1,800.00

The Style 39 had a scene showing a splashing fountain.

Mandolin PianOrchestra—Style 40

This instrument in the new and popular Colonial design is certain to prove one of the most sensational sellers of the year. Simple, yet massive in outline, it combines many of the architectural features of the most expensive styles built, and looks the part of a $5,000.00 concert style instrument.

To meet the popular demand of the moment, Style 40 contains one of the most attractive motion picture effects which we have yet produced. A typical Roman fountain in a delightful sylvan setting, plays with the most interesting realism. Three distinct motions are seen in the fountain's action. First the water issues from the apex of the fountain. It bubbles over, and in two successive steps or falls reaches the bed of the lake, where to all appearances it breaks into a myriad of shining particles.

Above this picture, which is startling in its vivid realism, is a beveled plate oval mirror in three sections, surmounted by a semi-circle of seven frosted electric lights. These shed a soft yet brilliant light upon the scene beneath, and give it an added charm.

Style 40 is regularly made in the handsome and original silver gray finish, but any other finish of wood can be furnished if desired. The decorative feature is Colonial throughout, notably in the plain yet heavy top piece and the carved pilasters at the ends, and the full length fluted columns on either side of the center panel. All carving is the finest hand work. The glass door in the lower section opens to the music roll compartment, and at the same time affords a view of the wonderful roll changing device in operation.

This instrument contains all the late Wurlitzer improvements, and musically will prove a perfectly satisfactory substitute for a large orchestra of finished musicians. It can be played by means of nickel-in-the-slot boxes, any number of which may be distributed through a house, or it may be played independently as a free attraction, as the owner may prefer.

The Automatic Roll Changing Device, which holds six rolls of music, containing from 20 to 35 selections, and automatically changes same, affords a constantly changing program of an hour and a half to three hours' duration.

INSTRUMENTATION :

A High Grade Piano with Mandolin Attachment.

42 Violins.	*Kettle Drum and Cymbals.*
12 Violas.	*Triangle.*
30 Violoncellos.	*Tambourine.*
Xylophone, 30 bars.	*Castanets.*
Bass and Snare Drums.	

All music for this style, as well as for the other Wurlitzer PianOrchestras, is arranged by the leader of one of the foremost orchestras of the world. It is largely owing to this fact that the playing of this and similar Wurlitzer instruments is so often mistaken for the work of a first-class human orchestra.

Height, 10 ft. Width, 6 ft. 7 in. Depth, 3 ft. 6 in.

PRICE—Including Automatic Roll Changing Device, 6 Rolls of Music and 1 Slot Box . . .$2,200.00
This style may also be had without Roll Changing Device price. 2,000.00

Style 40. Wurlitzer gave its copy writers ample journalistic license. Note the claim that "All music for this style, as well as for the other Wurlitzer PianOrchestras, is arranged by the leader of one of the foremost orchestras of the world . . ." Early Wurlitzer catalogues were a combination of beautiful pictures and elaborate descriptions. Added to these were many testimonials and charts showing the profits which could be expected from a Wurlitzer machine. Added together these features made the Wurlitzer catalogue irresistible to the owners of public places. Modern advertising writers could learn a thing or two by reading these early Wurlitzer booklets.

"It was just like listening to a Real Orchestra"

THE WURLITZER PIANORCHESTRA

Provides Musical Entertainment of the Cabaret Variety at a Fraction of the Cost

NOW LOOK INSIDE FOR THE BIG STORY

With two "wonder lamps," a peacock with revolving colored tail and a diorama featuring a steamboat and zeppelin racing in a thunderstorm the Style 47 Mandolin PianOrchestra never failed to get applause from the audience, according to the above advertisement. The Style 47 which sold for $4050.00 in 1920 was one of the very latest PianOrchestra models to be made. As they were introduced at the tail-end of the market only a few were sold.

The Wurlitzer PianOrchestra provides high-class entertainment that makes business hum

One thing is certain— you want more business!

A Wurlitzer PianOrchestra will get you more business

Wurlitzer PianOrchestras are right now getting *more* business for 762 other men in your same line almost everywhere the sun shines. (Testimonials by the basketful.) What a PianOrchestra has done for others it will do for you.

The Wurlitzer PianOrchestra will give you entertainment of cabaret variety—at practically no cost.

The public drops the coins that play the music, thereby putting the instrument upon a basis that is self-paying.

You have heard the beautiful music of a 10-piece orchestra and have seen couples dance the fox trot, one step and hesitation, and you wished perhaps, that *you* could afford to employ a 10-piece orchestra and make *your* place just as attractive.

We can place a *PianOrchestra* in your establishment—give you practically the same volume and quality of music as a 10-piece orchestra, and you can add these entertainment features or dances and draw just as big crowds.

SPECIAL OFFER FOR IMMEDIATE ACCEPTANCE

You know that everybody likes music and if you can provide the music that they like best, you are *bound* to make your place more attractive.

ENCLOSED YOU WILL FIND A RETURN POST CARD. If you will fill in and mail back this card AT ONCE we will write you a *personal* letter and make a special offer for immediate delivery of a Wurlitzer Style 47 PianOrchestra, upon terms that will make it practically self-paying.

All you do is install it. We will not only show you a way to get your money back, but a way to make the instrument an *extra source of income.*

Our *Style 47 PianOrchestra*, here illustrated, is only one of many attractive styles.

It will cost you only a one-cent stamp to get our beautiful *art catalogue in five colors,* and a great variety of other high-class literature, which you will find very interesting reading.

Our proposition to you is an exceptional one. Do not toss this circular aside. Mail back the card now and hear the proposition anyhow!

The Wurlitzer PianOrchestra provides just the entertainment that everyone likes

There is as much difference in the quality of its music and the "music" of a majority of automatic musical instruments as between a human orchestra and a hurdy-gurdy. The Wurlitzer PianOrchestra is so nearly a "Human" Orchestra as to defy detection.

There is nothing of the mechanical in its playing. Seated in another room, and not knowing of the existence of this instrument, you would never question but that it is a real flesh and blood organization of ten trained musicians.

The music rolls which it plays are cut by a new process. The selections are all up to date.

The Wurlitzer PianOrchestra is equipped with the wonderful AUTOMATIC ROLL CHANGER

that makes it possible for it to play as many as thirty different selections without change or attention—classical, operatic, dances, songs, and all the national airs. A musical program of from one and a half hours' to three hours' duration, can be arranged without attention.

Every feature of this Automatic Roll Changer is patented by the Rudolph Wurlitzer Company, and cannot be found in any other instrument.

Now Read the Special Offer Below

THE RUDOLPH WURLITZER CO.

121 E. FOURTH ST.

ALBANY, N. Y., 17-19 Green St.
BUFFALO, N. Y., 701 Main St.
BOSTON, MASS., 630 Washington Ave.
COLUMBUS, OHIO, 57 Main St.

329-331 S. WABASH AVE.
Just South of Jackson

CLEVELAND, OHIO, 800 Huron Rd.
DETROIT, MICH., 26 Adams Ave. W.
DAYTON, OHIO, 133 Ludlow St.
KANSAS CITY, MO., 1016 Walnut St.

LOUISVILLE, KY., 652 S. Fourth St.
MILWAUKEE, WIS., 133 Second St.
PHILADELPHIA, PA., 912 Chestnut St.
ROCHESTER, N. Y., 370 Main St. E.

113-119 W. 40th; 114-118 W. 41st.
Between Broadway and 6th Avenue

SYRACUSE, N. Y., 427 S. Clinton St.
ST. LOUIS, MO., 1109 Olive St.
SAN FRANCISCO, CAL., 985 Market St.

Wurlitzer Concert PianOrchestra—Style 32
With Wurlitzer Automatic Roll Changer
Instrumentation:

Piano	30 Flutes	26 French Horns
56 Violins	30 Piccolos	26 Bass Violins
30 Violoncellos	30 Clarinets	Chimes
30 Violas	30 Oboes	Bass and Snare Drums
26 Saxophones		Kettle Drum and Cymbals

Triangle
Tambourine
Castanets
Tremolo

Height, 11 ft. 3 in.   Width, 7 ft. 4 in.   Depth, 4 ft. 5 in.

Shipping weight, 3800 lbs.

Concert PianOrchestra—Style 32

The CONCERT PIANORCHESTRA, Style 32, is one of the most expensive styles built. It represents the best that human ingenuity has been able to create in self-playing musical instruments. No pains nor expense have been spared to make it all that the most critical and fastidious lover of music could desire.

The case is the handsome silver gray finished oak, with rich hand carvings, and artistic panels and mouldings. This style may be had in mahogany or magnificent white enamel finish, with gold leaf mouldings and trimmings. The doors on either side are embellished with the most costly stained art glass, set in brass pipings in the design of the harp. The center panel is made of beveled plate mirrors, subdivided and embellished with brass piping, lit up by electric lights. The whole exterior of the magnificent case reflects the art and skill of the master cabinet-maker's craft. Different instruments of this, as well as other styles of PianOrchestra, will show slight changes in case design, so that it is seldom two are seen exactly alike.

The imposing case design, however, is only a surface indication of the marvelous volume of rich, melodious harmony that pours forth from the 314 pipes, and accompanying instruments at the touch of a button, or dropping of a coin in a convenient slot box. Imagine a trained orchestra of thirty pieces playing in perfect harmony, under a skilled director, and you get a fair conception of the grandeur of its music.

This magnificent instrument contains 314 pipes, as follows:

INSTRUMENTATION:
A High Grade Piano.

30 Piccolos.	30 Flutes.	Xylophone, 30 bars.
30 Oboes.	26 Saxaphones.	Chimes, 13 bars.
56 Violins.	26 French Horns.	Triangle.
30 Clarionets.	26 Bass Violins.	Tambourine.
30 Violas.	Bass and Snare Drums.	Castanets.
30 Violoncellos.	Kettle Drum and Cymbals.	Tremolo.

Seventeen expression stops control the expression and solo effects the same as the orchestra leader controls his players by the wave of his baton. An automatic swell controls the volume, increasing and diminishing it as required, to give the perfect orchestral effect. The rendition of a grand opera overture, a popular ragtime selection or a standard classic by this magnificent instrument is equally enjoyable, and will delight and charm the most esthetic music lover.

Special Dance Music, arranged in perfect time, is cut for the Concert PianOrchestra. The rolls play about three minutes, with a minute and a half encore. For dancing, the Concert PianOrchestra is far superior to the ordinary human orchestra, because of its perfect time. It can be set to any desired speed, and will never vary until reset.

Owners of Hotels, Cafes, Restaurants, Nickelodeons, Dancing Academies and Pavilions should investigate the merits of this modern automatic orchestra. It will save them thousands of dollars, and prove far more attractive and efficient than a human orchestra.

This style is built with the Automatic Roll Changing Device, but may be had without it, if desired. By means of the Automatic Roll Changing Device, a program lasting from an hour and a half to three hours is rendered without the necessity of changing a roll or giving the instrument any attention. It holds six rolls of music, containing from twenty to thirty-five selections. This magnificent instrument, with its facilities for furnishing a long and diversified program, without attention, will prove a wonderful attraction in large Restaurants, Concert Halls, Cafes, etc.

The largest PianOrchestras were the Concert models. Various Concert PianOrchestras had from about two hundred pipes to nearly four hundred. The extra control perforations cut into the Concert rolls permitted more elaborate orchestral effects than were possible with the smaller Mandolin styles. List prices for the Concert PianOrchestras were mostly in the $3500.00 to $7500.00 range. The Style 32 Concert PianOrchestra shown at the top of the page incorporated the sound of nearly two dozen different orchestra instruments. To the left is shown a Style 32 Special Concert PianOrchestra which was made to order for a Wurlitzer customer. In addition to their use on orchestrions the Concert PianOrchestra rolls were used to operate certain large models of Wurlitzer photoplayers. The style H and K photoplayers shown on page 85 used Concert PianOrchestra rolls as did a number of others.

Wurlitzer Concert PianOrchestra—Style 31 A

With Wurlitzer Automatic Roll Changer

Instrumentation:

Piano	30 Flutes	26 Bass Violins	Triangle
56 Violins	30 Oboes	Chimes	Tambourine
30 Violoncellos	30 Piccolos	Bass and Snare Drums	Castanets
30 Violas	26 Saxophones	Kettle Drum and Cymbals	

Height, 10 ft. 6 in.   Width, 6 ft. 10 in.   Depth, 3 ft. 11 in.   Shipping weight, 3500 lbs.

Style 31-A Concert PianOrchestra.

Concert PianOrchestra

Style 32

Dimensions.—Height, 11 ft. 3"; Depth, 4 ft. 5"; Width, 7 ft. 4".

PRICE.—Including 6 Rolls of Music and 1 Slot Box $3,800.00
With Automatic Roll Changing Device 4,000.00

Style 32 Concert PianOrchestra. Instrumentation of this machine was identical to the Style 32 shown on the preceding page; only the case designs were different.

Concert PianOrchestra—Style 31

This is one of the finest types of PIANORCHESTRA built, and is a splendid example of the wonderful progress made in perfecting the self-playing orchestra. Its music closely resembles the best work of a fine human orchestra.

Some idea of the volume and beauty of its music may be gained from the fact that it contains 258 pipes, including Oboes, Violins, Piccolos, Flutes, 'Cellos, Saxophones and Basses. In addition there is a high-grade Piano, Bass, Snare and Kettle Drums, Triangle and Cymbals.

All these different pipes and instruments are under the control of fifteen automatic stops, which bring into play, at the proper time, the various pipes or sets of pipes required to produce the exact orchestral effect as written in the music. Not only is the playing exact, but the separate notes coming from the various pipes are so sweet and natural that one might easily imagine they were produced by a human orchestra. The beauty of the music of the Concert PianOrchestra is beyond the power of pen-and-ink description. To borrow a rather hackneyed expression: "It must be heard to be appreciated."

The elaborate case of this magnificent instrument perfectly harmonizes with its wonderful musical qualities. It is built of quarter-sawed oak, in the new silver gray finish, handsomely paneled and decorated with gold-leaf. It may also be had in white enamel finish, with gold-leaf mouldings and trimmings. In the center is an oval-shaped art glass panel, which is illuminated by electric lights placed in the interior of the instrument. A plate-glass door opens to the music roll in front, through which the music roll is seen in operation.

INSTRUMENTATION:

A High Grade Piano.

30 Oboes.	26 Bass Violins.
56 Violins.	Bass and Snare Drums.
30 Violas.	Kettle Drum and Cymbals.
30 Piccolos.	Chimes, 13 Bars.
30 Flutes.	Triangle.
30 Violoncellos.	Tambourine.
26 Saxophones.	Castanets.

Style 31 is operated by a noiseless electric motor, which is placed inside the instrument, where it is out of sight. Any number of nickel-in-the-slot boxes may be connected with the instrument, by which it may be played from any part of the house; or push-buttons can be used instead of slot boxes, where the owner prefers to give his patrons free musical entertainment.

SPECIAL DANCE ROLLS

Special Dance Rolls, containing selections for dancing, that play about three minutes, with a minute and a half encore, are cut for this style. The dance music is entirely different from the other music, being cut especially for dancing, the drums marking time all the way through. Nothing can equal this instrument for dancing, as the time can be quickly regulated, and once set to a certain speed, will not vary. The volume is much fuller than that of the ordinary orchestra employed for dancing.

This style is built with the Automatic Roll Changing Device, but may be had without it, if desired.

This wonderful device holds six rolls of music, containing from twenty to thirty-five selections, and automatically changes the rolls as they are played through and rewound, thus affording a program, without repetitions, lasting from an hour and a half to three hours. This style will be found especially adapted to the higher class public places, where orchestras are usually employed.

Description of Style 31 Concert PianOrchestra.

Wurlitzer Concert PianOrchestra—Style 31

With Wurlitzer Automatic Roll Changer

Instrumentation:

Piano	26 Saxophones	26 Bass Violins	Triangle
56 Violins	30 Oboes	Bass and Snare Drums	Tambourine
30 Violoncellos	30 Flutes	Kettle Drum and Cymbals	Castanets
30 Violas	30 Piccolos	Chimes	

Height, 10 ft. 6 in.   Width, 6 ft. 10 in.   Depth, 3 ft. 11 in.

Shipping weight, 3200 lbs.

Wurlitzer Concert PianOrchestra—Style 68 C
With Wurlitzer Automatic Roll Changer
Instrumentation:

Piano	30 Flutes	12 Bassoons	Xylophone
65 Violins	30 Piccolos	20 Bass Clarinets	Chimes
26 Violoncellos	30 Clarinets	10 Bass Violins	Bass and Snare Drums
15 Violas	24 Oboes	26 French Horns	Kettle Drum and Cymbals
26 Saxophones	Triangle	Tambourines	Tremolo and Castanets

Height, 10 ft. Width, 10 ft. 9 in. Depth, 4 ft. 4 in. Shipping weight, 4200 lbs.

Style 68-C had a greater width than height. With their impressive dimensions and large volume of sound only the largest public places — ballrooms, large dining rooms, etc. — were candidates for a Concert instrument.

Wurlitzer Concert PianOrchestra—Style 72 A
With Wurlitzer Automatic Roll Changer
Instrumentation:

Piano	30 Flutes	10 Bassoons	Chimes
70 Violins	30 Piccolos	10 Bass Violins	Bass and Snare Drums
30 Violoncellos	30 Clarinets	16 French Horns	Kettle Drum and Cymbals
18 Violas	20 Oboes	10 Trumpets	Tambourines
26 Saxophones	14 Bass Clarinets	Xylophone	Triangle
		Tremolo and Castanets	

Height, 12 ft. Width, 7 ft. 4 in. Depth, 4 ft. 3½ in. Shipping weight, 4000 lbs.

The Style 72-A Concert PianOrchestra stood an imposing twelve feet high and weighed two tons. It is no wonder that so few of these instruments were saved after their usefulness had ended!

Concert PianOrchestra—Style 43

The largest and finest style of PianOrchestra built. The case illustrated is a most imposing design, richly hand carved, with circular carved pilasters and capitols. In order to give every owner of this magnificent style something entirely exclusive, the case designs are made different. No two are alike, although all are equally as handsome as the style illustrated on the opposite page.

The panels on each side are set with heavy beveled-edge mirrors, and the central panel is of richly colored art glass, faced by a brass lattice work screen—an entirely unique treatment, producing a most artistic effect.

Set in each of the side panels, with mirror background, are handsome statues, with artificial flowers that are so natural looking that without close inspection they cannot be told from the fresh cut article. Intertwined with the flowers are small electric globes, which light up when the instrument is playing, producing a most gorgeous appearance.

In the center is a much larger figure, standing on a pedestal and holding a vase of drooping flowers interspersed with electric light bulbs, which light up when the instrument plays. The reflection in the mirrors at the back mingles the flowers with the lattice work, so that it presents a realistic picture, suggestive of a summer flower garden. The architecture, down to the minutest feature, is lavishly splendid, and fit to adorn the handsomest ball room in existence.

Naturally, one would expect something extra in the music of so fine an instrument, and on this point there will be no disappointment. 370 musical pipes represent as many different orchestral instruments. These are all under automatic control, more perfect and more rapid than any ever exerted by the director of a human orchestra. The playing of Style 43 so nearly resembles that of a large metropolitan Symphony Orchestra, that unless one sees the instrument, it is difficult to say whether the music is not made by a skilled human orchestra.

Our finest PianOrchestra contains all the latest improved Wurlitzer automatic features, especially the Automatic Roll Changing Device, which affords a continuous musical program of an hour and a half to three hours, without repetition or bother of changing the music rolls.

Special Dance Rolls, containing selections especially arranged for dancing, are cut for this style. This music is ideal for dancing, as the drum section marks the correct dance tempo, and when the instrument is set to perfect dance time, it does not vary a hairsbreadth.

With no other instrument, perhaps, can our nickel-in-the-slot boxes be used to such fine advantage. A liberal number distributed at tables in a restaurant or cafe would result in a continuous shower of money, for the excellence of the music is such that patrons would never tire of listening. Furthermore, numerous coins will be deposited for every tune heard, as the parties at the numerous tables would each pay to hear the different selections, and while each would receive full value, the owners of the instrument receives several coins for each selection played.

This refers, of course, to its operation by nickel-in-the-slot. Where the music is used as a free attraction, it will unquestionably prove the greatest trade magnet ever devised. Patrons will flock to listen to a concert by the most magnificent automatic orchestra ever built.

Study carefully the following list of instruments, which PianOrchestra, Style 43, represents. The instrumentation is by far the most ambitious and pretentious ever attempted in an automatic musical instrument.

INSTRUMENTATION:
A High Grade Piano.

30 Violins.	*30 Saxophones.*	*26 Brass Trombones.*
30 Violas.	*30 Clarionets.*	*Xylophone, 20 Bars.*
30 Violoncellos.	*30 Oboes.*	*Chimes, 13 Bars.*
26 Bass Violins.	*26 French Horns.*	*Bass and Snare Drums.*
30 Flutes.	*26 Flageolets.*	*Kettle Drum and Cymbals.*
30 Piccolos.	*26 Bassoons.*	*Triangle, Tambourine and Castanets.*

Also a *Tremolent* for producing the tremolo effect in the music and an *automatic swell* to produce shading and expression.

Height, 11 ft. 9 in. Width, 7 ft. 10½ in. Depth, 5 ft. 7½ in.
PRICE—Including Automatic Roll Changing Device, 6 Rolls of Music and 1 Slot Box...$7,500.00
This style may also be had without Roll Changing Device. Price...........7,300.00

The Style 43 was one of the most elaborate Concert PianOrchestras. The installation of one of these would provide the owner with a "continuous shower of money" according to the above description.

Wurlitzer Concert PianOrchestra—Style 32 A

With Wurlitzer Automatic Roll Changer

Instrumentation:

Piano	30 Flutes	26 French Horns	Triangle
56 Violins	30 Piccolos	26 Bass Violins	Tambourine
30 Violoncellos	30 Clarinets	Chimes	Castanets
30 Violas	30 Oboes	Bass and Snare Drums	Tremolo
	26 Saxophones	Kettle Drum and Cymbals	

Height, 8 ft. 7 in.   Width, 7 ft. 9 in.   Depth, 6 ft.   Shipping weight, 4000 lbs.

The Style 32-A Concert PianOrchestra cost $5750.00 in 1920. A specimen in the author's collection has art glass instead of mirrors and a statue instead of the scene on the front.

Coin Slot Boxes

For playing Wurlitzer Automatic Musical Instruments from any part of the house

By placing this ingenious slot box on the walls, at tables and other convenient locations, our instruments can be played from any part of the house.

It is equipped with our Coin Detector Slot, which will disclose at all times the last three coins deposited.

One nickel can be deposited at a time for playing a single selection. The slot cannot become clogged up.

The box is made of oxidized metal in two pieces. The front is tastefully ornamented with *fleur de lis* figures in relief, and the edges overlap the sides and effectually prevent prying off.

Fitted with best four-tumbler Yale lock.

Dimensions: Height, 11 in. Width, 6 in. Depth, 3½ in.
PRICE—.................$8.00 each.

Wurlitzer wall box made by the Monarch Manufacturing Company of Cincinnati. Monarch made wall boxes of similar design for Seeburg, Welte and others.

Chapter 8

The *Encyclopaedia Britannica* notes that the violin "is perhaps the best-known and most widely distributed musical instrument in the world." There is no disputing that the violin is indeed well-known. Ask a schoolboy to name a famous artist and he may name Rembrandt, Picasso, Goya, Gaugin ... or one of many others who have achieved fame. Ask him to name a famous maker of musical instruments ... and the chances are that Antonio Stradivari will be the one chosen. Stradivari, the violin-maker, has endured as a public legend while the names of pianoforte, harpsichord and other instrument manufacturers have disappeared in the cloak of time ... at least as far as the public is concerned.

Likewise, the violin received much attention from the manufacturers of automatic musical instruments. Many attempts were made to construct mechanical violin players. With the exceptions of the Mills *Violano-Virtuoso* and the Hupfeld *Phonoliszt-Violina* all were commercial failures.

HE VIOLANO-VIRTUOSO is introduced at this time, to the music trade and to music lovers generally, somewhat earlier than the management had intended.

Since the Alaska-Yukon Exhibition at Seattle in 1909, the instrument has been the subject of constant study, and many improvements have been made, for it has been and is the policy of the management not to offer the Violano-Virtuoso to the public, until both the violin and the piano attachment have been made as nearly perfect as possible.

The opportunity presented by the Piano Trade Exhibition however, for the demonstration of the Violano-Virtuoso, is one that we can not neglect particularly as we have been urged to avail ourselves of it by a vast number of music lovers who have heard the instrument in the last two years.

We have therefore taken space at the exhibition and shall be glad to go into the fullest detail of explanation and demonstration of the Violano-Virtuoso, both here and, after the exhibition closes, at our music room, Suite 601, Fine Arts Building, Chicago, Ill., bespeaking for ourselves however, a possible further indulgence of a few weeks in the matter of deliveries to purchasers.

By that time, in view of the rapid progress now being made in certain projected improvements, we are confident that we shall be able to fill all orders promptly and to the better satisfaction both of ourselves and our customers.

Respectfully,

THE VIOLANO-VIRTUOSO CO.

Chicago, June 1, 1911.

Leaflet first offering the Violano-Virtuoso for sale to the public. The Violano-Virtuoso, an improvement upon the Mills Automatic Virtuosa, was first publicly displayed at the Alaska-Yukon-Pacific Exposition in 1909.

The first model of the Mills *Automatic Virtuosa* appeared about 1905 or 1906. In contast to the later *Violano-Virtuoso* models, the *Automatic Virtuosa* played the violin alone ... without piano accompaniment. Evidently these first machines were strictly limited-production items.

In 1908 or 1909 a piano was added to the *Automatic Virtuosa,* and it was rechristened the *Violano-Virtuoso.*

In 1911 the *Violano-Virtuoso* was first offered for sale. Accompanying its introduction were many publicity releases, catalogues and flyers. Excerpts follow:

"The Violano-Virtuoso is today the result of ten years of constant experimenting and inventing and represents an outlay of more than $150,000.00. Thus far it has not been offered for sale for it is only lately that it has been brought to its present high stage of perfection.

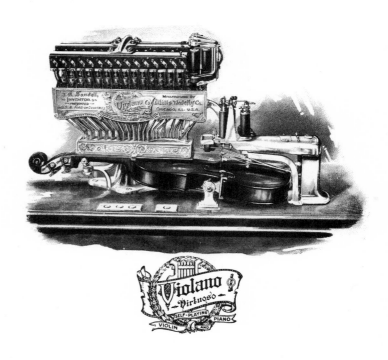

Violin and playing apparatus from the Mills Violano-Virtuoso. The style shown is early; later the playing mechanism was simplified and reduced in size.

A Teacher of Teachers

He who wishes to master the violin as the great performers have mastered it can call to his aid at any moment the world's music masters, with all their personality faithfully reproduced.

Or, should he desire a skilled piano accompanist, he has but to push a lever that stills the violin and permits the piano to play alone.

The pianist who wishes the help and inspiration of the violin, can have always at his call this rare performer.

The pianist, too, who wishes to acquire the touch of the Masters, needs but listen to the Violano-Virtuoso.

For teachers, for accompanists, for advanced performers on either piano or violin, the Violano-Virtuoso is an ever-present, ever-willing aid.

Professional musicians evidently could learn a thing or two by listening to the Violano-Virtuoso! This was Mills Novelty Company advertising at its finest.

The instruments, therefore, which were exhibited under the auspices of the U.S. Government at Seattle, Omaha and Chicago, represented not as perfect development, but in spite of that, they made so marked an impression upon all who heard them that the mails of the Violano-Virtuoso Company were filled with voluntary expressions of wonder and delight from Senators, Governors of States, Editors, Musicians and Teachers of Music...

What the wonderful discovery (of the mechanical piano player) has done for the piano, the invention and development of the *Violano-Virtuoso* have done for the violin. Until now this great instrument, the King of all musical instruments, has baffled every attempt to compel it to yield its treasures to any but the individual performer... Think now of an instrument which, without the touch of the human hand, produces by real bowing and real

The Mills Viol-Cello, combined a mechanically-played violin and cello. See page 68 for a larger illustration.

The Royal Violista shown above was manufactured around 1910 by Professor Wauters who worked for the Automatic Musical Company (the predecessor of the Link Piano Company) of Binghamton, New York, and who was later employed by the Rudolph Wurlitzer Company. The above model, shown with the violin removed from the playing mechanism, was one of at least two different case designs made. These machines were not commercially successful.

fingering, upon a real violin, effects beyond the reach of any but the greatest masters. And this is exactly what the *Violano-Virtuoso* does—playing not only the violin with the most exquisite shading and fautless technique, but as well, a perfectly tempered and adapted piano accompaniment..."

The advertising of the Wurlitzer Company during this period was outstanding...as we noted previously. But in the Mills Novelty Company they had a real competitor. Mills advertising, especially that for the *Violano-Virtuoso,* is sprinkled with many gems of copy writing...such as the statement that the violins used in the machines actually *increase in value* after they are purchased! To wit:

"When we first began building the *Virtuoso* we bought violins from the greatest violin makers, at an average cost of $300.00 apiece; but even these were not good enough — so we set about making better ones ourselves... These violins are of the famous Stradivarius model, having a beautiful, rich soft tone... Every *Violano-Virtuoso* therefore not only **has** a "trained" (by playing it at the factory **before** installing it in the machine) violin, but also one

Modell geschützt.

Hupfeld
Phonoliszt-Violina
Mod. A
the first and only Violin-Piano with Original Violins.

The instrument consists of three Violins arranged within a rotating horsehair bow and an artistic player piano "Phonoliszt", which accompanies the Violin playing in an artistic manner and which can also be used as Solo instrument by using the extensive Phonoliszt repertory.

This selfplaying Violina is not only a marvel technically but also absolutely perfect in musical respect. What **was** considered as impossible has been reached by Violina: to master the Violin by technique and inspire into its playing Soul and Emotion.

The tone of the Violina is well balanced in all positions, the peculiarities of the personal playing such as bowing up and downward, legato, staccato, vibrato, glissando etc. are so natural that one believes to listen to real artists. César Thompson, the Belgian Joachim, admired Violina and expressed his heartfelt congratulations.

The Phonoliszt-Violina has been awarded two of the highest prizes in 1910. the Grand Prix with the felicitations of the Jury at Brussels and the highest State Medal at the International Hunting Exposition at Vienna.

The tuning of the Violina is so simple that any layman can do this without any difficuly, in fact the tuning is easier than with hand playing instruments.

Dimensions:
Height about 7' 8" — width about 5' 2" — depth about 3' 1".
Weight: net about 770 lbs. — gross about 1550 lbs.

Hupfeld
Phonoliszt-Violina Mod. B.

The first self-playing Violin, operated by a horse-hair bow in connection with the masterplayer piano Concert-Phonoliszt.

The Phonoliszt-Violina is provided with three genuine high grade violins placed within a rotating circular horse-hair bow. In rendering the different pieces (from highest classics to popular music) all the delicacies and paculiarities of the human playing are maintained; in fact the variation in playing staccato, legato, glissando, vibrato, tremolo &c. in its most artistic execution commands true admiration of every connoisseur. Such beautiful effects have so far been possible by individual playing only and never before in the way of imitation.

All Violin pieces are accompanied by the Concert-Phonoliszt in the most perfect manner, this representing another most appreciable feature in addition to the amaging invention of the selfplaying violin itself. Another excellent quality of the Phonoliszt-Violina consists in being able to play the piano alone at any time, either by hand or by inserting perforated music-rolls of which we keep a well selected and extensive assortment on hand at all times.

Franz Mikorey, conductor of the Court Orchestra in Dessau writes about Phonoliszt-Violina:

Your Violina is a marvellous invention which must be admired by every professional musician. It gives me great pleasure to express to you my sincere felicitations upon so brillant a success after 25 years of strenuous work.

Dessau, May 27th, 1909. ———— (signed) **Franz Mikorey.**

Dimensions:
Height about 8', width about 5' 6", depth about 2' 7".
Weight: net about 1000 lbs., gross about 1320 lbs.

Modell geschützt.

Piano aus der Hofpianoforte-Fabrik Carl Rönisch, Dresden.

The Hupfeld Phonoliszt-Violina was a success. Unlike Mills, Hupfeld never mastered an automatic tuning device. The owner of a Phonoliszt-Violina had to have the machine tuned constantly, an annoying problem. Hupfeld also manufactured a deluxe model of the Phonoliszt-Violina with six violins, however very few of these were made. Each of the three violins in the regular Phonoliszt-Violina had only one working string, so the combined volume of the three violins was less than that of Mills' Violano-Virtuoso which had one violin but which could play all four of its strings simultaneously.

that continues to improve until, after a year or more of use, the violin which at first was worth only $300.00 may well be valued at $1,000.00."

The *Violano-Virtuoso* was an oustanding commercial success. The aggregate retail value of the 4,000 or so machines sold during the 1910 — 1930 era was probably on the order of eight to ten million dollars.

The Rudolph Wurlitzer Company had two main entries in the field of machines which imitated the violin; the *Solo Violin Piano* and the *Paganini Violin Piano*. Both of these machines simulated a violin through the medium of wooden pipes carefully made and tuned to imitate violin tones almost perfectly . . . in the same manner as the violin family stops on a pipe organ.

The first Wurlitzer machine introduced was the *Paganini Violin Piano*, a machine which was imported from Philipps of Bockenheim, Germany; maker of the *PianOrchestras*.

Basically, the *Paganini* (named, of course, after the famous violinist) was a reproducing piano to which one or more ranks of violin pipes were added.

Some of the larger models had a set of reeds in addition for greater foundation of tone. Still larger models were known as *Paganini Violin Orchestras* and possessed a full range of orchestra instruments including violin pipes, piano, reed organ, several ranks of pipes imitating wind instruments, xylophone, orchestra bells, cymbals, drums, triangle, tambourine and castanets.

WURLITZER
Reg. U. S. Pat. Off

PAGANINI

ROLL No. 334

1. The Sheik (Of Araby) Fox Trot . . . *Snyder*
2. By The Old Ohio Shore, Waltz. *Mary Earl*
3. Wimmin (I've Got To Have 'Em
    That's All) One step . . *Cantor & Fisher*
4. Ka-Lu-A, Fox Trot—from "Good
    Morning Dearie". . . . . *Jerome Kern*
5. In Maytime (I Learned To Love You)
    Waltz . . . . *Jack Snyder*

Made in U. S. A.

Paganini Violin Piano—Style 1

With Wurlitzer Automatic Roll Changer

Represents a Piano in combination with a Violin.

Height, 8 ft. 8½ in.   Width, 6 ft. 6 in.   Depth, 3 ft. 3 in.   Shipping weight, 1400 lbs.

Paganini Violin Piano—Style 2

With Wurlitzer Automatic Roll Changer

Represents a Piano in combination with 2 Violins.

Height, 9 ft. 4½ in.   Width, 6 ft. 6 in.   Depth, 3 ft. 5½ in.   Shipping weight, 1500 lbs.

Two of the Wurlitzer Paganini styles. A label from a Paganini roll is shown at the above right.

The Paganini Violin Piano

A Wonderful New Musical Instrument

This instrument is the latest Wurlitzer triumph and the very highest type of refined musical instrument.

The work of the Paganini Violin Piano will be best appreciated by musical persons who understand and appreciate good music. This instrument reproduces the actual playing of a piano and violin by artists of the highest rank, the violin leading and the piano playing the accompaniment.

The Paganini will play everything in music from the popular hits to the big classical numbers with a correctness of technic and musical shading that will positively amaze the listener.

Take a position in another room or turn your back on this new musical wonder and you will find it impossible to say that you are not listening to the best work of a finished pianist and violinist, thoroughly accustomed to playing together in concert.

The Paganini has been tried out in the very finest places and in every case it has caused a sensation, so *different* is it in every respect.

A visitor in a fine cafe or hotel restaurant of today notices that the music comes drifting in, so to speak, not loud, but in soft, delicate strains that can be plainly heard and enjoyed by those who wish to stop their conversation to listen, while it is so soft as not to interfere with low conversation by those who wish to talk.

The Orchestra usually is hidden in such places, and as said above, the music seems to *drift* in.

That is the exact niche the Paganini fills. It really seems made to order for just such refined places. Put the Paganini in the place of the hidden orchestra and your diners will never know but that they are listening to the finest violinist and pianist they ever heard. When they discover that the artist musicians are entirely automatic, their interest deepens. The charm of the music grows and grows with repeated hearings.

In a word, the Paganini Violin Piano is a thoroughly dignified, refined musical instrument of the highest grade, suitable for the finest metropolitan hotels and cafes. It will not only make good under the most exacting conditions, but it is no exaggeration to say that it will *carry the most critical audience by storm.*

An excellent assortment of music rolls is ready for the instrument. These include the latest popular music of the day and the classical standards which possess popular flavor.

In addition to the regular music rolls we have others for piano only. They are known as "hand-played rolls". An artist performer sits down to the piano and plays the composition which is copied exactly and later this perfect record serves as a *master record* from which duplicate music rolls are struck off.

The cases of the Paganini Violin Pianos are chastely elegant. They conform in every particular to the class of music the instrument produces.

Description of the Paganini from a Wurlitzer catalogue.

If desired, the piano in the *Paganini* could be played alone. For this purpose Philipps *Duca* rolls and Wurlitzer *Special Hand-Played Piano Music for the Paganini Violin Piano* rolls were available. When the piano was played alone it imitated the actual playing of famous pianists, as a reproducing piano.

Wurlitzer and Philipps were both very much aware of the success that the *Violano-Virtuoso* and Hupfeld *Phonoliszt-Violina* were enjoying. To counter the appeal of a *real violin* in a machine the *Paganini* literature was quick to point out that in order to work properly the owners of such machines should have a professional musician on hand *at all times* to keep the violin in tune and working properly!

In practice the *Violano-Virtuoso* kept in tune for long periods of time due to an ingenious system of tuning arms and weights which exerted constant tension on the strings regardless of changes in the temperature or humidity. The Hupfeld *Phonoliszt-Violina* was a different story. It had to be tuned constantly. Despite the fact that Hupfeld assured the prospective buyer that "any layman can do this without difficulty, in fact the tuning is easier than with hand playing instruments" this factor was probably a deterrent to many would-be-buyers.

Paganini Violin Piano—Style 2

With Wurlitzer Automatic Roll Changer.

Represents a Piano in combination with 2 Violins.

Height, 8 ft. 8 in.   Width, 6 ft. 3 in.   Depth, 3 ft. 1 in.

Shipping weight, 1300 lbs.

Paganini Violin Piano—Style 1

With Wurlitzer Automatic Roll Changer

Represents a Piano in combination with a Violin.

Height, 8 ft. 8 in.   Width, 6 ft. 3 in.   Depth, 3 ft. 1 in.

Shipping weight, 1200 lbs.

Solo Paganini Violin and Piano

Installed in The Famous

Poodle Dog Restaurant

San Francisco

The Poodle Dog Restaurant is a high class place, and caters to a fashionable money-spending trade.

Nothing can gain admittance to the exclusive "Poodle Dog" that is not superlatively fine.

The fact that Mr. A. B. Blanco, proprietor, after considering all other forms of musical attraction, selected the Wurlitzer Paganini, proves that the Paganini is the only instrument that meets the requirements of a high class Restaurant.

Mr. Blanco writes:

"I consider my Wurlitzer Paganini one of the wonders of the age." I cannot recommend it too highly. It is the most wonderful and pleasing musical instrument that money can purchase."

View of Interior of
Poodle Dog Restaurant and Hotel,
San Francisco

Note that the Paganini Violin Pianos were equipped with automatic roll changers. The Poodle Dog Restaurant used a Paganini for background music.

Lest a prospective purchaser think that the *Paganini* with its wood pipes would not sound *exactly* like a violin the following challenge was made: "Take a position in another room or turn your back on this new musical wonder and you will find it impossible to say that you are not listening to the best work of a finished pianist and violinist, thoroughly accustomed to playing together in concert."

It was further asserted that the *Paganini* would "carry the most critical audience by storm."

Despite Wurlitzer's sales efforts the *Paganini Violin Piano* was not a particularly good seller. It is doubtful if more than a few hundred in all were sold. Although they were imported from Philipps only from about 1910 to 1914 enough unsold machines remained on hand that they were listed in Wurlitzer price lists as late as 1920 and 1921.

Paganini Solo Violin Piano—Style 3

With Wurlitzer Automatic Roll Changer

Represents 2 Violins with Organ and Piano accompaniment.

Height, 8 ft. Width, 6 ft. 3 in. Depth, 3 ft. 1 in. Shipping weight, 1800 lbs.

A case style variation of the Paganini Style 3. The word "Solo" was occasionally added to Paganini catalogue descriptions. More often than not, these machines were known as Paganini Violin Pianos ... without the "Solo" adjective.

Paganini Violin Piano—Style 3

With Wurlitzer Automatic Roll Changer

Represents a Piano in combination with 2 Violins and **Organ.**

Height, 8 ft. Width, 6 ft. 3 in. Depth, 3 ft. 1 in. Shipping weight, 1400 lbs.

The Style 3 Paganini Violin Piano illustrated above is similar to the machine in the author's collection. Movable swell shutters in the top of the machine provide for expression variations. The Paganini used an exceptionally wide roll, 130 perforations wide, to provide for the many piano, pipe and reed organ expression and on-off controls plus orchestration for drums, xylophone and other instruments. The various extra instruments provided for on the roll were used only in the Paganini Violin Orchestra (see page 177) and were not in the regular Paganini styles.

The Wurlitzer Company tried its best to sell the *Paganini Violin Pianos.* The August, 1914 issue of the *Wurlitzer Booster* notes that "Surely every office has a *Paganini* on the floor, but the other styles sell so much better that you've all sort of forgotten it ..." In the same article the Wurlitzer dealers were admonished: "Don't, Don't, Don't overlook this beautiful instrument. Get your interest in it refreshed, see that yours is in good shape; give it a good place on your floor; then go at it again ..."

Undoubtedly most would-be-buyers who wanted a violin-playing machine bought a Mills *Violano-Virtuoso* instead. Another factor against the *Paganini's* popularity was that the most popular styles, the 1, 2, and 3 sold for $3,500.00, $3700.00 and $4250.00 respectively. Most people who wanted to spend $3500.00 to $4250.00 for an automatic musical instrument probably bought a *PianOrchestra* instead, as these machines were infinitely more attention-getting. These factors left the *Paganini* with a small and indefinite market.

A contemporary view of the Paganini is provided by a pencilled note which the author obtained as the "pedigree" of the *Style 3 Paganini Violin Piano*

The WURLITZER BOOSTER

GET SOME OF THE SPIRIT.

Geo. W. Gillins, President of Kohler-Campbell, Inc., piano builders, in a recent interview states:

"To one who studies fundamentals, every condition in this country points to the beginning of the greatest era of prosperity we have ever had!

"The dealers who will reap the harvest this fall are those who have on their floors the right goods in sufficient numbers to meet a demand that will come quick, and the manufacturers who begin now to prepare for the fall rush will be those who will profit by it.

"The depression which every business has experienced in the past year has not been confined to this country alone, but has been world-wide and the crop outlook for Europe and South America is equally as promising as it is here, and has its beneficial effect here at home."

Begin to believe it yourself, don't *think* any other way; believe that it is here now, get full of that spirit, go out and shoot some of it into *that* prospect, but stop talking occasionally long enough to let him say "all right, I'll take it!" Give him a chance to sign an order.

HOW'S YOUR PAGANINI?

Surely every office has a Paganini on the floor, but the other styles sell so much better that you've all sort of forgotten it.

Now this is absolutely wrong—in Germany (you know they are progressive there in the automatic line) instruments of the Paganini type prevail—all the really good places, cafes, theatres, etc., use them, and an instrument filled with drum cymbals and *crash* devices, is not in evidence.

The possibilities of the Paganini are different, its musical interpretation is superior to anything else we have, and there must be some trade in your vicinity—trade that *would not* consider an automatic instrument that *can* be interested in a Paganini.

You know the music rendered by a Paganini is soft, sweet and refined. The expression devices are so keenly adjusted that it is almost impossible to recognize its playing as anything but the actual performance of skilled musicians, skilled to an extreme, for the Paganini never makes any mistakes.

Don't, Don't, Don't overlook this *beautiful* instrument. Get your interest in it refreshed, see that yours is in good shape; give it a good place on your floor; then go at it again.

Be careful during your demonstration of it that you have quiet in your warerooms. Let everyone in your employ know that when the Paganini starts its an invariable sign for quiet. See that this rule is carried out *absolutely*. This you *must* do, unless your warerooms are such that you can have yours in a separate room.

ABOUT YOUR BULLETIN BOARDS.

Don't neglect your board, keep the interest in them up, and remember to get your copy of same in for the Booster. The writer has been working over the Booster cards for the past year, trying to figure out some records for your interest, but finds many months where some one office omitted altogether getting in its card. Be more careful this year, *please*. We know the compiled yearly record will be interesting. Last year S. Winter, of our Chicago office, was in the hundred point class every month but *two*, and Huennekes of New York, we believe would run way up high, did we have all the cards.

Now don't ask the editor to dig all this out from the auditor's books. Those are not public property and your blackboard should be correct. Any actual valuable difference or error of course, can be corrected or verified by our books.

Let your card be accurate then so we can depend on it alone in awarding such prizes, favor, etc., as this year may bring forth. Remember that $300 on one you know, for the 100 points each month. Sam Winter wouldn't have missed those two last year had this been on there, would you Sam?

HOW MUCH ARE YOU WORTH?

If you tip any scale at one-fifty pounds you are worth just seven-fifty per;

So a scientist says and I s'pose he knows, so I to his statement defer.

But this worth is based on the element parts of what your body contains.

And does not consider the value to you of what you can find in your brains.

You are made up of salt, of iron and lime, a little albumen and fat.

A bit of phosphorus, some sugary stuff and a little amnesia on that;

This collect of compounds represented in a man is what he could sell for junk.

But are you contented to sit down and feel that you'd sell for a figure so punk?

Are you selling yourself at a bargain store price, are you pleased with this seven-fifty per?

Or are you to show that the price has gone up, that you are really a man, not a cur?

Don't measure your worth in this physical way, if you do you will cheapen the bid.

What a man's worth is settled this way: By what he has under his lid.

WHEN YOU GO TO THE FACTORY.

When you have occasion to go to the factory with a customer, or send one, there are several things you should remember and consider.

First of all the factory may not have assembled those instruments you desire to see, so find out first, and make an appointment whenever possible.

When arriving in Buffalo it is better to telephone out to the factory and let them know you are there. They can best direct you how to reach the factory. You know it takes about one hour on the Interurban to get to the factory from Buffalo, and a certain car must be taken. The factory can tell you or your customer just *when* and *where* to get that car.

If you have made an appointment to be met in Buffalo, remember the factory man has the same time to consider in getting into Buffalo, and be definite about your time of arrival. If you expect to reach Buffalo at 7 A. M., and be met at 8 A. M., he has got to get out early. Should you find after making such an appointment you will be delayed until noon, don't send any *night* telegram about it, it would reach the factory too late—send a *regular* message even though it be after five P. M. That message will be delivered to Mr. Farny Wurlitzer or Mr. DeKleist at their residence, and stop that early trip and save a half day.

Address all telegrams, letters, etc., to the Rudolph Wurlitzer Mfg. Co., North Tonawanda, N. Y., and not to individuals—mark your letter inside for attention of those whom you may wish to reach personally.

When you send customers there, give them their instructions—and notify the factory of their coming. This will expedite matters, save unavoidable delays, and *keep appointments.*

A page from the August, 1914 issue of the Wurlitzer Booster. "How's Your Paganini" implores Wurlitzer dealers to get busy selling these machines.

Wurlitzer Paganini Violin Piano, Style 3,

In THE GRELL CAFE, 3338 State St., ROCHESTER, N. Y.

Do *You* know there are 10,000 Wurlitzer Instruments Now In Use?

From coast to coast, from the Gulf to the Lakes, no matter where you go, you will *invariably* be entertained with *Wurlitzer Music*.

Have you ever heard *a real* Wurlitzer Automatic Musical Instrument? Do you know of our profit sharing plan on which we install them?

Have you ever seen the Wurlitzer Automatic Roll Changer that plays 30 to 40 different selections without any attention whatever?

Have you heard the Wurlitzer Paganini Violin Piano, the most remarkable instrument of the times, which reproduces the playing of a fine violinist accompanied by a piano?

Did you ever hear our hand played music rolls, that will deceive the trained musical ear of any critic?

Come in and learn of all these *vital* facts, and let us show you how one of these instruments will help you in your business. No obligation of course.

E. W. KELLEY

Distributor of Wurlitzer Automatic Musical Instruments

22-24 Elm St.,   -   ROCHESTER, N. Y.

This advertisement, probably circa 1914 indicates that 10,000 Wurlitzer instruments of various kinds were then in use.

Paganini Violin Orchestra—Style 10

Violins, Flageolets, Flute Clarionets, Piccolos, Cellos, Baritone or Cornet, Xylophone, Orchestra Bells, Bass Drum and Cymbal, Crash Cymbal, Snare Drum, Kettle Drum, Triangle, Tambourine, Castanets, Piano and Organ.

Height, 11 ft. 4 in.   Width, 8 ft. 10 in.   Depth, 6 ft.   Shipping weight about 4200 lbs.

Price, with Electric Motor and 6 Music Rolls $10,000

Priced at $10,000.00 the Paganini Violin Orchestra was the most expensive Wurlitzer orchestrion listed in any of the Wurlitzer catalogues. This mammoth machine, like other Paganini instruments, was made by Philipps of Bockenheim, Germany. The Style 10 Paganini Violin Orchestra (also known in another Wurlitzer catalogue as Style 7) was available with oval wood panels in place of the art glass, if desired. Most of the Paganini machines were not coin-operated. They were intended to provide background or mood music for exclusive restaurants, country clubs and similar places. Paganini instruments were not listed in Wurlitzer catalogues until 1913-1914. Due to the World War, importation from Philipps was discontinued in 1914, thus accounting in part for the scarcity today of this type of machine. Also, the market for the Paganini was limited as noted in the text.

ORCHESTRION-CONSTRUCTION owes its existence to the principle of supplanting manual technique with mechanical appliances. The first instruments constructed by individual inventors did not sufficiently satisfy the requirements demanded by critics then consulted, but the road to a perfection of the new undertaking was eventually smoothed by patience and industry. Ideas succeeded ideas, new inventions superceded obsolete systems, the mechanism itself suddenly experiencing a radical change. Air, both suction and pressure, being enrolled in the service of the Orchestrion, and pinned rollers abandoned in favour of pneumatic construction throughout, one was able to employ paper notation-rolls for musical performance. But even this new acquisiton displayed considerable unproficiency, for concurrent with the ardour for mechanical improvement the ethics of music were somewhat lost sight of, resulting in instruments being placed on the market, which, to a sensitive ear, very often left much to be desired. The manufacturers, however, without intermission, endeavoured to remove these drawbacks which are unavoidably connected with an industry then in its infancy, with all possible speed, their undivided attention, long, being devoted to the capabilities of the instrument from a musical standpoint.

The era of inharmonic and noisy instruments ought to be really characterized as merely a transitory period extending up to the time when the success which attended unremitting labour and diligence, raised the capabilities of the orchestrion to its present undoubted high standard of excellence and artistic merit.

Great demands are now made on orchestrions, their task being to exemplify complete orchestration, and although at the present time, the best instruments, meet all requirements in this respect, the spirit of invention in industry, accepts of no restriction. It has always set itself higher ideals, the same being successively achieved.

For instance, the violin, possessing the noblest and most melodious qualities as solo instrument, has hitherto been beyond the range of possibility for mechanical, artistic reproduction,

But this, the most soul-inspiring of all instruments, which, in the hand of the master, laughs and weeps, ought and must be successfully exorcised into the répertoire of the pneumatic instrument. Many attempts were made to obtain this end, but very few met with any degree of success. The equipment with real violins, which is worthy of every recognition owing to the beauty of the instrument itself in the hands of a virtuoso, suffers from the great disadvantage that violins, like all other instruments, remains but a very short time in tune. The thing that stands in the way of friends and purchasers of these instruments is that either one must be at the trouble of continually tuning the violin oneself or engage a professional man for that purpose.

Having obtained such extraordinary success with our "Duca Reproduction Piano" we attempted to try a combination which should represent performance on a real violin. We considered this instrument from a truly artistic standpoint, and spared no pains to obtain a corresponding musical performance, which with the aid of a first-class staff of artists we eventually succeeded in accomplishing in a most satisfactory manner.

These instruments, which, on account of their splendid rendering of violin music, we have named after the greatest and most fascinating of violinists, "Paganini". The period between the earliest forms of instruments in mechanical combination, and the capabilities at the present time of instruments of the greatest artistic perfection and beauty, now placed on the market by manufacturers, is full of importance in the history of pneumatic instruments.

The greatest difficulties in this respect have been overcome, the real violins being abandoned on account of their sensitiveness and the consequent work and vexation entailed upon their owner, the problem being solved in another way: our Paganini Instruments not only give a representation of violin-playing, but even perform the finest nuances, the slightest vibrato, and a crescendo and diminuendo, full of soul, being represented in a perfection of beauty.

As in the case of our Duca-Piano, our first object has been to produce music of an artistic nature, no expense being spared to achieve this end. The wonderful performances of duettes on violin and piano by virtuosi in the concert hall as well as in private circles have ever been a source of great joy and satisfaction: these renderings may now be reproduced in absolute perfection of tone, expression and brightness on our Paganini Pianos.

We were aware that this problem would meet with the sharpest criticism on the side of musical celebrities, and therefore did not omit to submit our first model, immediately on its completion, to a thorough and critical examination at the hands of the foremost professional experts.

The recognition of a startling beauty of reproduction in violin-tone together with a highly artistic accompaniment on a Duca Piano, was unanimous. We place the Paganini model on the market with the consciousness that we are offering an instrument of a very high-class order.

As in the past our principle has ever been to evolve the best from the good, so it will be found that the models submitted in the following pages, not only meet the highest musical demands, but also in quality and workmanship, will keep up our old reputation for turning out first-clas instruments only. We have not a moment's doubt that our faithful circle of clients, who have ever taken an active interest in all our novelties, will also give our Paganini Pianos and orchestrions a sympathetic welcome. Our endeavours to eradicate the old prejudices against mechanism meets with considerable support, in that only the very best instruments are placed on the market, thus proving that the era of loud and noisy models has entirely passed away. On the other hand, our Industry can look back with pride upon really artistic achievements.

PHILIPPS-PAGANINI-VIOLINS-PIANOS AND PAGANINI-ORCHESTRIONS

Description of the Paganini instruments from an original Philipps catalogue.

**PHILIPPS
PIANELLA PAGANINI-ORCHESTRION
MODEL No. 1**

WITH REVOLVING MECHANISM

Elegant oak-case with beautiful carving and glass decorations. The centre front panel is filled with a valuable tapestry, and facetted mirror decorations are interspersed. Violin-playing is reproduced in a most perfect manner, with suitable pianoforte accompaniment. An instrument worthy of all praise, equally applicable for private rooms as for Cafés and first-class restaurants.

Height . . . . 8 ft. 4 in.
Breadth . . . . 6 „ 4 „
Depth . . . . 2 „ 8 „
Net weight . . . . 1430 lbs.

Music-rolls bear the mark P. P.
Selections according to our Paganini Lists.

The listener is most agreeably surprised by the marvellous performances on our Paganini-Orchestrions, the same meeting the highest requirements of musical connoisseurs.

price charged for the regular Wurlitzer *Violin Piano*, a *65-Note Player Piano* with a rank of violin pipes added.

The violin solo arrangement which provided for "all the expression and accent necessary to play the best classical music" was evidently not enough of an incentive to induce many to part with $2100.00 for the *Solo Violin Piano* is a very rare machine today. Also a factor was the price of rolls. A four-tune *Solo Violin Piano* roll cost $6.75, over three times the $2.00 cost of a five-tune *65-Note Player Piano* roll. The music repertoire of the *Solo Violin Piano* was limited. Only a few hundred different roll titles were ever produced.

in his collection. The note reads, in part: "The Paganini. Built in Leipzig, Germany by Philipps. Brought to Los Angeles for display by Wurlitzer's agent, Mr. William L. Glockner, at 917 South Broadway. It remained there until 1919 when it was moved to New High Street (now Spring Street) near the Federal Building. In 1922 it was sold at auction for $375.00. The original price paid was $4200.00."

The *Paganini Violin Orchestra* with its $10,000.00 price tag was the most expensive and the most intricate automatic musical instrument marketed by Wurlitzer. This tremendous orchestrion played with perfect expression and reproduced the music of a symphony orchestra "in a faithful and artistic manner"...according to the catalogue.

The quantity of *Paganini Violin Orchestras* sold is nowhere recorded in the Wurlitzer archives. There are, however, extant photographs and catalogue illustrations which seem to indicate that at least *three* machines were imported into this country. We will probably never know the exact figure.

The sales of the *Paganini Violin Orchestras* in Germany were a different story entirely. Philipps catalogues illustrate a wide variety of these (many of which are reproduced in this book) sold as *Pianella-Paganini-Orchestrions* indicating that sales must have been worthwhile.

The other violin-imitating machine sold by Wurlitzer was the *Solo Violin Piano*. First introduced around 1917 or 1918 the *Solo Violin Piano* was a mechanical upright piano with fifty one wood violin pipes attached to the back of the sounding board. Through a special system of perforations the music was arranged to play the violin as the solo instrument with the piano in accompaniment.

The *Solo Violin Piano* was priced at $2100.00... about the same price charged for the popular *BX*, *CX* and *LX* orchestrions, and $600.00 more than the

**PHILIPPS
PIANELLA PAGANINI-ORCHESTRION
MODEL No. 2**

WITH REVOLVING MECHANISM

The exterior of this instrument displays simple elegance, being tastfully decorated with musical emblems. The centre panel is filled with a beautiful piece of tapestry of a favourite design, to the left and right there being ebony columns with metal ornaments. The musical equipment gives a rendering of a string trio. Owing to the great compass of tone possessed by the violin equipment, no limit is placed to its powers in the reproduction of violin pieces.

Height . . . . 7 ft. 8 in.
Breadth . . . . 6 „ 3 „
Depth . . . . 3 „ — „
Net weight . . . . 1496 lbs.

Music-rolls bear the mark P. P.
Selection according to our Paganini Lists.

The best classical music is reproduced on our Paganini models, representing the finest lights and shades in effective performance.

**PHILIPPS
PIANELLA PAGANINI-ORCHESTRION
MODEL No. 3**

WITH REVOLVING MECHANISM

Oak case, prettily decorated with beautiful metal ornaments, and mirrored panels, forming an ornamental piece of furniture. It possesses a perfect and artistic equipment incl. Violin, Piano, Harmonium — 44 tones — (also with Harp, at extra cost, see price list) and occupies a worthy position amongst the Paganini Models, in respect to its wonderfully accurate reproduction of individual-technique. The revolving mechanism secures a continual, musical performance, the music-rolls being changed automatically.

Height . . . . 9 ft. 2 in.
Breadth . . . . 5 „ 8 „
Depth . . . . 2 „ 11 „
Net weight . . . . 1628 lbs.

Music-rolls bear the mark P. P.
Selection according to our Paganini Lists.

No instrument offers so many practical and musical advantages as our Paganini-Orchestrion with revolving-mechanism.

Paganini instruments from the Philipps catalogue. Wurlitzer imported a number of these models and sold them under the Wurlitzer name.

PHILIPPS
PAGANINI-VIOLON-ORCHESTRION
MODÈLE No. 7
À MÉCANISME-REVOLVER
ORCHESTRION PNEUMATIQUE
:: DE MUSIQUE À CORDES ::

Splendide orchestrion avec musique artistique admirable. L'emploi d'une invention ingénieuse pour la reproduction de la musique à cordes en fait pour le présent **le chef-d'oeuvre du genre.** Ce Paganini est pour l'expression et l'instrumentation une merveille.

Sa composition est celle d'un orchestre complet de musique à cordes avec batterie, consistant en grosse caisse, tambour, timbales, tambourins, cymbales de différentes grosseurs, castagnettes, triangle, carillon et xylophone. Le piano à lui seul équivaut pleinement au jeu d'un artiste.

Les instruments à cordes, violon, alto, violoncelle, flageolet, avec leur accompagnement de flûtes, petite flûte, clarinettes, basses, basson, cornets, harmonium etc., combinés avec résonateur de construction spéciale et par vibrateur, donnent un ensemble où tous les artistes et dilettantes ne peuvent voir que l'idéal du genre.

Le Paganini remplace intégralement un orchestre d'instruments à cordes de premier ordre et est par suite indispensable aux cafés, hôtels, salles de concert, restaurants etc.

Hauteur	3,54 mètres
Largeur	3,20 „
Profondeur	1,76 „
Poids net	1900 kilos

Les rouleaux de musique sont marqués P. P.
Choix d'après notre liste Paganini.

PIANELLA PAGANINI-ORCHESTRION
MODEL No. 4

PHILIPPS
PIANELLA PAGANINI-ORCHESTRION
MODEL No. 8

PHILIPPS
PIANELLA PAGANINI-ORCHESTRION
MODEL No. 6
WITH REVOLVING MECHANISM

The most fastidious taste in respect to appearance as well as musical capabilities is catered for in the construction of this model. Elegant mahogany case fitted with columns, the intervening panels being decorated with real bronzes in the empire style. Mirrored panels run parallel with the side columns, a valuable tapestry occupying the centre. The specification is arranged for select chamber-music consisting of a first-class piano, harmonium, violins with flageolet tones, flutes, clarionets and percussion instruments: the equipment therefore gives a most effective and natural representation of a full symphony-orchestra.

Height	11 ft. 2 in.
Breadth	7 „ 8 „
Depth	4 „ — „
Net weight	1804 lbs.

Music-rolls bear the mark P. P.
Selection according to our Paganini Lists.

The finest string-band is reproduced by our Paganini Orchestrions, since they perform the music of symphony-orchestra in a faithful, natural and artistic manner.

PHILIPPS
PIANELLA PAGANINI-ORCHESTRION
MODEL No. 5
WITH REVOLVING MECHANISM

Very elegant, dark-brown, oak case with inlaid panels of a lighter colour on each side. Facetted mirror in centre panel with a cornucopia of artificial flowers, and to the right and left flowers in bronze relief. The numerous carvings and beautiful columns supporting the top are also worthy of mention. The specification and musical equipment is the same as model No. 6, securing a perfect musical representation.

Height	11 ft. — in.
Breadth	7 „ 6 „
Depth	4 „ — „
Net weight	1848 lbs.

Music-rolls bear the mark P. P.
Selections according to our Paganini Lists.

We are confident of our Paganini Violin Orchestrions obtaining unbounded admiration.

Paganini Violin Pianos from the Philipps catalogue. Many of these were called "orchestrions" in the German catalogue even though they only contained piano and pipes. In America the term "orchestrion" was applied to machines containing SEVERAL different orchestra instruments, especially drums and traps. It is not known whether all of the Philipps Paganini styles illustrated on this page and on the preceding page and following page were imported by Wurlitzer. Photographs and catalogue illustrations in the Wurlitzer archives indicate that Philipps models 1, 2, 3, 4, 5, 6 and 7 were among those brought to the United States. Other Philipps models not listed in the particular Philipps catalogue we had available were also imported as our Wurlitzer Paganini illustrations indicate.

PHILIPPS
PIANELLA PAGANINI-ORCHESTRION
MODEL No. 9

WITH REVOLVING MECHANISM

A magnificent case in white and gold with "Luxus" fittings. Artistic hand-carving, beautifully decorated candelabra with torches, whilst during performance it is illuminated inside by means of two crystal globes, which tend to make the instrument a work of art. The artistic performance of the Orchestrion is in keeping with its beautiful exterior, possessing full instrumental equipment.

Effect and music as the preceding models 7 and 8.

Height	12 ft. 6 in.
Breadth	10 „ 8 „
Depth	5 „ 10 „
Net weight	3630 lbs.

Music-rolls bear the mark P. P.

Selections according to our Paganini Lists.

Such instruments speak for themselves!

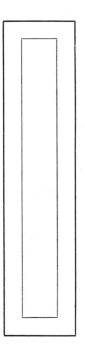

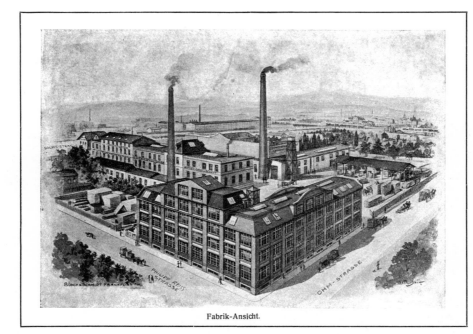

Fabrik-Ansicht.

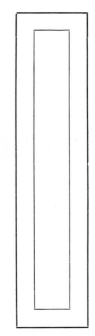

FRANKFURTER MUSIKWERKE-FABRIK
J. D. PHILIPPS & SÖHNE A.-G.
FRANKFURT AM MAIN-BOCKENHEIM
FILIALEN IN BERLIN, LEIPZIG, ESSEN (RUHR), WIEN UND BRUSSEL.

Factory of J.D. Philipps & Sohne located at Bockenheim, near Frankfurt-am-Main, Germany.

WURLITZER

SOLO VIOLIN PIANO ROLLS

Price, Per Roll, Without Spool, $6.75; Metal Spools, $1.00 Extra

ROLL No. 7172

Dear One—Fox Trot...........Fisher, Richardon & Burke
Bring Back Those Rock a-Bye Baby Days—Fox Trot....
....Silver & Bernine
What Did I Get By Loving You—Waltz...............Reid
Eliza—Fox Trot ....Fiorito

ROLL No. 7173

Oh Peter—Fox Trot..............Wiedoeft, Rose & Stafford
Charley My Boy—Fox Trot................Kahn & Fiorito
Memory Lane—Waltz.....................Spier & Conrad
Bagdad—Fox Trot.........................Yellen & Ager

PAGANINI ROLLS

Price, Per Roll, with Spool, $8.00; without Spool, $6.75
Extra Spools, $1.25 Each

ROLL No. 368

Follow the Swallow—Fox Trot...................Henerdson
Oh Peter—Fox Trot..............Wiedoeft, Rose & Stafford
Honest and Truly—Waltz...........................Rose
Charley My Boy—Fox Trot................Kahn & Fiorito
Go Long Mule—Fox Trot...............Creamer & King

WURLITZER

NET PRICE LIST OF

AUTOMATIC INSTRUMENTS

EFFECTIVE MARCH 1, 1920.
This list cancels all former price lists.

Style	Catalogue Page No.	Price
Pianino	7	$ 575.00
Violin-Flute (Pianino) ..	8	750.00
S	9	900.00
I	11	1100.00
IX	12	1200.00
AX	14	1500.00
DX	15	1700.00
BX	16	1900.00
CX	17	2100.00
Solo Violin Piano..........		2100.00

Price, F.O.B. Factory

Page from a 1925 Wurlitzer roll catalogue lists new selections available for the Solo Violin Piano and for the Paganini. This and other contemporary catalogues indicate that only one or two rolls per month were released for these machines. The March 1, 1920 price list at the above right prices the Solo Violin Piano at $2100.00 — the same price charged for the CX Orchestra Piano.

This 1919 photograph taken at Wurlitzer's North Tonawanda factory shows a Solo Violin Piano being assembled. The gentleman at the left is working with the pneumatic stack from the piano. The individual pneumatics, one for each playing piano note, each collapse when the appropriate perforation passes over the tracker bar causing the piano note to sound.

WURLITZER Solo Violin Piano
Coin Operating Attachment

The Solo Violin Piano combines practically a full eighty-eight-note piano with a scale of Violin Pipes, having a range of fifty-one notes. This combination provides for all the expression and accent necessary to play the best classical music.

This instrument is equipped with the WURLITZER Patented Automatic Roll-Changer.

The music is arranged to play the Violin as solo, and the Piano as accompaniment. Write for special catalog.

Height, 4 ft. 10½ in. Width, 5 ft. 1¼ in. Depth, 3¾ ft. Shipping weight, 1250 lbs.

The Wurlitzer Solo Violin Piano provided all the expression and accent necessary to play classical music according to the above catalogue description. The Solo Violin Piano was not one of the more popular Wurlitzer models, hence they are very rare today.

Drop a Nickel and fill the air with beautiful Music

THERE'S A **WURLITZER** Instrument Here

Wurlitzer placards such as this were hung on the front of machines or displayed in a prominent place to attract more nickels. A dozen or so different varieties of these cards were produced.

Chapter 9

Sometime in 1905 Howard Wurlitzer wandered into a downtown Cincinnati cafe. There, confronting him, was a most unusual musical instrument — a self-playing harp! Upon hearing it play Howard was impressed with its soft and melodious tones. It was just the thing to add to the Wurlitzer line!

Diligent inquiry revealed that J. W. Whitlock & Company of Rising Sun, Indiana (located about thirty-five miles distant) had made a few of these self-playing harps as an experiment and had put them on location in Cincinnati, the nearest large city.

The Rudolph Wurlitzer Company lost no time in contacting Whitlock. An agreement was made whereby Wurlitzer agreed to sell the harps on an exclusive basis. A contract for the purchase of one thousand harps was signed. On the strength of this contract J. W. Whitlock & Company constructed a new wooden factory building and set up production line manufacturing facilities.

The new machine was immediately re-introduced as the *Wurlitzer Harp*. One of the initial catalogue descriptions read:

THE WURLITZER HARP

After nine years of constant labor, at great expense, we have succeeded in perfecting the *Wurlitzer Harp,* a most refined musical instrument for places where the piano cannot be used on account of its being too loud.

This beautiful instrument is conceded by everyone who has seen and heard it to be the most wonderful as well as the sweetest musical instrument ever produced.

The Harp contains sixty strings which are picked by automatic fingers (almost human in their operation), and produces a volume of soft, sweet music equal to several Italian Harps played by hand. The face of the instrument is covered by a large harp-shaped plate glass, showing the interior lit up by electric lights and the wonderful little fingers picking the strings. This feature gives the instrument an exceedingly attractive appearance...

As a money-maker in fine hotels, cafes, restaurants, cigar and drug stores the harp has proven itself to be the King of them all; its soft,

THE WURLITZER HARP

A Refined Musical Attraction, with Nickel-in-Slot Attachment and Operated by Electricity

Style A Wurlitzer Automatic Harp.

sweet music making it exceptionally popular in places where other instruments would be too loud.

Price including motor and 1 roll of music... $750.00

Extra rolls containing six selections, each... $6.00

One or two years later a new type of Wurlitzer *Automatic Harp* appeared, the *Style B.* Unlike the regular *Style A* model which was rectangular in outline, the *Style B* had the profile of a real harp. At the time of its introduction the *Style B* was offered for $600.00 which was $100.00 more than the then-current retail price ($500.00) for the Style A. Only a few of the *Style B* machines were ever made.

During the years from about 1905 to 1915 additional orders for two or three thousand harps were placed with Whitlock. These re-orders plus the original order for one thousand placed the total number made at three to four thousand.

Demand for the *Automatic Harp* dwindled as the novelty wore off. The retail price was reduced from $750.00 to $650.00, then to $500.00 and then, in 1916, to $375.00. Shortly thereafter the *Automatic Harp* was dropped from the Wurlitzer line. A few years later the sale of rolls (also made by Whitlock) for the machines was discontinued also.

The Wurlitzer Automatic Harp—Style A

Height, 6 ft. 6 in. Width, 3 ft. Depth, 2 ft.

PRICE—Complete with Electric Motor and 1 Roll of Music containing 6 selections.....$500.00
Extra Music Rolls, 6 selections each.................................... 4.50

Shipping Weight, 515 pounds.
Net Weight, 280 pounds.

The Automatic Harp was manufactured by J.W. Whitlock & Company of Rising Sun, Indiana. Wurlitzer became exclusive distributor in 1905. In addition to selling harps Wurlitzer maintained a large route of harps on location in the Cincinnati area. One employee of the Cincinnati office had as his sole duty changing rolls on these harps and emptying money from their coin boxes.

The Wurlitzer Automatic Harp

A Refined Musical Instrument for the Best Places.

The Wurlitzer Automatic Harp is one of the most wonderful self-playing musical instruments ever invented. The picking of the strings by little automatic fingers, almost human in their action, is a marvelous operation. It took eight years of constant study and unremitting effort to perfect the mechanism that operates these wonderful little fingers.

The Automatic Harp fills a niche in the field of music that cannot be filled by any other musical instrument. The Harp has always been the "Symbol of Music" even in the most select circles, because its sweet, mellow notes appeal to the lovers of soft, refined music as do those of no other instrument.

It is now nearly six years since we placed the Automatic Harp on the market. When it was first introduced, it created a sensation wherever seen and heard. Since then it has proved itself the best attraction and money-getter ever introduced in first-class public resorts where soft, refined music is required.

We are now building two styles of the Harp, Style "A," which is the original, and Style "B," the new style. The case of Style "A" is the straight front, with the harp-shaped plate glass and fancy scroll work decorations. (See illustration.) Style "B" is the new design, built on the lines of the original Italian Harp. This new-style case is very artistic and greatly enhances the appearance of the instrument.

The cases come in beautifully figured quarter-sawed oak in a variety of finishes, such as Golden, Weathered, Antwerp, Flemish, and silver gray.

DESCRIPTION OF THE AUTOMATIC HARP

The Automatic Harp is operated by an electric motor and a nickel-in-the-slot attachment. The music is produced by perforated paper music rolls, containing six selections each. The paper rolls are automatically rewound at the end of the last selection, in a few seconds, by the Automatic Music Roll Rewinding Device, and are then ready to repeat the program.

The Automatic Music Roll Rewinding Device is one of the features of all of our automatic musical instruments, and is the only practical method yet devised for taking care of the music roll on self-playing instruments.

The slot device on the Harp is the patented Magazine Slot, which will hold nickels enough at one time to run the entire music roll of six pieces through, and cannot be "worked."

The Harp has a new patented Tracker Bar Adjusting Screw, by means of which the Tracker Bar is quickly adjusted in case the paper music roll is not tracking properly. All metal parts are nickel-plated.

The entire mechanism of the Harp is surprisingly simple, being similar to that of the Electric Piano. Anyone of ordinary intelligence can easily master the working parts of the Harp and take care of it.

The Harp requires tuning more frequently than other automatic musical instruments, but the quickness and ease of tuning, more than offsets the difference between the attention it requires in this respect and that of the ordinary electric piano.

In tuning the Harp there is only one string to be brought up to pitch, whereas in tuning a piano, there are three strings that must be brought into unison. For this reason it takes an expert to tune a piano, while anyone with an ordinary ear for music can tune the Harp, after being shown how.

Original catalogue description of the Wurlitzer Automatic Harp. The description is continued on the following page.

One of the peculiarities of the Harp (and it is just being fully realized), is the fact that the older the instrument gets, the better the tone. This is accounted for by the same principle that makes a violin and other stringed instruments sweeter in tone as they grow older. The Harp is a stringed instrument, built on the same lines as the smaller stringed instruments that are played by hand.

This beautiful instrument has been the means of introducing the self-playing musical instrument into the very best class of public resorts—places where, previous to the advent of the Harp, no music at all was used. Weekly receipts taken from them during the past few years prove the Harp to be without question one of the most profitable investments ever placed in public places.

Any number of our nickel-in-the-slot boxes can be used in connection with the Harp, as with the PianOrchestra, so that it may be played from any part of the house.

Interior of a Style B Automatic Harp.

The Wurlitzer Automatic Harp—Style B

Height, 6 ft. 6 in.   Width, 3 ft.   Depth, 2 ft.

PRICE—Complete, with Electric Motor and 1 Roll of Music, containing 6 selections.....$600.00

Extra Music Rolls, 6 selections each.. 4.50

Shipping Weight, 545 pounds.
Net Weight, 310 pounds.

The Style B Automatic Harp with its ornate Italian case was introduced several years after the Style A. Harps were waning in popularity then, so only a few Style B machines were produced.

"THE MECCA," 431 Walnut St., CINCINNATI.

R. W. GRUBER.   FRED. B. SALMAR.

"The Mecca"

431 WALNUT STREET.
GRUBER & SALMAR, Proprietors.

Aged and Select Whiskies.

The Best Grades of Imported and American
Wines, Liquors and Cigars.
Telephone, 2394 Main.

Cincinnati, Jan 16-1906. 190

The Rudolph Wurlitzer Co.,
            City.

Gentlemen:-

            Ours was the first Cafe in Cincinnati to secure your
famous Automatic Harp, having had it almost nine months. The fact
that it has almost paid for itself in that short time, is the best
evidence of its wonderful popularity. We regard it as the greatest
musical entertainer for first class Cafes ever produced.

            Yours truly,

            Gruber & Salmar
            The Mecca.
            #431. Walnut St.

Judging from this letter the first Automatic Harp was installed in a Cincinnati restaurant in April or May, 1905. The information on this and the next four pages is taken from a 1906 Wurlitzer catalogue of automatic musical instruments that devoted 14 of its 20 pages to the then new Automatic Harp.

NIEMES', 5th and Vine Sts., CINCINNATI.

Above: John Niemes' cafe was one of the first in Cincinnati to secure an Automatic Harp.

Below: A listing of some of the locations in Cincinnati which had Automatic Harps in 1906. A total of 135 Harp locations were listed! Only about half are shown here.

A FEW OF THE REPRESENTATIVE PLACES IN CINCINNATI THAT ARE USING OUR INSTRUMENTS.

Name.	Address.	Kind of Inst.
Kramer, Chas. F.,	5th and Elm.	Harp
Kinzel, M.,	McMillan St.,	Harp
Koehler, John,	181 Fairfield Ave., Bellevue,	Harp
Kollmer, Anna,	Spring Grove & Amen Aves.,	Harp
Kreinebaum, Gustav,	500 E. 12th St.,	Pianino
Lackman Hotel,	Vine St.,	Harp
Litke, J. R.,	135 W. 5th St. (Indiana Hotel),	Harp
Lemker, Lawrence	514 Madison Ave., Covington,	Harp
Lampe, Wm.,	4th and York Sts., Newport,	Harp
Linchinger, A.,	1904 Vine St.,	Pianino
Le Grant,	600 Reading Rd.,	Harp
Lemmel, Paul,	Poplar and Western,	Pianino
Leonard & Weichering,	Clark and Linn,	Harp
Luebke, F.,	Gest and Freeman.	Pianino
Leesman Bros.,	1029 Freeman Ave.,	Harp
Locke, W. O.,	4937 Main Ave., Norwood,	Harp
Lucas, Henry W.,	2225 W. Clifton Ave.,	Pianino
Macke, R.,	517 Walnut St.,	Harp
Mecklenberg, Louis,	Highland & University Aves.,	Harp
Mackzum, R. G.,	4915 Main Ave., Norwood,	Harp
Mohr, M.,	513 Walnut St.,	Harp
Mecca,	413 Walnut St.,	Harp
Majestic,	526 Vine St.,	Harp
Mulligan, Jas.,	5th and Central,	Harp
Mulligan, Jas.,	516 Central Ave.,	Pianino
Miller,	1918 Madison Ave., Covington,	Pianino
Mueller Bros.,	Gilbert and McMillan,	Harp
Marqua, Chas. E.,	McMillan and Gilbert,	Harp
Meidel, M.,	Vine and Charlton,	Harp
Meister, Conrad,	2019 Central Ave.,	Harp
Martin,	5th and Baymiller	Pianino
Munroe Hotel,	27 W. 7th St.,	Harp
McGarvey,	1514 Russell St., Covington,	Pianino
Nougaret, A.,	231 E. 4th St,,	Harp
Niemes, J.,	9 W. 5th St.,	Harp
Nieberg & Shaefer,	8th and Madison Ave., Covington,	Harp
Osterholt, J. H.,	1916 Madison Ave., Covington,	Harp
Oehler & Renner,	1026 Gest St.,	Pianino
Oliver, E. W.,	Spring Grove, opp. Winton Sta.,	Harp
Parmerton & Robinson,	515 Walnut St.,	Harp
Pflamm, B.,	Pearl and Butler.	Harp
Prunello, Louis,	641 Walnut St.,	Harp
Parnell,	112 6th Ave., Dayton,	Pianino
Pittner, Jake,	619 College St.,	Pianino
Parmerton, Scott,	635 Central Ave.,	Harp
Pohlar, D.,	1600 Vine St.,	Harp
Page, H.,	1205 Vine St.,	Harp
Peterson, A.,	12th and Vine,	Harp
Poppe, G.,	7th and Carr	Pianino
Pfitzer, John,	Liberty and Freeman	Pianino

Name.	Address.	Kind of Inst.
Renner, Joseph,	520 Main St.,	Harp
Rand Hotel,	W. 5th St.,	Harp
Roehl & Crone,	11 E. 5th St.,	Harp
Rudd, Eugene,	414 Central Ave.,	Pianino
Robinson, T. & Bro.,	415 Central Ave.,	Pianino
Rinkenberger, Louis,	9th and Plum,	Harp
Ritte, Henry,	Main and Southern Latonia,	Harp
Roskopf, John C.,	2444 Gilbert Ave.,	Harp
Renner, H.,	1810 Vine St.,	Harp
Reichrath,	3720 Spring Grove Ave.,	Pianino
Rolfes, Ignatus,	654 Freeman Ave.,	Pianino
Sands, Wm. A.,	840 Bank St.,	Pianino
Sickenger, Chas. S.,	Pearl and Butler,	Harp
Smith, A. F.,	6 E. Front St.,	Harp
Starck, A. J.,	1121 Madison, Covington,	Harp
Schneider, Wm.,	11th and Brighton Sts., Newport,	Harp
Smith, E. W.,	Taylor and Walnut Sts., Bellevue,	Harp
Schmiesing, Fred.,	1640 Blair Ave.,	Harp
Storck, W. J.,	1216 Vine St.,	Harp
Stross Hotel,	24–26 W. 12th St.,	Harp
Schiller, Dan.,	Spring Grove and Platt,	Pianino
Smith, J. A.,	Bank and Freeman	Pianino
Silber, Chas. B.,	6th and Plum,	Harp
Schaefer, Jacob,	1500 Elm St.	Harp
Schmidlin,	4902 Main Ave., Norwood,	Harp
Seegmueller, Wm.,	137 Elder St.,	Harp
Spreen, Mrs. H.,	Betts and Baymiller,	Harp
Schupick, Louis J.,	Richmond and Freeman,	Pianino
Steinkamp, Edw.,	2829 Woodburn Ave.,	Pianino
Stratford Hotel,	636 Walnut St.,	Harp
Suhre, G.,	5th and Baymiller,	Harp
Schroerluke,	968 W. 5th St.,	Pianino
Thomas, E. H.,	415 W. 5th St.,	Harp
Terrany, Jake,	Court and Vine	Harp
Van Camp,	31 W. 6th St.,	Harp
Wulftange, Wm.,	35 E. 5th St.,	Harp
Wuebben, Herman,	714 E. Pearl St.,	Harp
Wyss, Joseph,	Elm and George,	Harp
Wright, E.,	George and Central	Pianino
Woest, H. C.,	615 Main St., Latonia,	Harp
Wuebben, Henry,	1113 Main St.,	Harp
Winzing, Tony,	East End,	Pianino
Wermil, Wm. J.,	2153 W. 8th St.,	Pianino
Wilhelm, A.,	Bank and Coleman,	Pianino
Willis, A.,	1035 Central Ave.,	Pianino
Walter, J.,	1011 Liberty St.,	Pianino
Wrede, B.,	Court and Baymiller,	Harp
Yunk, C. H.,	8th and Main, Covington,	Harp
Zoo Club House,	Zoo,	2 Harps

"THE BISMARK," 430 Walnut St., CINCINNATI.

"MUSIC HATH POWER TO SOOTHE THE SAVAGE BREAST."

PROBABLY no truer saying was ever quoted to illustrate the power music exerts over the human race. What must be its influence in our advanced civilization if it has power to touch a tender spot in the breast of the untamed savage? No man can answer.

Go back through the dark ages from the beginning of history and we find that all nations and tribes at all times had their musical instruments of some kind or other and so it will be in the generations to come as long as the race exists, music will continue to play its important role in the affairs of man.

Notwithstanding the fact that music is as old as humanity itself, it has never been so popular among all classes of people as it is at the present time.

The perfecting of instruments that play automatically is propably responsible more than any other one cause for this great popularity. The ability to produce good music at will, by the pressing of a little button or the dropping of a coin in a slot without the expense of a musical education or the hiring of trained musicians, enables us all to gratify our love for music.

MUSIC IN PUBLIC PLACES.

With the great stride forward in the production of automatic instruments, has come a popular demand for music in all public places where people congregate for social intercourse, or, to while away an idle moment, so that today it can be safely said, that no public place is complete without its music of some kind. Nothing is more attractive in a public place of recreation or amusement than music, and the general public is not slow in showing their approval by opening their pocket books to pay for it as is amply proven by the great success of our automatic musical instruments. We have over two hundred instruments in the best Hotels, Cafes and Restaurants of Cincinnati, and their popularity is fully attested by the testimonials of some of the representative cafe owners, found in this booklet.

CINCINNATI, OHIO, January 20, 1906.

THE RUDOLPH WURLITZER CO.,
CITY.

Gentlemen:—
    The Wurlitzer Automatic Harp, placed in our Cafe a few months back has proven a wonderful success as an entertainer and money maker, so that today we regard it as an absolute necessity for first-class cafes.
                              Yours truly,
                              THE BISMARK CAFE CO.
                                   EMIL SCHMITT, Mgr.

The Bismark Cafe furnished Wurlitzer with a testimonial for the Automatic Harp. Evidently Wurlitzer's copy writer liked the theatre, for he quotes from William Congreve's play "The Mourning Bride," Act 1, Scene 1, written in 1697.
    "Music hath charms to soothe the savage breast, to soften rocks,
        or bend a knotted oak."

EIMER'S, 532 Walnut St., CINCINNATI.

AUTOMATIC MUSICAL INSTRUMENTS AS MONEY MAKERS.

THOUSANDS of dollars are spent now days by up-to-date hotel, cafe and restaurant owners in decorating and beautifying their places, for the pleasure and comfort of their patrons, but of all the works of art, beautiful frescoes and modern conveniences, nothing adds more to the patrons' pleasure than the sweet strains of music, or brings larger returns on the investment, if it is one of our automatic instruments. We can show many instances where our automatic instruments have been the means of increasing the bar trade from 10 to 25 per cent. Aside from this increase of the bar trade there is positively no legitimate investment that can be made in connection with the cafe business, that will pay such heavy dividends. Receipts from many of our instruments show as high as 300 per cent on the investment and never less than 50 per cent. As an example, there are a number of our automatic harps in Cincinnati, that have taken in their cash price in nine months, and would undoubtedly have taken 50 per cent more if they had been owned by the proprietors and received the same close attention given to their bar trade. Where on earth can such a rate of interest be made on a safe legitimate investment?

WHY OUR AUTOMATIC MUSICAL INSTRUMENTS ARE SO SUCCESSFUL.

In the first place we are the largest manufacturers of automatic musical instruments in America. We have devoted many years to developing and perfecting a line of automatic instruments that lead the world.

We have succeeded in eliminating the complicated mechanisms usually found in all automatic instruments, thus making our instruments so simple that any one of ordinary intelligence can understand and take care of them without the help of expert mechanics.

By reason of the enormous sales of our automatic instruments, we can afford to cut and supply a greater variety of new music which is the most important factor (after a good instrument) in its success as a money maker. We cut about 12 new selections per week, or over 500 per year, this means we give our patrons every good selection composed.

We have a splendid organization of expert mechanics trained in the automatic business to tune, regulate and keep our instruments in perfect condition. We keep in close touch with each one of our city customers through a special telephone operator in our exchange who calls up daily, to see that they are getting perfect service, such as tuning, change of music, repairs, etc.

Complete records are kept in our office showing the exact time every telephone call is made, where from, who answered, what was wanted the repairman's number, when trouble was remedied and other general information.

The above details will give the reader some idea of why the house of WURLITZER is conceded to be the leader in the automatic musical business.

THE RUDOLPH WURLITZER CO., CITY.   CINCINNATI, OHIO, January 28, 1906.

    Gentlemen:—

        The Wurlitzer Automatic Harp placed in my cafe a few months ago has proven such a great success as an entertainer and money getter that we would not be without it.   Yours truly,

                                                                                WILLIAM EIMER.

The above text notes that 12 new selections (2 rolls as there were 6 tunes per roll) were cut for the Harp each week. Telephoning each of the Wurlitzer customers in Cincinnati daily must have been a tremendous task.

THE "WURLITZER HARP."

AFTER eight years constant labor and one year thorough test, the Wurlitzer Automatic Harp is now ready for the general market. This beautiful instrument is conceded by all to be the most wonderful as well as sweetest musical instrument ever produced. It is one of the latest additions to our automatic line, and as a refined musical attraction has no rival. The harp contains 60 strings in full view, being covered with plate glass, showing the operation of the almost human fingers as they pick them. It is operated by perforated paper rolls containing six tunes each.

The soft sweet music of the harp makes it especially desirable where a piano cannot be used, on account of its being too loud.

As a money maker, the "Wurlitzer Harp" has proven itself the king of them all.

DESCRIPTION.

CASE: Handsome quarter-sawed oak with carved panels. HEIGHT: 6 feet 6 inches. WIDTH: 3 feet. DEPTH: 2 feet.

The perforated music rolls are only 8½ inches wide, contain six tunes each, and are automatically rewound in 30 seconds when the end of the roll is reached. A dial, with numbers from 1 to 6, always indicates the number of the tune that is being played. An electric light on the inside just above the strings, proves an attractive feature. A most important feature is the new coin detecting slot by which every coin dropped in the instrument can be seen; thus preventing the use of spurious coins and slugs to operate it.

Price $750.00
INCLUDING ONE ROLL OF MUSIC.

Extra Rolls . . . . $7.50 each.
LIST OF MUSIC ON REQUEST.

THE HARP IS FURNISHED WITH EITHER DIRECT OR ALTERNATING CURRENT MOTORS.

SOLD FOR CASH OR ON EASY PAYMENTS.

A Refined Musical Attraction, with Nickel-in-Slot Attachment and Operated by Electricity

One of the earliest advertisements for the Automatic Harp.

Below: Businesses within the city limits of Cincinnati, Covington, Newport, Bellevue and Dayton could install a Harp or Pianino on a percentage basis.

A BUSINESS PROPOSITION.

MOST BUSINESS MEN with money to invest are glad to find a safe investment that will net them 6 per cent on their capital. If you have money to invest and a Cafe or Public Resort, where you do even enough business to make a fair living, we can prove to you before you invest one cent, that one of our automatic musical instruments will pay you at least 50 per cent on your investment in actual receipts, taken from the instrument, to say nothing of the increased bar receipts it will bring you.

If you have no money to invest, or do not care to, we are perfectly willing to invest for you and place one of our automatic harps or pianinos in your place on per cent and let it pay for itself out of its receipts, provided you are not outside of the city limits of Cincinnati, Covington, Newport, Bellevue or Dayton. Thus you are enabled to become the owner of a fine musical instrument and a great money maker without any cost to you.

If you want to keep up with the march of progress in your business you can not afford to be without a good instrument, and we have made the terms and conditions so liberal, that every cafe or public resort in this city can and should have one of our instruments.

If you have any doubts as to the benefits of music in your place, just look over the list on another page of representative cafes and saloons using our instruments, and read what some of them have to say concerning them, then call and see us, or drop a postal and our representative will call on you. Do this today, don't wait until tomorrow. A good musical instrument will help your business more than anything else you can lawfully have in your place.

The original J. W. Whitlock factory as it stands today in Rising Sun, Indiana. In this factory the first Automatic Harps were built.

Stewart Whitlock, son of J. W. Whitlock, examines a style B Automatic Harp, one of three Harps (a Style A and two Style B machines) he sold the author in 1965. The Harps were in "mint" condition and had been stored on the Whitlock premises since their manufacture over half-century ago. A few rolls and spare parts were also acquired — all that remained from the once-extensive Harp manufacturing facility.

This larger factory also stands today in Rising Sun. This factory was built in order to provide facilities to fill Wurlitzer's order for one thousand Harps. (see text, page 185).

THE J. W. WHITLOCK COMPANY

Rising Sun, Indiana is a pleasant little community located on the west bank of the Ohio River about thirty-five miles downstream from Cincinnati, Ohio. The author travelled there in 1965 and talked with Stewart Whitlock and his sister, both of whom had many recollections of the days of the Automatic Harp.

After a year or so of experimenting J. W. Whitlock patented the Automatic Harp in 1899. In 1905 an agreement was signed with the Rudolph Wurlitzer Company of Cincinnati whereby Wurlitzer agreed to buy one thousand machines. A new building was built to provide the space to manufacture these. On the second floor of the new building the rolls for the Automatic Harp were produced. The rolls were arranged by two women (one of them Mrs. J. W. Whitlock) who marked and edited pieces of sheet music and then played the tunes on a recording device which cut a master roll. The roll perforator then made copies from the masters. In later years the perforating machinery was sold for scrap metal.

After the original order for one thousand Harps was filled Wurlitzer ordered an additional thousand. Demand for the Harps waned and the total number produced from a second order was only five hundred or so machines. (This account as given from the recollections of Mr. Stewart Whitlock differs from Mr. Farny Wurlitzer's recollections of orders for 3 or 4 thousand Harps.)

Following his success with the Automatic Harp J. W. Whitlock experimented with a violin-playing machine. A prototype which used bowing discs (similar to the Mills Violano-Virtuoso) was produced, but the device was not successful.

In later years the J. W. Whitlock Company engaged in a number of other ventures including the manufacture of radios, race-horse amusement machines and other items. Today the J. W. Whitlock Company is active in the boat and furniture business.

An "Annual Clean-up of Factory Rebuilt Wurlitzer Automatic Musical Instruments" held by the Dayton, Ohio branch store about this time featured an *Automatic Harp* for $62.00 and another one for just $45.00.

The Wurlitzer coin-operated *88-Note Player Piano* was an ephemeral addition to the Wurlitzer line. Appearing first in catalogues about 1906 it was listed only for six or seven years after which it was dropped.

A 1907 Wurlitzer catalogue described this machine as follows:

"The Wurlitzer *88-Note Player Piano* is another recent addition to our line. It is the first and only complete automatic piano ever constructed; by complete we mean a full-sized keyboard piano, playing the entire scale of 88 notes with expression and operated either by the touch of a button, nickel-in-the-slot device or played by hand in the usual way.

To more clearly explain why it is the only complete piano it must be understood that no other automatic piano plays more than 65 notes, or about two-thirds of the standard piano scale, and has no means of regulating the expression . . .

The Wurlitzer 88-Note Player Piano—Style A

Playing the Full Keyboard of 88 Notes.

Height, 4 ft. 9 in. Width, 5 ft. 3 in. Depth, 2 ft. 4 in.

PRICE—Complete, with Electric Motor, and 1 Roll of Music, containing 5 selections......$800.00

Extra Music Rolls, 5 selections, each...................................... 4.50

Shipping Weight, 1,025 pounds.
Net Weight, 755 pounds.

The Wurlitzer 88-Note Player Piano was the first Wurlitzer roll-operated coin piano with a keyboard. Introduced about 1906 it was supplanted within a year or two by the 65-Note Player Piano. The 88-Note model was discontinued a few years later.

The Wurlitzer 88-Note Player Piano—Style B
Designed Especially for Home Use

This instrument is operated by a push button instead of nickel-in-the-slot, and is designed for home use. Otherwise, the general description of Wurlitzer 88-Note Player Piano—Style A, on page 25, applies to this style.

This Player Piano for home use has a very great advantage over the ordinary instrument operated by foot-power. It is only necessary to push the button, and the owner may sit back and enjoy as fine a performance of any musical selection as any artist can produce by expert hand-playing. There is no tiresome pumping or foot-pedaling; no bother with intricate control features. In short, no skill nor exertion is required to produce an artistic performance.

Everything is entirely automatic when the electric current is turned on. At other times it serves as an excellent high-grade piano for hand-playing.

Height, 4 ft. 9 in. Width, 5 ft. 3 in. Depth, 2 ft. 4 in.
PRICE—Complete, with Electric Motor and 1 Roll of Music, containing 5 selections.....$850.00
Extra Music Rolls, 5 selections each..................................... 4.50
Shipping Weight, 1,025 pounds.
Net Weight, 755 pounds.

The Style B 88-Note Player Piano was intended for use in private homes. Like the coin-operated model the Style B was a short-lived type.

The Wurlitzer 88-Note Player Piano—Style A

The only AUTOMATIC ELECTRIC PIANO, playing the entire keyboard of 88 notes with real musical expression.

Ever since self-playing pianos were invented, efforts have been made to perfect a piano that would play with expression, the same as a human performer plays. Little progress was made along this line, however, until we succeeded in perfecting our new 88-Note Player Piano.

This wonderful piano not only plays with expression, but plays the entire keyboard of 88 notes as well. To thoroughly appreciate these advantages, it must be understood that no other automatic piano built plays the entire 88 notes, and has the means of regulating the shading and expression. So superior is the new Wurlitzer 88-Note Player Piano to all other pianos operated by electricity, that it cannot be compared with anything else of its kind.

It is the first complete and perfect automatic piano playing the entire keyboard of 88 notes ever built, and is, beyond all question, the best any amount of money can buy. It is intended for fine hotels, private apartments and homes, and all other first-class places where a high standard of musical excellence is required.

Those seeking the very best in a self-playing piano, that can also be played by hand in the usual way, have only to hear this latest triumph in a self-playing piano to realize how far it is ahead of any other automatic piano ever built.

GENERAL DESCRIPTION

The Wurlitzer Player Piano is a strictly high-grade piano in every respect. It is constructed of the very best materials, assembled by expert piano builders. Besides containing all the important improvements found in our 65-Note Player Piano, it plays the entire keyboard of 88 notes with real musical expression, the same as a skilled human performer playing by hand.

The cases are double veneered mahogany, quarter-sawed oak and silver gray ash of very artistic design, with rich mouldings and panels. The oak cases come in golden, weathered, Flemish, and silver gray finishes.

The mechanism by which the instrument is operated is the simplest ever devised, and can not give trouble. It is operated by our new Direct Drive Gear, which transmits the motive power direct, without the use of troublesome belts and pulleys. It has our patent Speed Regulator, by which the tempo of the music is adjusted to any desired speed; our Magazine Coin Detector Slot; our Automatic Music Roll Rewinding Device, by means of which the paper music rolls are kept in shape; a metal tracker bar and metal tracker frame, and our new patent tracker bar adjusting screw, by means of which the tracker bar is quickly adjusted in case the paper music roll is not tracking properly, and the adjustable Music Roll Flange for lengthening and shortening the music roll. All metal parts are nickel-plated.

No one desiring a high-grade piano, that may be played either by electricity or by hand, in the usual way, would have anything else after seeing and hearing this modern instrument.

Any number of our nickel-in-the-slot boxes can be used in connection with the 88-Note Player Piano, as with the PianOrchestra, so that it may be played from any part of the house.

The new Wurlitzer *Player Piano* will undoubtedly bear out our unqualified claim as the finest and best Automatic Player Piano ever built."

A year after the above *88-Note Player Piano* description was printed the *65-Note Player Piano* made its entry. Although according to the above description it was an "incomplete" piano the *65-Note Player Piano* with its limited scale of notes became the sales leader. The *65-Note* roll, as mentioned earlier, was versatile and could be used on a wide variety of machines. Accordingly, the *88-Note* model was phased out.

Like other Wurlitzer automatic musical instruments built before 1909 (with the exception of the *Automatic Harp* and the *PianOrchestras*) the early *88-Note Player Pianos* were made by Eugene De-Kleist at North Tonawanda. After 1909 production continued under Wurlitzer's ownership with Farny Wurlitzer in charge of the operations. Assisting him until 1914 was Eugene DeKleist's son, August.

One of the most lively Wurlitzer musical machines ever made was the *Mandolin Quartette*. Anyone listening to one of these machines today cannot help but agree with the Wurlitzer catalogue description of over half a century ago, "The music is much louder than that of any piano or other instrument of its size, and the trilling of the mandolins, together with the piano accompaniment, produces a charming musical effort that cannot fail to delight the most fastidious music-lovers."

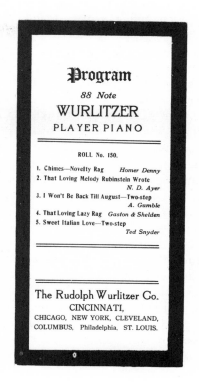

Program card for the 88-Note Player Piano.

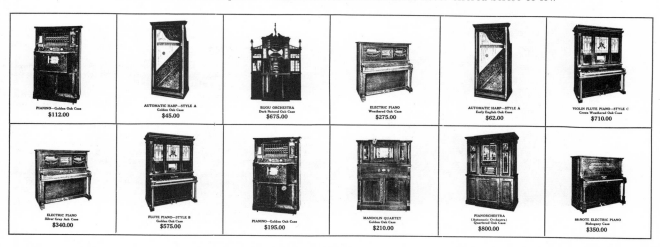

An interesting array of rebuilt used Wurlitzer machines offered for sale by the Dayton branch store. What coin piano collector today wouldn't give an eyetooth to buy machines at these prices of fifty years ago!

The *Mandolin Quartette* consisted of a 34-note piano section and a 27-note mandolin part. The mandolin effect was produced by small wooden hammers vibrating against the metal piano strings by means of a revolving cam.

The *Mandolin Quartette* made its debut around 1906. An early catalogue description read:

THE MANDOLIN QUARTETTE

The *Mandolin Quartette* is the latest addition to our automatic line. It is the result of several years' experiment and effort to produce something entirely new and different from anything else on the market. To say it is a success, is but mildly expressing the praise it has received from those who have seen and heard it.

The *Mandolin Quartette* is a combination instrument producing the beautiful trill of mandolins with piano accompaniment so naturally that it at once delights and fascinates the music lover. It is hard to convey in cold type an adequate idea of the charming musical effects rendered by this wonderful instrument, suffice it to say, it has created a sensation wherever it has been heard...

As a money maker the *Mandolin Quartette* bids fair to break all records, and those fortunate enough to secure the first of these instruments in their locality will simply coin money."

Early Mandolin Quartette case design. This design with beveled oval glass windows was used from about 1906 to a few years later when it was replaced by the design shown below.

The Mandolin Quartette

Height, 5 ft. Width, 3 ft. 11 in. Depth, 1 ft. 7½ in.

PRICE—Complete, with Electric Motor and 1 Roll of music, containing 5 selections.....$650.00
Extra Music Rolls, 5 selections each.................................... 4.50

Shipping Weight, 705 pounds.
Net Weight, 490 pounds.

The Mandolin Quartette is a recent addition to our line of self-playing musical instruments, and is one of the most desirable musical instruments ever invented. It is a combination of mandolin effects accompanied by a piano. The music is much louder than that of any piano or other instrument of its size, and the trilling of the mandolins, together with the piano accompaniment, produces a charming musical effect that cannot fail to delight the most fastidious music-lovers.

The Mandolin Quartette has scored one of the biggest hits ever made by any kind of self-playing musical instrument, not musically alone, but as a money-getter as well. It has frequently taken in as high as $10.00 per day in nickels. What stronger proof of its popularity could be asked?

DESCRIPTION OF MANDOLIN QUARTETTE

The Mandolin Quartette comes in beautiful quarter-sawed oak, mahogany and silver gray ash cases, of handsome and attractive design. The oak cases come in golden, weathered, Flemish and silver gray finishes.

The top panel is divided into three sections, of which the middle section is a plate glass door on hinges, that may be readily opened to change the music roll or regulate the tempo of the music. On either side of this plate glass door are small glass openings, through which the coin detecting slot and the program are seen.

The number of each selection is stamped on the music roll, which may be seen through the plate glass door in front. By consulting the program, the next selecttion to be played is shown, thus enabling customers to know what they are going to hear next.

The instrument is constructed on the same simple principle as the Pianino, the difference being in the action, which is divided, thirty-four notes for the piano and twenty-seven notes for the mandolin part.

It contains our new Direct Drive Gear arrangement, which transmits the motive power direct from the motor, and eliminates the troublesome belts and pulleys; our Magazine Coin Detector Slot, which will hold nickels enough at one time to run the roll of five selections through, and our Automatic Music Roll Rewinding Device, by which the music roll is always kept wound on its two spools, so that it cannot get out of shape from the effects of the atmosphere.

The Mandolin Quartette has a metal tracker bar and metal tracker frame. All metal parts are nickel-plated. It also has a patent tempo regulator, which perfectly controls the time of the music.

Another valuable feature is the new patented tracker bar adjusting screw, by means of which the tracker bar is quickly adjusted in case the paper music roll is not tracking properly, and the adjustable flange for lengthening or shortening the music roll.

The tempo of the music on the Mandolin Quartette can be quickly regulated to any desired speed by means of a small patent speed regulator in front of the music roll.

The interior is lit up with electric lights while playing, showing the piano and mandolin action in operation.

Any number of our nickel-in-the-slot boxes can be used in connection with the Mandolin Quartette, as with the PianOrchestra, so that it may be played from any part of the house.

The Mandolin Quartette imitated the trilling of mandolins. Those who heard the Mandolin Quartette were charmed by its music.

Interior view of the Mandolin Quartette. This illustration is from a salesman's catalogue of Wurlitzer machines owned by Joseph Bacigalupi whose father owned Peter Bacigalupi & Sons, leading automatic musical instrument dealer in San Francisco during the first few decades of the 20th century. Peter Bacigalupi & Sons were distributors for Wurlitzer, Cremona and North Tonawanda Musical Instrument Works machines.

The Mandolin Sextette

Height, 4 ft. 9¼ in.   Width, 3 ft. 11½ in.   Depth, 1 ft. 10¼ in.

PRICE—Complete, with Electric Motor and 1 Roll of Music, containing 5 selections.....**$850.00**

Extra Music Rolls, 5 selections each.................................... **4.50**

Shipping Weight, 750 pounds.
Net Weight, 525 pounds.

The Mandolin Sextette. These were strictly a limited production item and were on the market for only a short time.

The Mandolin Sextette

The Mandolin Sextette is another new and exceedingly attractive addition to our great line of nickel-in-the-slot musical entertainers. The music of the Mandolin Sextette is a decided novelty, being different from that of any other musical instrument ever invented. It closely resembles a small orchestra of Violins and Mandolins, with Piano accompaniment. The beautiful trilling of the mandolins, mingled with the strains of the violins, and the piano rounding out the melody, produces a musical attraction that is bound to make a hit wherever heard.

The Mandolin Sextette is built in cases of remarkably handsome design, in beautifully figured mahogany veneers, light and dark weathered, golden, Flemish and the new silver gray oak and ash. The top panel is divided into three sections, the middle section being a plate glass door, giving access to the music roll. On each side are glass panels, showing the magazine coin detector slot and the program. In the center of the bottom panel is a large plate glass through which is seen the violin pipes. Over the plate glass is a handsome scroll in the form of a lyre. The interior is lit up by electric lights while playing.

The mechanism of the Mandolin Sextette is very simple, in fact, practically the same as that of our automatic pianos, expect that the piano action is divided into two sections, one section of 34 notes for the piano, and the other of 27 notes for the mandolin.

The violin pipes are set in the front at the bottom of the case, with a bird's-eye maple panel behind them, making a very neat background for the pipes, and at the same time hiding the interior mechanism.

It contains our Direct Drive Gear, Magazine Coin Detector Slot, metal Tracker Bar and Tracker Frame (all metal parts handsomely nickel-plated), Patent Tracker Bar Adjusting Thumb Screw, Patent Tempo Regulator, and all our modern improvements, making it a practical coin operated musical instrument that cannot fail to give universal satisfaction.

The Mandolin Sextette is operated by perforated paper music rolls, containing five selections each. The music rolls are the same as the Mandolin Quartette rolls, and can be used on both instruments.

Any number of our nickel-in-the-slot boxes can be used in connection with the Mandolin Sextette, as with the PianOrchestra, so that it may be played from any part of the house.

WURLITZER Electric Piano—Autograph Style

The WURLITZER Autograph Piano renders an absolutely true reproduction of the individual interpretations personally played by many of the world's renowned artists. The Autograph Piano is a distinct departure from any instrument ever manufactured for use in supplying musical entertainment in public places, especially designed to play the most difficult classical compositions COMPLETE. This Piano is to the PUBLIC PLACE of business, what the REPRODUCING PLAYER GRAND PIANO is to the PRIVATE HOME.

This instrument is equipped with the WURLITZER Patented Automatic Roll-Changer. Height, 4 ft. 9 in. Width, 5 ft. 1 in. Depth, 2 ft. 4¾ in. Shipping Weight, 1050 lbs.

AUTOGRAPH REPRODUCING ROLLS
Price, Per Roll, Without Spool, $3.75
Extra Spool, $1.25

ROLL No. 70079

Ukulele Lady—Fox Trot..............................Kahn & Whiting
Played by Max Kortlander
Some Day We'll Meet Again—Fox Trot..............Van Loan
Played by Kortlander & Arden
The Midnight Waltz..............................Donaldson
Played by Harold Scott
The Flapper Wife—Fox Trot......................Carl Rup
Played by Scott & Watters
Moonlight and Roses—Fox Trot..............Black & Moret

The Autograph Reproducing Piano was listed in Wurlitzer catalogues in the 1920's. Like other Wurlitzer pianos of this era it was equipped with the roll-changing mechanism. Unlike other types of Wurlitzer coin piano rolls, the Autograph Reproducing rolls were recorded by famous pianists.

Introduced at $750.00 the price of the *Mandolin Quartette* dropped a few years later to $650.00.

A few *Mandolin Quartettes* containing a rank of violin pipes were produced. At first these were sold as *Mandolin Quartettes* with pipes added for $200.00 extra. Soon the name was changed to the *Mandolin Sextette* and the machine was given a separate catalogue designation. In the 1912 Wurlitzer catalogue (portions of which are reproduced in this book) the *Mandolin Sextette* was described as resembling "a small orchestra of Violins and Mandolins, with Piano accompaniment."

Only a few *Mandolin Quartettes* survive today. Most of those which do may be traced to a hoard unearthed several years ago by John and Stella Ragan of Caledonia, Wisconsin. Like the Providence, Rhode Island, Roehl hoard mentioned earlier the Ragan find consisted mostly of earlier machines. Included in the group were several *Mandolin Quartettes*, a number of *Pianinos* and other coin pianos of the pre-Prohibition era. The old timer from whom they purchased the pianos had operated them on a route many years earlier. Incidentally, it was the Wurlitzer *Pianino*, he said, that was the most consistent money maker for him in those days.

Last but not least in the Wurlitzer line-up was the Wurlitzer coin-operated *Autograph Reproducing Piano* which was, as the name implies, a reproducing piano intended for commercial use.

The advertisements for the *Autograph Reproducing Piano* proclaimed that "This piano is to the PUBLIC PLACE of business what the REPRODUCING PLAYER GRAND PIANO is to the PRIVATE HOME."

Evidently the intended place for *all* reproducing pianos was the private home . . . for the *Autograph Reproducing Piano* found little success in the marketplace. Wurlitzer was not the only manufacturer to have this experience. Seeburg, with its competing *Style X Expression Piano* billed as having been "designed for locations demanding a reproducing instrument," met with similar diffidence. The patrons of honky-tonks, taverns and the like preferred *There'll be a Hot Time in the Old Town Tonight* or some other toe-tapping melody to the classical selections which made up most of the *Autograph Reproducing Piano's* repertoire.

Also, the *Autograph Reproducing Piano* missed the heyday of coin-piano sales ... it was not introduced until the 1920's.

Here concludes our chronicle of machines made by Wurlitzer and other manufacturers.

One unfortunate aspect of a book on this subject is that neither the printed words nor the illustrations can convey *exactly* what these machines sounded like. Capitol Piano and Organ Company said of its *Jazz Concert Orchestra:* "Your customers will go wild about it ... People passing your doors will stop to listen to the sweet music and will drop in ..." Wurlitzer, describing one of its *PianOrchestras,* came up with this question, "What can be more fascinating than to feast the eye on the rich carvings, while from the interior are conjured forth the rich vibrating tones of the instruments, which commingly dissolve into enchanting melody filling the soul with rapturous delight?" What a thrilling question this was!

In 1920 your curiosity could have been satisfied by visiting the nearest Seeburg, Wurlitzer, Welte or other showroom ... or a local speakeasy, ballroom or hotel. Today, however, is a different story. These machines are an extinct species. The only surviving ones are those carefully preserved by collectors and museums.

Listening to early coin operated pianos and orchestrions today is spine-tingling experience. Every machine has its own personality. The difference between a *Mandolin Quartette* and a *PianOrchestra* or the difference between a *Seeburg G* orchestrion and a Mills *Violano-Virtuoso* is the difference between day and night. Every machine has its own distinctive features which separate it from all others.

We will probably never know what a *Paganini Violin Orchestra* or a *Capitol Jazz Concert Orchestra* or an Engelhardt *Banjorchestra* did sound like ... we can only wistfully contemplate the sounds which once were regarded as commonplace, as none of these particular machines have survived the sands of time. The same is true of many others.

Some machines do survive. Many of these, some restored and others untouched as yet, are illustrated on the pages which follow. Our photo album shows some of the machines which remain from the one hundred thousand or more which were once scattered all across America, from the biggest cities to the smallest country crossroads.

Other machines survive ... but no one recognizes them. They are behind plaster walls, covered with dusty props backstage in a theatre, in the loft of a tumbledown barn or in any of a thousand different other places. If you chance to find one, and may Lady Luck be with you, you will have not just an ordinary antique ... but one which will *come to life* with the drop of a nickel and reward you with the long-forgotten tunes of yesteryear.

 PHOTO ALBUM

— COIN-OPERATED PIANOS AND ORCHESTRIONS —

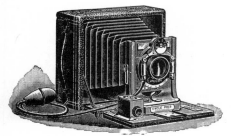

On the following pages are photographs of a few of the coin-operated pianos and orchestrions preserved by collectors today.

Right: This WurliTzer Pianino was rescued after having spent many years in a leaky Rhode Island barn. With its veneer peeling, glass broken in and general poor condition it will present a challenge to restore.

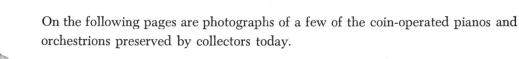

Top: John Lemmer of Chicago is shown with his Wurlitzer coin piano — a machine somewhat similar to the DX pictured on p. 125. Left: Regina Sublima piano (also sold by Wurlitzer as the Wurlitzer Tremolo Piano). This machine operates mechanically (rather than pneumatically) and produces a trilling sound not unlike a Wurlitzer Mandolin Quartette — but of lesser volume. Following its success with music boxes Regina sought to diversify its business. Entering the coin-operated piano field the firm produced several different styles including the Regina Sublima and a 65-note pneumatically-operated piano which used a standard "A" roll.

This section of William Allen's music hall in Santa Ana, California displays (left to right): Nelson-Wiggen "A" roll cabinet piano with xylophone and orchestra bells, Wurlitzer photoplayer with side chest (uses Wurlitzer 65-note Automatic Player Piano rolls), Cremona Orchestral K orchestrion and Seeburg KT orchestrion.

This duplex "Electrotone" piano was manufactured by the North Tonawanda Musical Instrument Works. For many years it saw hard service in the Grand Opera House in Meridian, Mississippi (see inset). In 1956 Leslie Hagwood of that city learned of the machine in the theatre which had been vacant since the 1920's. After many letters and telephone calls to the theatre owners the machine was acquired. Today the machine is once again pounding out ragtime tunes and show music.

Peerless orchestrion in the collection of Ed Zelinsky of San Francisco, California. Sometime during its life this machine was converted to play Cremona "M" rolls instead of Peerless rolls. Conversions were not unusual, especially when rolls for a particular type of machine were discontinued. However, the practice was far more prevalent with band organs than with coin pianos and orchestrions.

Jerry Cohen, a music box and coin piano collector from Studio City, California, admires a Style B Wurlitzer Harp (see pp. 188-189) at Svoboda's Nickelodeon Tavern in Chicago Heights, Illinois.

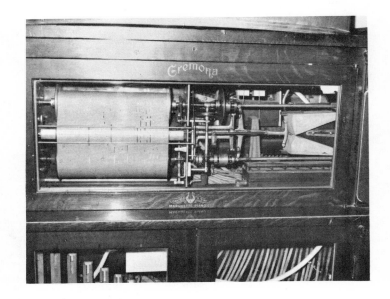

A rare cabinet style Cremona coin piano in Svoboda's Nickelodeon Tavern. Note the rank of violin pipes in the lower part of the case. This machine uses the style "M" roll and was originally equipped with the Cremona Tune Selecting Device (see p. 44). Unlike the machine shown above most Cremona coin pianos had a keyboard.

National Automatic piano from the collection of Gary Sage, Seaside, California. This machine features a ferris-wheel type of roll mechanism under the keyboard. Each roll contains one tune. The desired tune may be selected by dropping a coin into the appropriate coin slot (there is a separate slot for each roll). National Automatic pianos are fairly plentiful on the West Coast and were originally distributed mainly there.

Jerry Doring of San Gabriel, California is shown holding the motor of his fine Wurlitzer orchestrion. Using the long-frame type 65-note Wurlitzer Automatic Player Piano roll this machine contains a piano with mandolin, flute pipes, bass drum, snare drum and triangle as accompaniment.

This Wurlitzer Style L Orchestra Piano in the Sage collection is similar to the Clark machine illustrated on page 135. The Sage machine has the long roll frame device rather than the roll changer.

Early Peerless coin piano owned by Gary Sage of Seaside, California. Like certain other early coin pianos the Peerless shown above has the roll mechanism in a box attached to the back of the piano. This system was not met with favor in its day as the owner of such a piano would have either to put it out two or three feet from a wall or else move the piano every time a roll change was needed.

Above and left: Seeburg "Grayhound" piano in the collection of Pete Schaeble of Queens, N.Y. A pack of greyhound dogs race as the music plays. When the music stops the winner is the dog nearest the striped pole. As with the Mills Race Horse Piano the Seeburg machine provided tavern patrons with visual as well as musical entertainment. Western Electric Piano Company, the Seeburg subsidiary, marketed a similar device called the "Derby."

Bill Stackhouse of Napanoch, New York is the proud owner of this fine Peerless Arcadian orchestrion (see p. 22). This machine uses the rare Peerless "O" roll and contains a wide variety of orchestra instruments. Note the striped grain design of the quartered oak. Quartered oak was the most popular wood veneer of the 1900-1930 era.

Wurlitzer Style 153 band organ in the collection of Harold Shaner of Cumberland, Maryland. The 153 was one of the most popular Wurlitzer styles (see p. 88).

Above left: The Peerless factories in St. Johnsville, N.Y. as they appear today — the present home of the Little Falls Felt Shoe Co.
Above right: Ed Freyer of Flemington, New Jersey is shown with his Acme perforator. Ed provides collectors all over the country with quality recuts of "A", "G" and Link rolls.

The Miles Mountain Musical Museum of Eureka Springs, Arkansas is one of several United States tourist attractions which feature restored coin pianos and orchestrions. Above, Floyd Miles explains the operation of a Coinola X orchestrion (see p. 48).

Automatic musical instruments are always a delight to the younger set. The young tot shown above listens intently to the output of a Coinola piano with mandolin and solo xylophone. Some collectors have just a single machine — the star attraction of a game room, den or living room. Others have built extensive collections — starting with a basic "A" piano roll or Wurlitzer 65-note piano and adding other types as they become available.

This is how you find them. This Wurlitzer Mandolin Quartette, property of the Mission Piano Company of San Francisco, awaits restoration.

Above: Violano-Virtuoso in a restaurant in Montana's famous Virginia City. It is doing today what it did many years ago — taking in coins by the hundreds.

To the right: Oswald Wurdeman, curator of the Virginia City automatic musical instrument collection, examines the perforations in a band organ master roll. He is an old timer, having first entered the business in the 1920's when his father owned the Electric Violin Company of Minneapolis, a distributor and operator of Mills, Western Electric and other machines.

The steam schooner "Wapama" which was active for many years in the coastal lumber trade now is part of the California Maritime Museum near Hyde Street Park in San Francisco. The Peerless 44-note piano entertains visitors when they come aboard. (photos courtesy of Harry Dring, superintendent)

On this page are shown machines from the collection of Jacob DeBence of Franklin, Penna. The top and lower right photos show a Coinola Midget Orchestrion with a piano, mandolin and two ranks of pipes — wooden flute pipes and metal violin pipes. Using the Coinola "O" roll the pipes play solo melodies. At the lower left is shown a Berry-Wood A.O.W. orchestrion (see pp. 52, 53). This machine originally saw service for many years in a tavern near Rochester, New York. It was "discovered" by Richard Reis who restored it and sold it to the DeBence collection. The A.O.W. was the largest orchestrion in the Berry-Wood line.

Larry Givens of Wexford, Penna. operates a piano roll perforator. Using equipment originally in the Ampico factories in East Rochester, N.Y. Larry Givens and his partner, John Gourley, produce a line of 88-note home player piano rolls (MelOdee brand) as well as recut reproducing piano and coin piano rolls.

This large cylinder-operated Welte orchestrion in the Givens collection was originally on a staircase landing in the palatial Mellon home in nearby Pittsburgh.

Larry Givens acquired this beautiful Seeburg H in Toronto, Canada. With a sizeable inventory of H rolls to play this orchestrion provides "background music" for the various roll cutting activities of the Givens-Gourley Company. The decorative carved wood statues which were originally on each side of front were missing when this machine was acquired. Shortly after this photograph was taken a pair of original statues was acquired — completing the case.

This Wurlitzer IX piano (see p. 117) in the collection of Murray Clark gives forth with lively melodies — just as it did years ago in the "good old days." This machine was obtained from a New Haven, Connecticut piano dealer who had acquired it as a curiosity. Murray has made a specialty of Wurlitzer machines and their operation. Among the fine restorations to his credit is the LX shown on page 135.

This National (Peerless) case looks attractive from the outside, but the insides are completely missing — the way John Gourley found it. Xylophones, drums and other parts were often stripped from orchestrions years ago when these machines had little value.

Other machines in the Clark collection include the Electrova shown above at the left and the Seeburg mortuary organ shown above at the right.

Above and left: Robert Johnson of The Collectors' Exchange, Rossville, Georgia, is shown standing by the chassis of a large Welte Concert Orchestrion. Like many Welte orchestrions this model originally had no cabinet but was built into a special room. Bob Johnson's musical interests are cosmopolitan and include coin pianos and orchestrions, theatre pipe organs and fretted stringed instruments. Bob, a talented musician, is a virtuoso on the five-string banjo and has made many radio and television appearances.

Above: Coinola orchestrion on display at Knott's Berry Farm, Buena Park, California.

To the right: Wurlitzer Style 32 Concert PianOrchestra (see p. 162) presently on view in the Penny Arcade in California's Disneyland. (Photograph from Player Piano Treasury)

On these two facing pages are machines restored by Oscar and Leonard Grymonprez of Gentbrugge, Belgium. The Grymonprez family business of building and repairing band organs and orchestrions traces its beginning to the 1880's. On this page: Above left and right is shown a magnificent Weber "Maesto" orchestrion. Standing in front of the machine (left to right) are Leonard Grymonprez, his father, Oscar Grymonprez and Josef DePlacido. At the left is an interior view of the top front of the Weber "Maesto". Measuring ten feet high and over eleven feet wide the Maesto was the largest orchestrion model in the line manufactured by Gebruder Weber of Waldkirch, Germany. Various swell shutters allow the many different instruments to play with realistic expression. Leonard Grymonprez, an avid student of European band organs and orchestrions, considers the Weber machines to be the finest orchestrions ever made on that continent. After hearing the Maesto play your author would not disagree. At the lower left is an unrestored Weber "Otero" orchestrion. Music rolls are stored on the shelves in the side wings. At the lower right is a Weber "Styria" orchestrion. Unlike the other Weber machines shown on this page the Styria has a keyboard. Note the swell shutters (for expression) at the top.

Above is a huge 121-key band organ manufactured in 1939 by Decap of Antwerp, Belgium. Originally the machine measured 27 feet wide and 17 feet high! Its present location is not sufficiently large so some of the top facade has been removed and stored. Above right: Leonard Grymonprez watches the folding cardboard music go through the key frame of the 121-key Decap. At the right is an 84-key Mortier band organ. Long one of the leading European band organ manufacturers Mortier remained in business until the mid 1950's. Below right is a large 101-key Mortier band organ which incorporates a 67-note accordion. This magnificent machine, restored by the Grymonprez enterprise, is now part of the fabulous collection owned by C. H. Hart of St. Albans, England. The wonderful music of these large machines must be heard to be appreciated. Once heard, it never will be forgotten. There is considerable interest in band organs and orchestrions in Europe today. In Holland band organs play concerts for tourists in the streets. In Belgium band organs are still a major source of music in dance halls and similar places. In England the Fair Organ Preservation Society numbers several hundred members — all devoted to the preservation of band organs (known as "fair organs" in Europe) and their music. Directly below is a large Weber "Solea" orchestrion. Its dimensions and interior contents are somewhat similar to the Weber "Maesto" shown on the preceding page.

The machines on this page are from the collection of Otto Carlsen of Monrovia, California. The two orchestrions in the above illustration are two of the finest still preserved in the United States. The orchestrion in the background is a Wurlitzer Style 40 Mandolin PianOrchestra (see p. 159) which was originally obtained in junk condition from a Florida collector. Now, hundreds of hours of effort later, it plays magnificently. In the foreground is a large Hupfeld orchestrion with an accordion in a glass case on the front. The Hupfeld is fully instrumented and has the Hupfeld single roll changer, a device somewhat similar to the Wurlitzer mechanism.

This Seeburg Phono-Grand in the Carlsen collection is a combination expression piano and phonograph. The top part of the case contains a record player under a hinged lid; the bottom section, an electric player piano. The piano part uses regular 88-note home player piano rolls as well as special Seeburg "XP" expression rolls. This compact machine was the ultimate in drawing room and parlor furniture about 1920 when it was introduced. The Phono-Grand must have been only a limited success as very few are known today. In 1965 Seeburg re-entered the mechanical piano field with the introduction of the "Serenada," an electrically-operated (via solenoids) player piano intended for use in the home.

Otto Carlsen listens to the Wurlitzer . . . as it comes to life after a silence of many years.

Mr. and Mrs. Carlsen in front of the Style 40 PianOrchestra. Note the 30-bar xylophone near the front in the upper part of the case.

Above: Restoration and repair shop at Sutro's, San Francisco. The two large partially disassembled machines in the background are a Hupfeld Phonoliszt Violina Model B and a Seeburg H orchestrion. Left: Wurlitzer orchestrion at Sutro's. Compare this one with the machine illustrated on page 132.

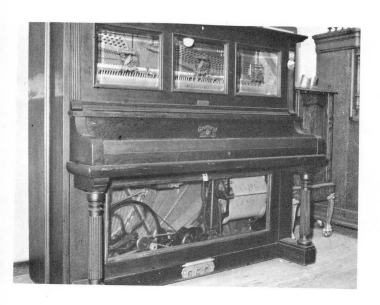

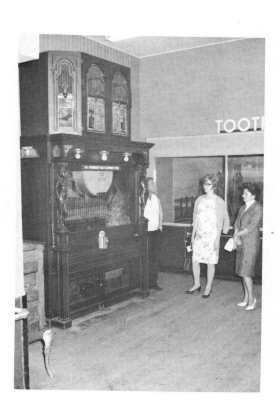

Above: Style 3 Cremona at Sutro's. As in many other mechanical music exhibits the machines at Sutro's may be played by anyone caring to put a nickel, dime or quarter in their slots.
Right: Sutro's has three Seeburg H orchestrions, one of which is shown above. The art glass has been removed from the front and placed on top. This permits visitors to watch the instruments in action when the machine is playing.

The private collection of Roy Haning and Neal White of Troy, Ohio is one of the most extensive in the country. Above, Roy Haning puts a coin into the slot of a fine Coinola CO orchestrion. Left, Neal White is shown with the chassis of a Style 15 Wurlitzer Mandolin PianOrchestra. This particular machine has the 12-roll automatic changer.

Seeburg KT Special orchestrion from the Haning and White collection. The KT Special, first marketed about 1925, was a latecomer to the automatic music field.

Interior view of the same Coinola CO shown at the top of the page. From a musical standpoint the CO is one of the most desirable orchestrions ever manufactured in the United States.

More machines from the Haning and White collection. They are (going clockwise): (1) Mills Race Horse Piano (see p. 66). This particular machine originally saw service in England and is equipped with a slot taking English pennies. It was part of a hoard of Mills machines located several years ago by Frank Holland of the Piano Museum in Brentford, Middlesex. (2) Nelson-Wiggen orchestrion with piano, xylophone, bass and snare drums and several other instruments. Like other Nelson-Wiggen orchestrions it uses a standard G (or 4X) roll. (3) Coinola C2 orchestrion which utilizes the "O" roll. A rank of pipes suspended in an inverted position in the bottom of the case behind the other instruments plays solo melodies. (4) Western Electric "A" roll piano showing the tune selector knob on the left front part of the cabinet. (5) Coinola Midget Orchestrion with piano, mandolin, xylophone, bass drum, cymbal, snare drum, wood block and triangle.

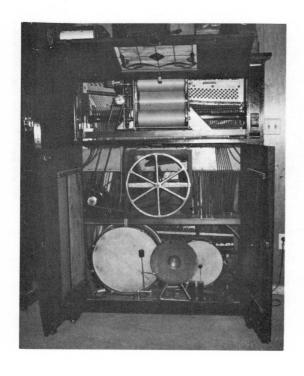

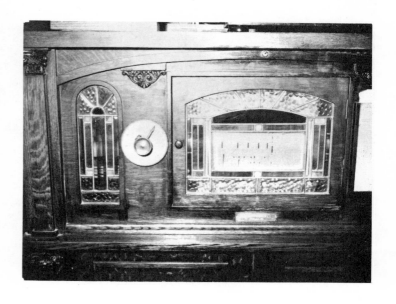

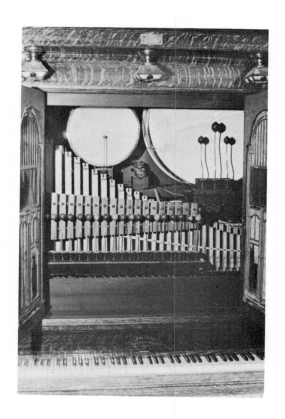

Seeburg H orchestrion in the Haning and White collection.

Seeburg H with the front doors opened.

Above: A Coinola X with a richly-figured quartered oak case is a highlight in the Haning and White collection. The X is flanked by two Nelson-Wiggen orchestrions.

Left: An Autoelectra, an early 44-note piano in the same collection.

The photographs on this page were taken at the Musical Museum in Deansboro, New York. Operated by the Sanders family this museum displays music boxes, coin pianos, orchestrions, band organs and other instruments. It has been a leading upstate New York tourist attraction for many years. (1) Above, Arthur Sanders is shown standing in front of an orchestrion that was manufactured in Germany and marketed in England by the Harper Piano Company. (2) Exhibit of music boxes and musical automata. In the background is a Welte-Mignon reproducing piano. (3) Coinola CO orchestrion. (4) Nelson-Wiggen orchestrion. (5) Wurlitzer Pianino (left) and an Engelhardt coin piano (right).

Mr. Edwin A. Link, son of E. A. Link (founder of the Link Piano Company) holds a portable keyboard which was originally used in the Link factory to tune keyboardless cabinet-style coin pianos.

Harvey Roehl and Ed Link examine the Link Style 2-E coin piano presently in the game room of the Link home in Binghamton, New York. The 2-E features a piano, mandolin effect, and xylophone.

AN AFTERNOON WITH ED LINK

During the preparation of this book the author had several conversations with Ed Link. During the autumn afternoon that the above pictures were taken the author, Murray Clark, and Harvey Roehl spent several hours with Mr. Link in his beautiful home. After many years of activity in other fields, Ed has revived his interest in the history of his father's firm by buying a fine Link theatre pipe organ and a Link Style 2-E coin piano, both of which are currently being restored.

Ed Link related many interesting facts concerning the "good old days" at the piano factory. Like many other manufacturers, they bought their pianos ready-made (including cases and art glass) from the Haddorff Piano Company of Rockford, Illinois, and then proceeded to add the roll mechanism, pneumatic stack, and the various instruments and controls. The factory capacity was about one automatic piano per day; about 300 instruments per year.

Arranging of the music rolls was done primarily by two men. One was Ray Deo (collectors of these machines will occasionally find a roll with a Deo Roll Company label on it, as he sold some rolls after the Link Company went bankrupt) and the other was Bill Sabin, a former first clarinetist with Sousa's band. Ed stated that Sabin arranged most of the pipe organ rolls, while Deo did most of the work on the piano and orchestrion rolls although he could not actually play the piano himself at all! Considering that Link rolls featured some of the best and most melodious arrangements, and that almost all the masters were designed mechanically on a drawing board, these men did a remarkable job.

About 80% of the Link instruments were sold to route operators rather than to individual business proprietors, and one operator, the Lockwood Piano Company of Rhode Island, had 300 Link machines! The route operators found that the endless rolls stimulated business as there was no pause for rewinding. The cumbersome job of changing a Link endless roll was no problem for an experienced route man. The operators also liked the Link pneumatic stack, because any individual pneumatic that was giving trouble could be unscrewed easily and another substituted quickly as a replacement. On machines of other makes the failure of a single pneumatic could entail dismantling the entire machine — a task of several hours duration.

Three perforating machines were kept busy turning out piano and organ rolls. Each machine could produce ten or fifteen rolls at a time, and each cutting of a particular roll took about two hours.

Most of the technical design of the various Link systems were made by the late George Thayer, who continued to his later years as a phonograph route operator. On the average the Link Piano Company employed 100 to 125 workers in the factory (now a paved parking lot — it was demolished several years ago) on Water Street in Binghamton, New York. One of the most interesting comments made by Mr. Link was that quarter and half-dollar slots were installed as original equipment on a number of Link machines, for expensive restaurants and other exclusive places where the proprietors were evidently not content merely to have the patron "put another nickel in."

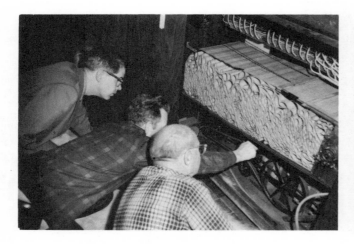

The author, Murray Clark and Ed Link examine the pump of the 2-E. Note the standard Link endless roll. Despite its appearance the endless roll works smoothly and doesn't become tangled.

Ed Link inspects the Link decal on the Link AX orchestrion in the author's collection.

Ed Link at the console of a fine Link theatre pipe organ. This instrument was taken from a Cleveland, Ohio theatre several years ago by an enthusiast in that area. In 1964 Mr. Link purchased it from him, and the instrument was being restored when these photographs were taken. It is destined to be presented to the Roberson Memorial Center, a cultural and historical center in Binghamton, New York.

A few of the hundreds of pipes in the Link organ. These and similar Link theatre organs were originally marketed under the name C. Sharpe Minor Unit Organ; C. Sharpe Minor was a well-known theatre organist who worked with the Link company and lent his name to their efforts. This particular organ originally cost about $30,000.00. Mr. Link noted that about seventy-five Link C. Sharpe Minor Unit Organs were sold over the years, mainly in the early 1920's.

In the late 1920's the Link Piano Company, like many other manufacturers of coin pianos and theatre organs, saw its market dwindle to virtually nothing. A few attempts at diversification were made, including the manufacture of a coin-operated automatic phonograph (Ed Link's first patent was on this device), and experimentation with sound systems for movies.

Finally, in 1929 the Link Piano Company was bankrupt, and Ed Link's father, E. A. Link, went to California where he operated a route of coin pianos for a few years.

Ed's interests had always been more in the field of aviation than in working at his father's factory, and he was able to combine his personal interests and knowledge of player pianos and pipe organs to develop a series of aviation devices which borrowed from both fields.

One venture was in aerial advertising. Ed took the Fairchild airplane shown above and equipped it with a set of "sky signs" suspended from the wings, which were able to spell out advertising messages in the night sky. This was done by means of lights in strategic places which would turn on and off in accordance with the ad copy punched in piano rolls! One airplane was equipped with a set of organ pipes voiced on high pressure; these also operated from a paper roll and played melodies as the craft flew through the skies! During this time the airplane was still a novelty to many people, with the result that the flying billboard was a success in attracting much attention.

Ed's greatest success, however, was in the development of the Link flying trainer, which actually used many player piano components. The advent of World War II brought fortune to the Link business, as training was needed for hundreds of thousands of pilots, and then after the war commercial airlines made extensive use of Link equipment to train their personnel.

A few years ago Ed Link sold his business, and it became a division of General Precision, Incorporated. Now Ed has achieved fame once again through his interest in undersea exploration. His activities concerning the salvage of buried treasure, survival of divers for long periods under the sea and other ventures have been the subject of many newspaper and magazine articles in recent years.

Just a few of the many fine machines in the collection of Harvey and Marion Roehl of Vestal, N.Y. are shown on these facing pages. In 1961 Harvey Roehl wrote and published "Player Piano Treasury," the first authoritative reference book on the subject. Clockwise, the photographs are: (1) Harvey Roehl works on a component from a Welte reproducing grand piano. (2) Link flute piano made many years ago in nearby Binghamton, New York. (3) Large Welte Philharmonic residence pipe organ. This impressive machine was rescued from a New York City mansion several days before it was slated for destruction. (4) The Seeburg G orchestrion now in the Roehl collection once entertained patrons of a Mobile, Alabama cafe.

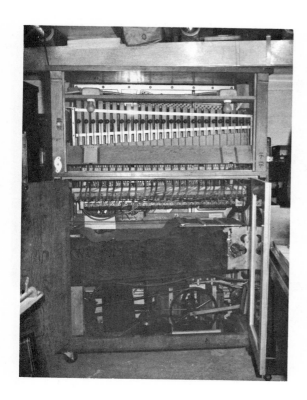

This Link 2-E piano in the Roehl collection contains a piano, mandolin attachment and xylophone. The 2-E was one of the most popular Link styles.

Marion Roehl assists with the restoration of a pump from a Seeburg KT Special orchestrion. A Chicago brewer acquired it in the late 1920's. It remained in the cellar of his Chicago home until 1965 when it was acquired by the Roehls. As this book was being written the machine was undergoing a complete restoration.

Harvey Roehl inspects the innards of his KT Special. The large machine in the background is a Style 25 American Fotoplayer, a cousin to the models illustrated on pages 31 and 32.

December 1965 —After several months' work the Seeburg KT Special is playing once again! This machine, first marketed by Seeburg in 1925, was one of the most sophisticated Seeburg machines built. Colored lights flash on and off in time with the music. (see original catalog illustration on page 39).

Above: Roll mechanism and front panel of a fine Coinola X orchestrion in the Roehl collection. During the 1920's this machine entertained the patrons of the Hollywood Tavern in Fleetwood, Pennsylvania.

Above left: Interior of the left side chest of the American Fotoplayer shown on the preceding page.

Left: This North Tonawanda Musical Instrument Works Style L coin piano (see page 54 for original catalogue description) awaits restoration.

Below left: This Seeburg Style E piano with mandolin effect and xylophone has been restored to factory-new condition.

Below: J. Lawrence Cook, well-known arranger of piano rolls, plays the Duo-Art reproducing piano in the Roehl music room.

Max Morath, one of the foremost exponents of ragtime music in America today, plays a restored American Fotoplayer now located in a Portland, Oregon, hotel.

Max Morath, on a visit to the Roehl home in Vestal, New York, plays ragtime music on a fine Julius Bauer Welte reproducing grand piano.

This European carousel, featuring a Hooghuys band organ, is representative of many merry-go-rounds with band organs in use in America and Europe today.

The proscenium or front of a Gavioli band organ.

How music is cut in Europe today. Mr. Eugene Peersman, renowned composer for mechanical organ music-books, showing some details of his craft.

Murtough Guinness and Hughes Ryder listen to the sounds as Al Hale turns the crank of his Dutch street organ. This machine was a feature attraction of the 1965 convention of the International Musical Box Society held at Lloyd Kelley's estate, Pin Oaks, at Barnstable on Cape Cod, Massachusetts.

In 1927 the proprietors of the Spring Mills Hotel in Spring Mills, Penna. purchased this Wurlitzer LX Orchestra Piano. Through the years it has remained in the same location. Today the Spring Mills Hotel has a small musical museum — and the LX is the featured attraction.

Collector Steve Lanick from Pittsburgh, Pennsylvania, admires the figurine on the front of the Dutch organ.

The North Tonawanda Musical Instrument Works building as it appears today. Compare this photograph with the factory illustration shown on page 55. The lettering, NORTH TONAWANDA MUSICAL INSTRUMENT WORKS, on the side of the building, is faintly visible today.

Lloyd Kelley, who purchased the remaining equipment of the Regina Music Box company a number of years ago, is shown making a metal music-box disc utilizing an original Regina disc perforator.

Close-up view of the front panel of the Bijou Orchestra.

Wurlitzer Bijou Orchestra in the collection of Terry Hathaway of Santa Fe Springs, California.

Front center panel of the 30-A Mandolin PianOrchestra.

Wurlitzer Style 30-A Mandolin PianOrchestra. This machine was found by Larry Givens in the abandoned ballroom of the Martin Hotel near Skaneateles Falls, New York, several years ago.

This Wurlitzer LX orchestrion looks small next to the huge 30-A PianOrchestra in the Hathaway home.

The machines on this page and through page 238 are from the collection of the author.

Upper left: Wurlitzer Style A Harp.

Upper right: The author's garage, like that of many other piano collectors, is cluttered with unrestored machines. A neighbor, M. P. Woodward, stands behind the Harp which has had the front and chassis removed from the case. By removing four screws the chassis may be lifted easily from the case, permitting easy access to the interior parts.

Lower left: Interior of the Harp showing rows of pneumatics above and the tracker bar and roll drive mechanism below.

Lower right: Close-up of the Harp strings showing the row of little "fingers" which pluck the strings.

Above: Automatic Roll Changer in the Wurlitzer Style 12 Pian-Orchestra.

Above right: Wurlitzer Style 12 PianOrchestra. Although this machine is quite large it is one of the smaller PianOrchestra styles. The original catalogue description of the Style 12 appears on page 142.

Below: Mills DeLuxe Violano Virtuoso with two violins. On the left of the Violano is the Violano Orchestra attachment. Unlike the regular Violano Virtuoso this machine uses a special Violano Orchestra roll which provides for the various drums and traps.

Below right: Wurlitzer Style 3 Paganini Violin Piano (see pp. 174, 179).

Above left and right: Cremona Orchestral J orchestrion (see p. 46). For many years this machine reposed in a Massachusetts restaurant. Now, fully restored, it plays lilting melodies from the Roaring Twenties once again.

Below right: Roll drive mechanism of the Cremona Orchestral J.

Below left: Coinola Midget Orchestrion similar to the Haning and White machine shown on page 215.

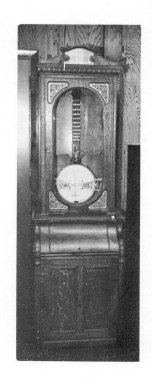

Above: Chassis of a Wurlitzer Style 32-A Concert PianOrchestra similar to the machine shown on page 165. At the time this photograph was taken the machine was stripped down for restoration of the individual components. Like many other large Wurlitzer Pian-Orchestras the 32-A chassis and case are separate. The chassis stands by itself; the ornate exterior case fits around it.

Above right: Encore Automatic Banjo. Over a dozen of these early machines are known in various collections in the United States. The Encore was first marketed around the turn of the century.

Below left and right: Exterior and interior views of a Seeburg G orchestrion. The art glass of this orchestrion style is particularly attractive.

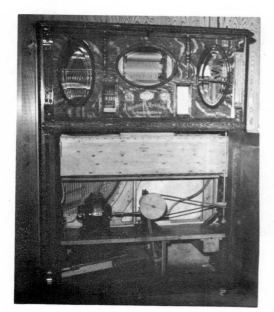

Above: The front of this Link flute piano is adorned with beautiful art glass.

Above left: Nelson-Wiggen Selector Duplex piano-pipe organ which once was located in a Pittsfield, Maine funeral parlor.

Left: Top front section of a Wurlitzer 32 Concert PianOrchestra similar to the machine shown on page 163. As the parts cluttering the interior show, the machine is totally unrestored.

Below left: Wurlitzer Mandolin Quartette with bottom doors open.

Below: Roll drive mechanism and coin slot apparatus of the Mandolin Quartette.

Above: The author's sons, Wynn and Lee, listen to "On Wisconsin" being played on an Empress Electric Y orchestrion.

Above right: Empress Electric Y orchestrion. The catalogue description of this machine appears on page 51.

Right: This huge Seeburg Pipe Organ Orchestra photoplayer was acquired by the author from the H. H. Robey Theatre in Spencer, West Virginia. Instrumentation includes piano, mandolin, oboe, bassoon, vox humana, cello, violin, diapason pipes, flute, chimes, xylophone, bass drum, snare drum, cymbal, tympani and over a dozen other traps and novelty effects.

Below right: Close-up view of the manuals of the Seeburg Pipe Organ Orchestra. The upper keyboard is for the organ pipes, the lower for piano (although the piano keyboard can be coupled to play organ also). The brass nameplate notes that the instrument was originally sold by the Seltzer Music Company of Pittsburgh, Pennsylvania, a leading distributor of Seeburg and Operators Piano Company products.

Below: Interior of a Link AX orchestrion (see p. 43). The sloping shelf at the top is used to hold the endless roll.

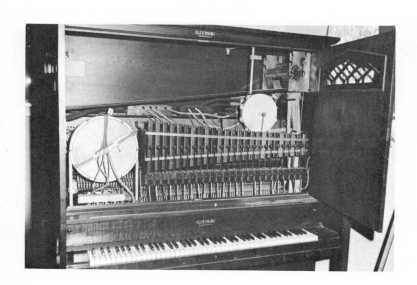

Wall boxes originally used with coin pianos. They are (left to right): (1) Seeburg wall box shaped like a miniature coin piano, (2) and (3) Wurlitzer wall boxes, (4) Link wall box with program card on front, (5) early Wurlitzer wall box (see p. 166), (6) early Seeburg wall box, (7) Mills wall box for use with the Violano Virtuoso, (8) Wurlitzer wall box similar to the one shown on page 202.

This angular view shows a large Wurlitzer photoplayer, model CU Duplex, acquired by the author in 1965. This machine, one of the larger Wurlitzer photoplayers, uses Concert PianOrchestra rolls. Instrumentation includes a full complement of pipes and percussion instruments. When new this instrument probably sold for about $4,000.00.

This Wurlitzer Style O theatre photoplayer was stored for many years in a West Virginia feed and grain store before the author "discovered" it. The style O was one of the smaller Wurlitzer photoplayers. Like other small Wurlitzer photoplayers, it used Wurlitzer Automatic Player Piano rolls. Like most other photoplayers that turn up today, this Style O is in need of restoration and has some parts missing. One of the author's sons, Wynn, and his grandfather, Dr. Raymond Masters, look on with interest.

Another view of the Wurlitzer CU Duplex theatre photoplayer shown above. When this picture was taken it was so closely packed into a Pennsylvania warehouse that a full-view photograph could not be made. A full set of metal orchestra bells extends across the front center of the left cabinet. The number of photoplayers of various makes that survive today is not known but probably is not more than a few dozen machines in all. These cumbersome machines could not be moved or stored easily, so most were scrapped and torn apart when their usefulness ended in the late 1920's.

The machines illustrated from this page through to the end of the book were in the collection of the late Mr. A. C. Raney of Whittier, California. This collection was dispersed in the early 1950's and formed the basis of the collection now on display at California's Disneyland. Other machines from the Raney Collection are now in various private collections throughout America. These photographs were taken in 1950. Above is a Seeburg H orchestrion (left) with the art glass removed to permit a view of the interior. To the right is a Hupfeld Phonoliszt-Violina, Model B (see page 170 for original catalogue description).

An Orchestral Regina music box (see p. 75) and an Encore Banjo.

The machine at the left features a piano and a large set of pipes. It was manufactured by Electrova and sold by Engelhardt of St. Johnsville, New York. This instrument is presently in the Disneyland collection. The machine at the right is a Wurlitzer Pianino.

"In the foreground is a Seeburg KT Special orchestrion with the art glass removed. The large machine in the center is an Imhof & Mukle orchestrion dating from the 1910 period. Partly obscured by the Imhof & Mukle is a Wurlitzer Style A Automatic Harp."

A Regina parlor-style music box with an automatic disc-changer is in the corner of this room. To the right is a fine DeLuxe two-violin Mills Violano Virtuoso.

Fully visible in the foreground is a rare Resotone Grand. To the right of it is a Regina Sublima piano, followed by a Cremona Orchestral K orchestrion and two Seeburg KT orchestrions.

Left to right: A cabinet-style Coinola machine with the art glass and door center panels removed; center, a Western Electric "A" roll piano; a Wurlitzer Violin Pianino (see p. 109).

Left, a Link Style 2-E piano with xylophone; center, a Seeburg G orchestrion with the standard G art glass; right, a Regina Orchestral Corona music box with automatic disc-changer. This type of machine uses a 27-inch diameter metal tune sheet.

A German-made Polyphon music box. The bottom of the machine provides space for storing extra discs. In the background is a Seeburg G with a rare style of art glass featuring sailboats on the center panels.

The Wurlitzer Style L orchestrion has the art glass removed. Note the striking grain pattern of the quartered oak case. In the foreground is a European Piano-Orchestrion with a painted scene on the front of the case.

This Style 32 Wurlitzer Concert Pianorchestra from the Raney Collection is now a featured attraction at Disneyland. See page 215 for another view of the same machine.

This beautiful Welte orchestrion from the Raney Collection is also now at Disneyland. Only a few large Welte orchestrions still survive in America.